MULTINATIONAL INDUSTRIAL RELATIONS SERIES

No. 12

EMPLOYEE FINANCIAL PARTICIPATION: AN INTERNATIONAL SURVEY

by

CHARLES R. PERRY

and

DELWYN H. KEGLEY

with

EDWARD J. OST

ROGER G. MCELRATH

BETTY J. SLOWINSKI

CHRISTIAN F. SCHNEIDER

INDUSTRIAL RESEARCH UNIT
The Wharton School, Vance Hall
University of Pennsylvania
Philadelphia, Pennsylvania 19104-6358

Copyright © 1990 by the Trustees of the University of Pennsylvania
Library of Congress Catalog Number 90-70588
MANUFACTURED IN THE UNITED STATES OF AMERICA
ISBN: 0-89546-077-7

Foreword

In 1972, the Industrial Research Unit began an ongoing research program dealing with various facets of multinational industrial relations. The program is now under the joint direction of Professor Richard L. Rowan, Director of the Industrial Research Unit, and Duncan C. Campbell, Associate Director of the Unit.

This study, *Employee Financial Participation: An International Survey*, is one of several studies that examine important industrial relations issues and compares their treatment in various industrialized countries. The reader of this study should be aware that it is a survey and not a detailed, analytical treatise covering financial participation on a worldwide basis. The study attempts to bring together in one place a description of all of the major group employee financial participation plans along with the economic and political background leading up to the current plans, an evaluation of these plans, and a discussion of trends for the future of employee financial participation.

The authorship of this study has been a true team project in the Industrial Research Unit. Faculty and professional staff have worked together to develop the findings that are presented in this study. Professor Charles R. Perry has served as general editor of the study, and much praise is deserved by Delwyn H. Kegley, a member of the professional staff, who provided outstanding assistance to Professor Perry. Others who played a major role in the study include Betty J. Slowinski (France), Christian F. Schneider (Germany and Switzerland), Roger G. McElrath (Employee Stock Ownership Plans), and Edward J. Ost (Gain Sharing). Their dedication and hard work in the project made it possible to complete the study in an efficient manner.

Kathryn E. Pearcy, editor at the Industrial Research Unit, assisted in all phases of the project and prepared the index; Mrs. Marthenia A. Perrin, business manager in the Unit, handled all of the various administrative matters involved with the work; Mrs. Sue A. Torelli, Unit librarian, assisted in many research questions; and Mr. O.P. Suri, Miss Rita M. Gorman, Miss Janice A. Reith, and Mrs. Veronica Robinson provided word processing assistance.

The study was financed by special contributions from corporate subscribers to the Unit's Multinational Research Advisory Group Information Services. The authors, of course, are solely responsible for the study's content, which should not be attributed to the grantors or to the University of Pennsylvania.

Richard L. Rowan, Director
Industrial Research Unit
The Wharton School
University of Pennsylvania

Philadelphia
May 1990

TABLE OF CONTENTS

PAGE

FOREWORD.. iii

CHAPTER

I. INTRODUCTION 1
Asset Accumulation Plans 3
Deferred Profit Sharing Plans 4
Employee Stock Ownership Plans 5
Cash Profit Sharing Plans 6
Gain Sharing Plans 6
The Role of Government 6
The Nature of the Study 8

II. GAIN SHARING IN THE UNITED STATES 9
Team-Based Pay: The Concept 9
Distribution of Gain Sharing 11
Team-Based Pay 12
Broad Team-Based Applications 13
Gain Sharing and Employee Participation 14
The Union Response to the Team Concept 16
Characteristics of Team-Based Pay in Union
    Environments 17
Team-Based Pay: White Collar Applications 21
    Financial Services Sector 22
    Industrial Firms 23
    Future of Team-based Pay in the
        White-Collar Sector 26
Gain Sharing Results 26
Integrating Gain Sharing and Profit Sharing 27

III. PROFIT SHARING IN THE UNITED STATES 29
The History of Profit Sharing 29
    Tax Advantages 32
    The Rise of Deferred Profit Sharing 33
Types of Plans 34
    Deferred Plans 34
    Cash Plans 39
    Combination Plans 40
Legislative Developments 40

ERISA	41
Impact of Regulation	41
Profit Sharing and Collective Bargaining	42
The Automobile Industry Plans	45
Steel and Aluminum Industry Plans	48
Other Industries	50
Profit Sharing Results	52
IV. Employee Savings Plans in the United States	57
Advantages and Disadvantages of Savings Plans	58
Savings Plan Features and Trends	59
Coverage	60
Eligibility	60
Employee Contributions	60
Employer Contributions	62
Voluntary Suspensions	63
Investment of Contributions	63
Investment Transfers	64
Vesting	64
Forfeiture Allocation	66
In-Service Withdrawals	66
Loans	67
Forms of Distribution	67
Trends	68
V. Employee Stock Ownership in the United States	69
Definition, Types, and Provisions	69
Types of ESOPs	71
Provisions	73
How ESOPs Are Used	77
Disadvantages of ESOPs	82
Performance of ESOP Companies	85
Ownership of Capital	85
Equity Financing	88
Economic Results	90
Worker Participation and Labor-Management Cooperation	92
Evaluation	95
Unions and Employee Stock Ownership	98
Contemporary Views of Organized Labor	98
Organized Labor's Criticisms of ESOPs	101
Potential Uses of Employee Ownership for Organized Labor	108

Table of Contents

VI. CANADA AND MEXICO 111
    Canada 111
        Profit Sharing Plans 112
        Equity Sharing 113
        The Union Reaction to Gain Sharing 115
    Mexico 116
        Profit Sharing Legislation 116
        The Role of Organized Labor 118

VII. UNITED KINGDOM 119
    Company Profit Sharing 119
        The Finance Act of 1978 and Amendments 119
        Profit-Related Pay (PRP) 121
        Evaluation 124
    Savings-Related Share Option Plans 128
        Features of SAYE Plans 128
        Tax Aspects 129
        Evaluation 129
    Employee Stock Ownership Plans (ESOP) 130
    Gain Sharing 135

VIII. FRANCE 137
    Background of Financial Participation 137
        1959 Profit Sharing Law (Voluntary) 137
        1967 Profit Sharing Law (Compulsory) 138
    The 1986 Legislation 139
        Compulsory Deferred Profit (Capital) Sharing 140
        Voluntary Cash Profit Sharing 142
        Savings, Share Ownership, and Share Option
            Plans 145
    Other Legislation 137
    The Public Sector 148
    Examples of Profit Sharing Agreements 148
        Kronenbourg 148
        EDF and GDF 149
        Other Agreements 149

IX. FEDERAL REPUBLIC OF GERMANY 151
    Development of State-Aided Asset Formation Plans ... 151
        First Asset Formation Law—"DM 312 Law" 152
        Second Asset Formation Law 153
        Third Asset Formation Law—"DM 624 Law" 153
        Fourth Asset Formation Law—"DM 936 Law" 154

Fifth Asset Formation Law 156
The Amended Fifth Asset Formation Law
   of 1989/90 159
Contractual and Codeterminational Aspects of
   Employee Asset Sharing 161
Forms of Employee Capital Sharing 163
Trade Unions and Employee Capital Sharing 172

X. SWEDEN 175
   Swedish Wage-Earner Funds 176
      Background 176
      Present Operation 178
      Results 179
   Voluntary Profit Sharing in Sweden 181
      Åkermans 183
      Svenska Handelsbanken 183
      Volvo 183
   Gain Sharing in Sweden 184
      Scan Väst 184
      Volvo Kalmar Plant 185
      Swedish Farmers' Union (LRF) 186
      Alufuor 187
   Trends in Sweden 187

XI. OTHER EC AND EUROPEAN COUNTRIES 189
   The Netherlands 189
      Statutory Savings/Profit Sharing Plans 189
      Company Profit Sharing 191
      Stock Ownership/Share Option Plans 192
      Collective Asset Formation Plans 192
   Belgium 193
      Profit Sharing Legislation 193
      Company Profit Sharing 194
   Italy 195
      Trade Unions and Politics 195
      Performance-Related Pay 196
      Employee Share-Ownership Plans 199
   Denmark 200
   Switzerland 201
      Development of Employee Financial Participation .. 201
      Present Situation 203
      Examples of Employee Share Plans 205
   The European Community 207

Table of Contents ix

XII. SUMMARY AND CONCLUSIONS 209

TABLES AND FIGURES

TABLE III-1: Employer Contributions as Percentage of Pay .. 36

TABLE III-2: Employer Contributions as a Percentage of
  Net Profits, 1980–1988 (All Plans) 36

TABLE III-3: Automobile Industry Profit Sharing
  Plan (1989) 46

TABLE III-4: Average Profit Sharing Payout to Employees of
  Chrysler, Ford, and General Motors, 1983–1989 46

TABLE III-5: Performance of Large Profit Sharing and
  Non-Profit Sharing Companies, 1987 53

TABLE III-6: Performance Comparisons, 1973–1976 53

TABLE IV-1: Employer Payments as a Percentage of
  Payroll for Selected Employee Benefits, 1987 59

TABLE IV-2: Employer Contribution Rates for Defined
  Contribution Plans 1986 and 1977 62

TABLE IV-3: Prevalence of Investment Funds Offered in
  Defined Contribution Plans, 1986 and 1977 64

TABLE VII-1: Growth of ADST Profit Sharing Plans,
  1979–1987 121

TABLE VII-2: Comparative Performance of Profit Sharing
  and Non-Profit Sharing Companies, 1977–1985 128

TABLE VII-3: Percentage of Employees Receiving
  Payment by Results Payments 135

TABLE VII-4: Payment by Results Payments as a
  Percent of Gross Average Earnings for Those
  Receiving Such Payments 136

TABLE VIII-1: Compulsory Profit Sharing
  Agreements 141

TABLE VIII-2: Growth of Voluntary Profit Sharing
Agreements 144

FIGURE IX-1: Financial Effects of a Company-Level
Participation Offer 158

TABLE XI-1: Number of Employees and Actual Participants
in Companies with Savings Plans 190

TABLE XII-1: Tax Incentives for Employer and Employee
by Country 211

CHAPTER I

Introduction

One of the most significant business initiatives in the 1980s was experimentation with employee participation in decision-making within the enterprise. At the same time, employers in countries with market economies increased their experimentation with employee financial participation. The concept of sharing profits or other assets with employees is necessarily related to the private enterprise system, so it is not surprising that the countries in which private enterprise is the strongest are generally the countries where financial participation has flourished. The most obvious example is the United States where profit sharing, gain sharing, savings plans, and employee stock ownership plans (ESOPs) have become relatively widespread on a voluntary basis with some government encouragement through the tax laws. In Europe, employee financial participation has been more influenced by government policies attempting to encourage asset accumulation, a wider distribution of the ownership of capital, or performance-related pay.[1]

This survey will examine the status of employee financial participation in those countries in which there have been significant developments in recent years. Although the countries included were selected on a somewhat arbitrary basis, each illustrates a different approach to employee financial participation. Included are the United States, Canada, Mexico, the United Kingdom, France, the Federal Republic of Germany, the Netherlands, Belgium, Denmark, Italy, Switzerland, and Sweden. The United States, Canada, and the United Kingdom represent a completely voluntary approach, while Sweden and Mexico represent a mandatory (but different) approach. France combines both voluntary and mandatory profit sharing plans with a wide assortment of other types of plans. Germany and the Netherlands have emphasized asset and equity accumulation plans. In Switzerland, share purchase plans have been very popular.

The exclusion of European countries such as Ireland, Norway, Spain, Portugal, and Greece does not signify that employee financial

---

[1]Jean Remus, "Financial participation of employees: An attempted classification and major trends," *International Labour Review*, Vol. 122, No. 1 (January-February 1983), p. 1.

participation does not exist in those countries, but that there is relatively little activity or few strong initiatives from either employers or governments. In a few other European countries there are signs of interest in employee financial participation that will bear watching during the coming years. For example, beginning in 1990, employers in Finland are encouraged by law to set up voluntary profit sharing funds with allocations to employees based on profitability or productivity.[2] Recent political changes in Eastern Europe may be the first step toward economic reforms and the possibility of an embryonic development of employee financial participation, particularly in the area of employee ownership. In 1989, the ESOP Association's annual convention in Washington, D.C., was attended by representatives from the People's Republic of China, the Soviet Union, and Poland, all of which have expressed varying degrees of interest in employee ownership. Poland probably offers the greatest potential for the growth of employee ownership because privatization to some extent appears to be inevitable and because Poland had a small successful exposure to privatization of a state-owned enterprise through the employee ownership method prior to World War II.[3]

South American countries such as Venezuela, Peru, and Chile (like Mexico) have had compulsory profit sharing for many years. Employee stock ownership plans, however, are rare in Latin American countries, with the possible exception of Chile where privatization of state-owned enterprises in the 1980s resulted in significant employee ownership.[4] Recent legislation in Argentina designed to facilitate privatization includes incentives to do this through employee ownership.

Governments and employers in most Asian countries have exhibited little interest in employee financial participation of the types common in the West. In the case of Japan, profit sharing plans such as cash and deferred plans similar to those in the United States and Western Europe, are relatively few.[5] Singapore must be mentioned

---

[2]"Voluntary profit funds start," *Industrial Relations Europe*, Vol. XVII, No. 203 (November 1989), p. 2.

[3]For a brief description of this privatization effort, *see* Krzysztof S. Ludwiniak, "Democratization of the Socialist Economy," paper presented to the ESOP Association, 12th Annual Convention, May 24-26, 1989, at Washington, D.C.

[4]*Ibid.*

[5]Bonus payments for all levels of employees in addition to base pay are common, however. Bonus payments in Japan constitute a significant portion, approximately 20 percent, of an employee's total compensation. In Japan, bonuses are treated statistically and practically as part of wages rather than as supplemental benefits and are

Introduction

as a nation which has provided a strong impetus to employers and unions to enter into voluntary "flexible wage" agreements.[6] It remains to be seen what the long-term results of these plans will be.

Employee financial participation plans recently introduced or currently developing in the leading countries generally are not new. There are five broad generic classifications (with overlap in some situations) into which these plans fall: asset accumulation, deferred profit sharing, employee stock ownership, cash profit sharing, and gain sharing.

ASSET ACCUMULATION PLANS

Asset accumulation plans provide for employees to set aside a portion of their pay, and perhaps to receive payments from their employer, in an account that is invested for a period of time before being made available to the employee. The most common examples are savings and thrift plans in the United States. There are similar plans in Europe, some including employer contributions and some not. Here the aim is to encourage employee saving while entailing little risk for the employee and to provide a relatively low-cost fringe benefit for the employer. There is virtually no direct incentive for an employee to work harder, faster, or smarter.

---

paid semi-annually in summer and in December. The amount of money made available for bonus payments is determined by negotiations each spring between the union, if any, and the employer after the financial performance of the company for the prior year is known. Somewhat indirectly, the bonus amount is based on the company's performance for the prior year and the general economic situation. Individual employees receive payments based on age, job, skill, and performance factors. The bonus does not appear to be treated as an incentive payment since the conditions for receiving the bonus are rarely stated in employee contracts. Japanese employees have come to rely on the bonus as a dependable source of income year after year. In that sense, it is similar to the thirteenth month's pay which is common in Europe. See Masanori Hashimoto, "Employment and Wage Systems in Japan and Their Implications on Productivity: A Transaction-Cost Perspective," in Alan S. Blinder (ed.), *Paying for Productivity: A Look at the Evidence* (Washington, DC: The Brookings Institution, 1990); Masahiko Aoki, *Information, Incentives, and Bargaining in the Japanese Economy* (Cambridge and New York: Cambridge University Press, 1988).

[6]Effective in 1988, employers and unions are able to negotiate flexible wage agreements which provide: (1) a basic wage reflecting the value of the job in the market; (2) a one month annual wage supplement; (3) a variable wage component based on the company's profitability or productivity and individual performance; and (4) a small increment of approximately 2 percent to recognize seniority, loyalty, and experience. As of September, 1988, approximately 40 percent of the companies monitored by the Labor Ministry had adopted a flexi-wage system. See "Flexible Response," *Far Eastern Economic Review*, September 8, 1988, p. 141.

DEFERRED PROFIT SHARING PLANS

Deferred profit sharing is a form of deferred compensation under which the allocated profit share is held in trust and is not immediately available to the employee. It is by far the most prevalent type of profit sharing plan in the United States. The Profit Sharing Council of America in its 1989 survey reported that 80 percent of its survey participants had deferred plans.[7] In Europe, cash plans (discussed below) are generally more common than deferred plans.

Generally, a deferred profit sharing plan must be approved by the tax authorities, particularly where tax concessions to employer or employee are involved. In fact, most countries regulate plan features such as eligibility, contribution rates, vesting, investments, distribution, etc.

The United States is unique in its use of deferred profit sharing plans to provide retirement benefits. Since most European nations have well developed public retirement plans, there has been less need for private, supplementary pension plans. Where there is no other company retirement plan in effect in the United States, a deferred profit sharing plan may be the primary retirement benefit provided by the employer. If there is another retirement plan, the deferred profit sharing plan may be a supplement to it. Because of the distinctive use in the United States of deferred profit sharing to provide retirement benefits, such plans have minimal value as employee motivators. The employee receives nothing more than a periodic statement of the amounts accumulated in his or her account and perhaps a projection of prospective retirement income. There is little to induce the employee to be more productive or to work harder or smarter. Obviously, the employee is receiving some degree of *future* financial security, but individual, immediate incentive value is probably minimal. The employer, on the other hand, may deduct from current income amounts paid into the trust up to specified limits, thereby reducing that employer's tax liability. Of course, employers may have other reasons for establishing deferred profit sharing plans, for example:

—to attract and retain high quality employees;
—to provide for capital accumulation through the tax exempt trust;

---

[7]Profit Sharing Council of America, *1989 Profit Sharing Survey* (1988 Experience) (Chicago: Profit Sharing Council of America, 1987), p. 2. The PSCA data is confirmed by a BLS survey. *See* U.S. Department of Labor, Bureau of Labor Statistics, *Employee Benefits in Medium and Large Firms, 1988*, Bulletin 2336, August 1989, p. 106.

Introduction

—to provide an inducement to employees to identify with the company;
—to serve as a part of a total participatory culture within the company.

EMPLOYEE STOCK OWNERSHIP PLANS

As its name implies, an employee stock ownership plan is any plan that provides for employees to become shareholders of the company by which they are employed. An employee may always choose to become a shareholder of his or her employer if the company's shares are publicly traded. The purpose of specific plans, therefore, is to enable employees as a group to accumulate shares more rapidly under favorable conditions. (Stock bonus plans and stock option plans limited to top executives are excluded from this study).

Employee stock ownership plans have acquired a specific meaning in the United States where they have grown tremendously over the last ten years, largely as a result of favorable tax considerations for companies which establish them. The chief difference between ESOPs and other stock ownership plans is that ESOPs make possible a greater share ownership for employees. The United Kingdom seems poised to move in much the same direction, although the tax advantages there have not attained the level they have in the United States.

From the point of view of the employee participant there is little difference between an ESOP and a deferred profit sharing plan, at least to the extent that the profit sharing trust invests in stock of the sponsoring employer. In neither case does the participant (in the U.S. model) receive any stock (or cash) until distribution at some future time. The ESOP participant, like the deferred profit sharing participant, may receive a periodic statement of amounts accumulated in his or her account. Incentive to the employee to improve performance is diffused and generalized in both cases. For most ESOP participants, little is gained in the way of participation in company desision-making because of the ESOP itself.

From the employer's standpoint, the ESOP offers the possibility of additional tax benefits over a deferred profit sharing plan. Employers may also establish ESOPs in hopes of realizing many of the same indirect advantages as those listed above for deferred profit sharing plans.

CASH PROFIT SHARING PLANS

Although deferred profit sharing and cash profit sharing have some common features, the differences are more significant than the similarities. The most important difference from the point of view of the employee participant is that the reward from a cash profit sharing plan is paid much closer in time (and in immediate cash) to the performance being rewarded than it is with deferred profit sharing. This ordinarily would be expected to increase the incentive value of the payment, but it also means that the amount received is taxable in the year it is paid to the employee. In the United States, the employer has no particular encouragement for tax purposes to establish a cash profit sharing plan. Such plans do not require IRS approval and are relatively easy to establish and administer.

GAIN SHARING PLANS

Gain sharing is usually considered as a productivity improving or cost reducing activity not directly related to profit levels. Gain sharing also provides for payments to participants much closer in time to the performance that is being rewarded, and is often organized on a unit-wide basis while profit sharing usually is company-wide. Gain sharing is closer to a true incentive plan than cash profit sharing, and is certainly closer than deferred profit sharing, savings plans, or ESOPs.[8] A given employer may have one or more of all of these plans designed to meet particular company objectives.

THE ROLE OF GOVERNMENT

In many countries, governments have considered to a greater or lesser extent that the aims of profit sharing, stock ownership, and asset formation plans are desirable. They have, therefore, frequently made tax concessions available for plans to encourage their wider utilization. This has often made the support of such plans a political issue. Thus, the compulsory profit sharing system in France owes much to Gaullist views of social order. In 1978, tax concessions for profit sharing were secured by the Liberal party in the United Kingdom as one of the prices for its continued support of the minority

---

[8]Excluded from this study are piecework (individual incentive) plans which are at the high end of the employee incentive scale. They are designed to induce the individual worker to work harder or smarter to increase output and consequently the reward which follows relatively quickly.

Labor government; and in 1987 the Conservative government introduced profit-related pay with the hope of making pay more flexible.

Where tax concessions to employers or employees are involved, the government must weigh the current and future loss of revenue against any benefits that accrue to the public from employee financial participation plans. There always exists the danger that short term revenue needs will dominate considerations for tax advantaged plans; where that occurs the value of the plans to the national economy becomes secondary. It is easy to lose sight of the fact that in many countries, particularly the United States, these plans only *defer* tax liability—they do not eliminate it. It is also easy to forget that in most countries a relatively small percentage of the workforce receives direct benefits from employee financial participation plans making it particularly important that benefits to the minority are not granted at the expense of the majority.

In Europe, a number of countries have seen employee financial participation plans as a useful source of funds for investment. The problem of the generation of investment in welfare-oriented societies is a major issue to which this study will return. Both in Europe and in the United States persistent shortages of private investment have been a major economic problem, and the creation of mechanisms for small investors to accumulate savings has been seen as one way of offsetting this difficulty.

There have been proposals in a number of European countries, particularly the Netherlands, Sweden, West Germany, and Denmark, for legislation to establish collective profit sharing or asset formation plans. The proponents of such measures have justified them partly by the need to generate additional funds for investment. Critics, however, have pointed out that such plans usually include trade union control over the investment funds. As such, they are seen as a means of enhancing the political and economic power of unions and not as a means of meeting individual economic aims.

Such arrangements have often been classified generally as profit sharing, but in addition to the direct union control, they differ from most profit sharing plans in two fundamental respects. First, they are multiemployer plans and draw on the profits of many companies to set up large composite funds. Second, they limit the holding of the individual, either partially or wholly, to a stake in the central fund rather than a holding directly with his own employer. The plans are also compulsory, with all companies above a certain size required to participate. Their aims are also quite different from individual company profit sharing plans. They seek to alter the balance of economic power in favor of unions and to modify the existing economic system by redistributing wealth from stockholders to collective funds.

THE NATURE OF THE STUDY

The reader will easily see by the amount of space devoted to the United States in this study that employee financial participation is much more common in this country than elsewhere. Nevertheless, important developments in the field are unfolding in a number of countries in Europe and elsewhere, some patterned on U.S. plans and others substantially different. Because of the scope of the subject matter of employee financial participation on a world-wide basis, this study is necessarily a survey rather than an exhaustive analysis of the many and varied plans around the world. The additional detail and analysis devoted to plans in the United States does not signify that those plans are better or more effective than others. This study attempts to bring together in one place a description of all of the *major* group employee financial participation plans along with the economic and political background leading up to the current plans, an evaluation of those plans, and a discussion of trends for the future of employee financial participation.

CHAPTER II

Gain Sharing

Nontraditional compensation systems, particularly gain sharing, have grown significantly in popularity during the 1980s.[1] This chapter, based on a survey of 102 American firms[2] and a review of the current literature, examines the current status of gain sharing. Although gain sharing provides the basic principles that drive all team-based pay systems, the concept of gain sharing has evolved so rapidly in the 1980s that the use of the term, without making appropriate qualifications, can become very confusing. The discussion of the various definitions of gain sharing, how they have evolved, and the problems and opportunities that various forms offer, form the core of this chapter.

TEAM-BASED PAY: THE CONCEPT

All systems designed to deliver team-based pay incentives have the same basic premises. First, they always have one or more explicitly stated unit or firm level performance goals that can only be achieved through teamwork. Second, team-based incentive systems must always contain a reward component that is contingent on the successful performance of those goals. Third, to be effective, the reward that is granted must be perceived by the employee receiving it as resulting from contributions that he or she has made. Fourth, the reward granted must be perceived by the employee as a fair reward for the gain achieved. Fifth, and most important for the credibility of the program, the behaviors promoted and the rewards offered must produce a signal that unambiguously relays what precisely is meant by "good performance."

---

[1] Carla O'Dell, with the collaboration of Jerry McAdams, *People, Performance, and Pay* (Houston, TX: American Productivity Center, 1987), pp. 8-9.

[2] The survey of sixty manufacturing and forty-two service sector firms was conducted by telephone and mail to establish the extent and nature of pay for performance programs. Detailed, telephone and personal interviews were conducted with human resource executives, plant managers, and gain sharing facilitators in thirty of these firms.

Although there is no universally agreed upon definition of gain sharing,[3] there is a consensus in the literature on its parameters. All gain sharing programs are designed to develop as close a linkage as possible between cash awards and specific unit-wide productivity or financial goals.[4] Gain sharing is most commonly defined as a unit-wide bonus system designed to reward all eligible participants for improved performance. Gains are shared with all employees in the unit according to a pre-determined formula, and the payoff is dependent on the degree to which a unit achieves a gain in productivity.[5]

In small organizations, the entire company may be tied to a gain sharing program, while in large organizations individual plants, departments, or other sub-units typically use a variety of gain sharing plans tailored to their particular requirements. The most widely recognized types of gain sharing programs are the Scanlon, Rucker, and Improshare plans, although hybrid plans customized on the basis of one or more of these prototypes greatly outnumber the pure forms.

Scanlon plans are widely described in both the popular and academic literature.[6] Typically, a Scanlon plan includes a formula-based bonus system linked to some set of relationships between sales value and labor costs, and an employee suggestion program that is designed to operate through a series of interlocking committees composed of operating managers, supervisors, production employees, and, if the company is unionized, union representatives. The bonus formula generally uses an historical baseline period for setting the standard of performance that triggers bonus payments. There is wider variation in the types of bonus formulas used in Scanlon plans than in either Rucker or Improshare programs.

A Rucker plan is also based on a suggestion system, as well as a less elaborated committee system, and a bonus formula based on value added (labor costs/sales—cost of goods sold or value added/payroll). Generally speaking, the Rucker type of plan has a far less

---

[3]Edward E. Lawler, *Gainsharing Theory and Research: Findings and Future Directions* (in press); George Strauss, *Participatory and Gainsharing Systems: History and Hope* (Berkeley: University of California, Organizational Behavior and Industrial Relations Working Paper No. OBIR-17, 1987).

[4]For example, Lawler, *Gainsharing Theory and Research*; Edward E. Lawler, "Paying for Organizational Performance: Understanding the Approaches and Outcomes for employer and employee," *The Business and Economic Review*, No. 1 (Summer 1987), pp. 13-19; and Ezey M. Dar-El, *Productivity Improvement: Employee Involvement and Gainsharing Plans—Introducing SHRED COST, A New Productivity Improvement Approach* (Amsterdam and New York: Elsevier, 1986), among others.

[5]O'Dell and McAdams, *People, Performance, and Pay*, p. 96.

[6]Christopher S. Miller and Michael H. Schuster, "Gainsharing Plans: A Comparative Analysis," *Organizational Dynamics*, Vol. 16, No. 1 (Summer 1987), p. 44.

Gain Sharing

elaborated participatory structure than the Scanlon plan and is commonly used as an alternative to the Scanlon plan in firms attempting to move from a traditional style of management toward a higher level of employee involvement in decision making.[7]

An Improshare plan uses a bonus formula based on productivity standards that emphasize quantity and quality in relation to total labor hours expended.[8] Of the pure types of gain sharing program, Improshare appears to be the most frequently used form. Improshare programs stress quality and quantity goals derived from engineering standards. Although Improshare programs need not contain an employee involvement component, they can be and usually are combined with quality circles and/or work teams.

DISTRIBUTION OF GAIN SHARING

A 1989 survey by Hewitt Associates reported gain sharing plans in 16 percent of the 705 companies represented in the survey,[9] which can be compared with a 1987 study by O'Dell and McAdams which found gain sharing in 13 percent of the 1,598 firms surveyed.[10] Both surveys reported that gain sharing is more prevalent in goods-producing businesses (Hewitt—18 percent of manufacturing companies; O'Dell—20 percent of manufacturing companies) than in service companies (Hewitt—15 percent; O'Dell—8 percent).[11] Both surveys reported that gain sharing is more likely to be found in larger companies (1,000 or more employees). A more important consideration, perhaps, than company size is the types of employees participating in gain sharing. Although the Hewitt survey examined broader categories (e.g., exempt and non-exempt, salaried and hourly) than the O'Dell survey, both indicate that gain sharing is more likely to be used with managers and supervisors or other selected exempt salaried employees. Approximately one-third of the companies in both surveys include all employees in their gain sharing plans. Unionized employees were covered in only 11 percent of the companies in the Hewitt survey.[12]

Both surveys clearly show gain sharing as a new incentive program for many companies. The Hewitt survey reported that two out

---

[7]*Ibid.*, p. 45.
[8]*Ibid.*, p. 46.
[9]Hewitt Associates, *Compensation Trends and Practices, 1989* (Lincolnshire, IL: Hewitt Associates, 1989), p. 199.
[10]O'Dell and McAdams, *People, Performance, and Pay*, p. 8.
[11]Hewitt, *Compensation Trends*, p. 201; O'Dell, *People, Performance, and Pay*, p. 8.
[12]Hewitt, *Compensation Trends*, p. 199; O'Dell, *People, Performance, and Pay*, p. 36.

of three plans had been in operation less than three years. The O'Dell survey showed that 73 percent of the plans surveyed had been established five years or less.[13]

TEAM-BASED PAY

In order to understand why teamwork emerged in the 1980s as a tool for achieving greater productivity and how this affected the popularity of gain sharing and related incentive systems, it is useful to look at the four major factors which served as catalysts for change in this decade.[14] First, American industry came under enormous competitive pressure from Asian and Western European firms. Second, deregulation in such key industries as air and railroad transportation, communications, construction, and banking altered the business strategies, modes of operation, and the industrial relations systems of large numbers of firms that had previously enjoyed long periods of relative stability. Third, technological change had a heavy impact on a large number of both service and manufacturing enterprises. And finally, less obviously, but still to a significant degree, Japanese employee relations techniques created strong interest in the use of the team concept in the American business community.

All of these factors emerged in a period of industrial retrenchment marked by massive staff cuts that peaked in the 1980-82 recession. Increased use of part-time help, flexible staffing programs, and cost control measures designed to reduce costs while increasing productivity all gained considerable attention as a result. Incentive pay and employee involvement systems of all types came into vogue, and the principles that are the hallmark of gain sharing—pay for productivity, employee involvement, and the team concept—became central themes for regaining a competitive edge in the marketplace. Other nontraditional forms of pay, such as pay for knowledge and lump sum bonuses, also showed impressive growth in popularity in the 1980s.[15]

---

[13]Hewitt, *Compensation Trends*, p. 199; O'Dell, *People, Performance, and Pay*, p. 8.

[14]The Bureau of National Affairs, *The Changing Workplace: New Directions in Staffing and Scheduling* (Washington, D.C.: The Bureau of National Affairs, Inc., 1986), pp. 1-4.

[15]Nancy J. Perry, "Here Come Richer, Riskier Pay Plans," *Fortune*, Vol. 118, No. 4 (December 19, 1988), p. 51.

BROAD TEAM-BASED APPLICATIONS

If one trend stood out in the development of incentive compensation theory in the 1980s, it was the use of incentive pay to assist in meeting the needs of changing businesses. This trend was especially noticeable in gain sharing approaches, where employee participation is usually a centerpiece of action. Not only has employee participation served to reinforce the potential of profit sharing, employee stock ownership plans, and other innovative compensation programs as reward techniques suitable to the promotion of team-based performance, but it has also allowed gain sharing systems to evolve into more complex systems in traditional industrial environments.

One of the firms surveyed by the author presents an interesting example of the evolution of gain sharing from a narrow application to labor efficiency to one focusing on the success of the business strategy. This firm developed a gain sharing plan at a nonunion parts manufacturing plant in 1982 which at first achieved significant success, but then stagnated, and was finally phased out in 1987.

The plant had the lowest productivity level in its manufacturing group between 1981 and the beginning of 1983. At the end of 1983, after gain sharing had been in place for one year, productivity had increased by 22 percent, and the plant had become the top producer in its group. Between 1983 and 1984, however, productivity leveled out, showing no gains over the previous periods. By 1987, the plant's overall performance had dropped to the middle of the group. At this point, management discontinued the program and conducted an investigation to determine why progress in productivity improvement had ceased.

A careful analysis conducted by the management concluded that the program had failed to sustain improvement because it had emphasized the wrong performance factors. Eighty percent of the plan's performance equation was based on rewarding labor efficiency when it should have been targeted on customer satisfaction.

The executive interviewed pointed out that the workers loved the program, but the ideas that were needed could not be introduced into the system because the attention of the workers was focused in the wrong direction. The pay formula was based on the performance history of a process that had become obsolete.

The gain sharing program had succeeded in teaching employees to satisfy goals set up for them by management. What it did not do was lead to an examination of the validity of the goals when conditions changed. The program's performance measures were exclusively directed toward labor efficiencies in the production of a highly complex mix of products. When engineering-based procedures displaced the manually controlled production system, the pay formula proved to be both inappropriate and impossible to redesign. Maintaining market position required that the workforce turn its attention to developing a technical support system that satisfied customer needs. Management decided to switch from a narrow, industrial engineering focus to a more balanced view in which the business strategy would dictate the direction of the design effort. The new approach emphasized the development of a workforce with the capacity to understand the needs of the business and an evaluation of how well current production methods fulfilled those needs.

The use of team-based compensation to meet overall business needs forces adoption of performance objectives that have less definition and clarity than are used in gain sharing plans designed for more narrowly defined industrial processes. The employee is asked to contribute a great deal more insight to his or her work, and the definition of what good performance means is correspondingly more difficult to articulate. Technological innovation, particularly in information systems, is making possible the definition and monitoring of business goals that would have been impossible to track a few years ago. Placing such demands on employees in a rapidly evolving and unstable business environment, however, exerts tremendous pressure on the employee to adapt to these demands on the one hand, and on the capacity of management to maintain credibility and consistency when competitive pressures work at cross-purposes with their commitment to build an effective and stable organization on the other.

GAIN SHARING AND EMPLOYEE PARTICIPATION

Both in the author's survey and in the literature on gain sharing,[16] success in achieving teamwork appears to depend on a steady flow of relevant communication and a strong commitment to developing a participative culture.

The less successful approaches are marked by internal contradictions in which the commitment to participation is undercut by actions that frequently discredit the program in the eyes of the employee, or prove counterproductive in the eyes of operating management. Offering team-based incentives or employee involvement programs on a take-it-or-leave-it basis in labor negotiations, reward

---

[16]See, for example, Lawler, *Gain Sharing Theory and Research*.

systems that have no connection with productivity, and programs that do not provide employees with access to the decision making process are the most frequently encountered defects in failed programs.

Many programs have evolved from concessionary bargaining situations in which plants were facing imminent failure. Successful programs usually share two characteristics. First, management refrains from offering incentive pay before it can afford to do so. In the author's survey, three firms that had introduced gain sharing under concessionary bargaining conditions or in situations where an organizational unit faced serious economic problems had first developed and implemented participative strategies before offering a gain sharing reward system. Second, management convincingly demonstrates its commitment to the program. Each of the three firms that had successfully pursued this strategy possessed a cadre of managers who believed in a participative style of management, were highly committed to the success of their programs, and showed willingness to make a long-term investment in their employees.

A problem that frequently stalls gain sharing and similar initiatives is the need to overcome skepticism among line managers about the effectiveness of employee involvement. Approximately one-third of twenty-six managers interviewed who had substantial responsibilities for implementing employee involvement and gain sharing systems voiced concern over potential opposition from middle managers and supervisors to such programs. Managers and supervisors at these levels frequently seem to fear that gain sharing and other team management concepts will make them expendable.

Resistance among managers and supervisors is extremely difficult to detect, and is capable of inflicting widespread damage to a participative program. Advocates of gain sharing and employee involvement seem to agree that, in the long run, it is essential for operating managers and supervisors to be selected for their capacity to work in team environments, to be trained to understand and work with team building concepts, to be rewarded and recognized for their efforts, and to be assured that such programs are not a threat to their security.

An uncritical acceptance of employee participation is not likely ever to be achieved, however, nor is it necessarily warranted. Depending on perspective, there are some reservations about the use of participative management practices that cannot be easily discounted. For example, many managers interviewed in this survey who are generally supportive of gain sharing and employee participation programs voiced reluctance to yield to employees a level of involvement that threatens what they feel are legitimate management prerogatives, such as overall strategic control of the business. In addition, several managers expressed the opinion that employees neither can share in, nor want to share in the decision making process beyond a relatively narrow band of tasks.

Employees and unions have, in fact, frequently expressed doubts about the sincerity of management, concern over job security, and fear of what will happen to them if they cannot learn new skills as rapidly as management would like. As a result of resistance encountered when management installed an extensive retraining program designed to broaden the job skills of their work force, one of the firms surveyed now takes employee fear of change into consideration whenever new training or employee involvement programs are implemented.

Many of the older employees declined to participate in the training sessions offered because they feared that they would not be able to master the new skills. Two problems were felt to be the source of these anxieties, fear of loss of job security, and fear of loss of respect among their peers. To overcome these fears, management assured them that no employee would lose his or her job for not taking part in the new training program. They also pointed out, however, that the new approach would increase the plant's productivity, and that a more broadly competent work force was needed. Promotions and higher pay would depend on acquiring the new skills. The training programs were then introduced carefully, and every effort was made to remove from the atmosphere anything that might make the situation seem threatening to those who felt intimidated. As a result, most of the employees who had initially feared participating in the program were won over to the new approach.

THE UNION RESPONSE TO THE TEAM CONCEPT

In an increasing number of large corporations, unions now are participating in managerial information sharing and decision making processes to a degree that would have been unthinkable twenty years ago. A growing body of literature, however, indicates that there is considerable suspicion of management's motives for promoting the team concept among many union officials and scholars sympathetic to unions.[17] The substance of their critique is as follows:

---

[17]*See* especially, Charles Ellinger and Bruce Nissen, "A Case Study of a Failed QWL Program: Implications for Labor Education," *Labor Studies Journal*, Vol. 11, No. 4 (Winter 1987), pp. 195-219.

- The team concept does not improve conditions. Instead, it undermines union influence because it gives the appearance of collusion and can result in role and peer conflicts. Programs based on the team concept often place union members and officials who are team leaders in the middle of controversy, since they may be regarded as pseudo-supervisors without real authority on the one hand, and turncoats currying management favor by their former co-workers on the other.[18]
- The team concept has been forced on unions and workers by management, which uses unemployment as a club to force them to accept what is euphemistically called the team approach. In reality, the team approach is dictation of management terms that contain no elements of mutuality. The team concept is not conceived for the mutual benefit of the firm and the employee, but as a tool of management to further increase its control and to destroy the union.[19]
- The strategy for broadening job classifications and designing them around the firm's technologies is heavily weighted in favor of technical or productivity goals that outweigh the human factor. Broadening of job skills may benefit a relatively small number of workers, but this is at the expense of other, perhaps more highly skilled workers, whose jobs are made more restrictive and subject to tighter management controls. Workers rewarded with team leadership roles merely become agents of control, "foremen without ties."[20]
- The proof of management's cynicism is the large number of plant closings that have taken place over the last several years, job losses because of technological innovations, and the shift of industrial production overseas.[21]

CHARACTERISTICS OF TEAM-BASED PAY IN UNION ENVIRONMENTS

One survey respondent with a mixture of union and nonunion gain sharing programs supplied what is probably a typical profile of the differences that exist between gain sharing and related pay systems operated under union and nonunion conditions:

- Its two nonunion programs are based on the same essential model as its three unionized programs. In the two nonunion plants, however, 50 percent of the base wage is centered on productivity, while in union plants the gain sharing bonus is totally separated from the base wage.
- In the nonunion plants, the performance criteria are generated by employee members of the employee-management joint committee,

---

[18] Donald M. Wells, *Empty Promises: Quality of Working Life Programs and the Labor Movement* (New York: Monthly Review Press, 1987), pp. 78-101.
[19] Wells, *Empty Promises*, pp. 135-137; Mike Parker and Jane Slaughter, *Choosing Sides: Unions and the Team Concept* (Boston: South End Press, 1988), pp. 39-41.
[20] Wells, *Empty Promises*, pp. 142-143.
[21] Parker and Slaughter, *Choosing Sides*, pp. 39-40.

while in the three unionized plants the programs are designed by management. Employees in the two nonunion plants are much more heavily involved in plan design then their counterparts in the unionized plants.
- Eligibility thresholds to qualify for a payout are much higher in the nonunion plants. In unionized plants, 1040 hours of work qualifies, while in the nonunion plants 1700 hours are required. Since management was neutral on the issue, these figures reflect the wishes of the union leadership and its members for the former, the participating employees for the latter.

The lower requirements selected in the unionized plants tend to diminish the size of the bonus for individuals, but guarantee that more can share in the bonus pool. The higher requirement of the nonunionized plants restricts the number of participants, but increases the size of the bonus. Employees in nonunion environments tend to maximize the size of the bonus and actively work at keeping employee population to a minimum. By contrast, unions are sensitive to pleasing a varied constituency and try to avoid internal bickering and divisiveness. Fear of divisiveness was felt to be the chief reason motivating negative union reactions to gain sharing, according to this firm's managers.

Goal definition and development of teamwork can have both positive and negative effects in a union environment. Many of the unionized companies surveyed indicated that they do not want employees challenging management decisions, particularly where compensation practices are concerned. Several commented that they would not permit a situation to develop that allowed unions to challenge what they feel are management prerogatives. For example, while some managers expressed the view that workers were justified in questioning management compensation packages that were excessive, most were opposed to allowing unions to get involved in executive compensation, as Chrysler seemed to allow in its 1988 negotiations with the United Auto Workers (UAW). The agreement that resulted stipulates that executives would not be paid bonuses if workers did not receive anything from the profit sharing plan.[22]

On the other side of this issue, both unions and older workers have sometimes expressed reluctance to take on the decision making responsibilities implicit in team management. One company encountered difficulty in a major plant after having successfully introduced gain sharing into several plants in other areas of the country. In this plant, unlike in the others, the firm was not the dominant

---

[22]"Chrysler Suggests More Equity in Payment of Bonuses to Execs., Profit Sharing to UAW," *Daily Labor Report*, No. 76 (April 16, 1988), pp. A15-A16.

employer, and past management-union relations had not been as positive as they had been at the other locations. When the management team charged with developing gain sharing and employee involvement programs asked union officials to elaborate on their objections to gain sharing, their reactions reflected concerns centering on job security, mutual trust, and where accountability would lie if the program failed.

The union questioned the management team's assertions, explanations, and beliefs about the merits of contingency performance. Is gain sharing really good for business? Do management decisions affect the work plan under team conditions? For example, is it good business to rework scrap and recycle it? Can we be doing the wrong things efficiently in the name of teamwork? If management makes the wrong decision and the workers effectively execute it, whose responsibility is that, and who pays the penalty for failure? Will gain sharing shift the onus of business failure or poor decision making to the workers' shoulders and let management off the hook?

This firm's management feels that the union's response mirrors the difference in value orientations between management and the unions. These types of questions must be dealt with to the satisfaction of both parties if teamwork, employee participation, and pay systems based on gain sharing principles are to have a realistic chance of success. In the words of one human resources executive at this firm, "Unions don't want the monkey on their backs for failed business strategies. They do want productivity pay when objectives are achieved, but they don't want to be held accountable for management's mistakes."

Programs surveyed by the author that are successful or show promise of succeeding in union environments tend to share most of the following characteristics:

- The union and company have a history of good relations or are working at improving them. This may be more difficult to achieve with a local affiliated with an international than it is with an independent union, since the firm's position on labor-management programs may be at odds with the parent union's stance. The local of an international union in one of the surveyed firms did split with the parent union on such issues, however, where the interests of both the plant's management and the local's leadership and membership overrode the parent union's opposition to labor-management teams.
- The firm is a dominant employer in the area. This situation offers a short term advantage to the firm in that time is needed to resolve program inadequacies and to create a climate supportive of the necessary team process. The disadvantage is that management may

have a false sense of security about the program's positive reception because employees are reluctant to provide negative feedback.
- Both the union's leadership and employees are interested in the proposal itself. As the foregoing discussion on union reaction to participative programs indicates, however, conflicts will inevitably occur. When they do, they must be dealt with consistently and in a manner that will not dissipate initial feelings of goodwill.
- Management makes a commitment to avoid adjusting standards unless process or capital changes are truly required. If such changes are anticipated, they are openly discussed between management and the union. A joint management-union committee is usually created to handle such situations.

The differences between union and management perspectives on so many basic issues seem to indicate that we are not yet entering into an era of unquestioned increased union-management cooperation. It is a mistake, however, to see the importance of these issues as being solely dependent on union-management relations. They involve a complex interaction of economic and competitive forces that invite employees to examine their interests in light of their own bargaining positions, independent of either force. Product quality, shareholder interests, mergers and acquisitions, government regulation, and local economic conditions all affect the capacity of the firm to attract employees and to offer the kind of working environment that allows both the firm and the employees it selects to enter into a mutually beneficial agreement.

Management will always pursue its goals of turning a profit, maximizing shareholder returns, and improving employee relations. Unions will continue to impress on their memberships the value of protection from exploitation through work rule changes, and the union's ability to gain for them higher wages, better benefits, and more job security. It is the decision of the employee that is pivotal to the nature of the outcome. Employees have a vital interest in gaining more control over their careers and satisfying their individual aspirations, including the capacity to have a more direct influence over company performance and a fair return for their efforts.[23]

It is on these issues that the success of team-based pay and employee participation systems hinge. A destructive confrontation between union and management, bad faith bargaining, or manipulation on the part of either union or management produces no winners, only losers. Each side must be able to cope with the requirements of worker-management cooperation without forgetting that other stakeholders (such as the firm's customers) have considerable

---

[23]Timothy L. Ross, Larry L. Hatcher, and Dan B. Adams, "How Unions View Gainsharing," *Business Horizons*, Vol. 28, No. 4 (July-August 1985), pp. 15-22.

impact on the firm's survival and prosperity. In a competitive world, management vision and employee commitment must both be highly developed in order for a firm to make effective use of the team concept.

TEAM-BASED PAY: WHITE COLLAR APPLICATIONS

White-collar employees (those classified as executives, managers, professionals, sales, administrative, or support personnel), today account for approximately 55 percent of the American work force. Some observers suggest that figure could rise to 90 percent by the turn of the century.[24] Twenty-one of the firms surveyed by the author were found to have either developed or expressed an interest in developing team-based compensation systems for their middle management and administrative personnel.

Most of these programs were designed in the 1980s, and most combine features of their firms' executive pay programs with cost control provisions and the team concept commonly emphasized in gain sharing systems. Such programs contain business performance goals, unit efficiency and effectiveness measures, and provision for awarding either a group incentive, an individual incentive, or both.

In the white-collar sector, gain sharing seems to fare best in clerical applications where there is a reasonably strong tie between the effort expended and results achieved. For example, one insurance company has an Improshare-type gain sharing system for employees who process its group employee benefit claims. The plan includes 3,000 employees in widely scattered field offices, ranging in size from 50 to 150 employees. Statistical controls are natural to the claims adjusting process and were already built into the system when gain sharing was introduced.

This company uses quality circles in these operations. The quality circles had been installed prior to the introduction of gain sharing, however, and are not formally linked to the gain sharing program, although they made its introduction easier. According to the executive interviewed, quality circles had evolved naturally in the system, and were not consciously installed by management. Conceptually, this Improshare program stands alone, but fits into an environment that had already developed the necessary participative mechanisms to support it.

---

[24] American Productivity Center, *Participative Approaches to White-Collar Productivity Improvement* (Washington, D.C.: United States Department of Labor, BLMR 116, 1987), p. 1.

Financial Services Sector

In contrast to the industrial firms surveyed, which tend to install employee involvement systems prior to installing incentive pay formulas, firms in the financial service sector tend to back into employee involvement systems that have either evolved as a matter of necessity to support the pay incentive systems or have evolved independently of them. Rarely do financial service firms seem to make employee involvement a prime objective of the system in the same way that industrial firms do.

One result is that both the pay systems and the employee involvement systems that gain notice are being driven by financial objectives derived from automated information systems. Typical is the experience of a large bank located on the West Coast. Prior to 1979, this bank had used incentive plans almost exclusively in functional areas and branch operations where it was necessary to provide a competitive total compensation package. Today, it uses over thirty different incentive plans throughout the bank, and has several more in the design stage. The emphasis of the bank's approach to incentive compensation has shifted from providing a competitive pay package to engineering incentive pay packages that enhance performance.

Use of incentive pay programs has been growing in this bank since 1982, but the pace has quickened since 1985, when management began to feel the impact of deregulation in the form of intensified competition from both other banks and financial services firms. The development of a sales oriented culture, for example, has become a high priority not only because the bank must compete to seize new business opportunities, but because it must also defend traditional services and product lines that were formerly immune from competition.

The incentive programs favored vary from pure individual merit systems through individual incentive pay based on unit performance, to incentive plans that pay strictly group bonuses. The foundation of this bank's approach to compensation is a base salary system in which salaries may not exceed the mid-point of the pay range. Any compensation awarded that is above mid-point must come from its variable compensation systems. To fund these systems, set percentages of corporate or unit profits are fed into bonus pools. The programs are consciously designed to reflect the impact of employee performance on revenue production. Targets are based on product lines, and profits are calculated for each product. The stated objective is to structure the reward system so that the connection between product line and profitability achieved is as highly visible to the employee as possible.

An Eastern bank launched its first incentive programs in 1983. These programs gained new importance in 1986, when the chief executive officer gave his support to the use of incentive based pay. The programs are built around strategic business plans and emphasize team effort, combined with stress on individual contributions to the team effort. Two programs are tightly coordinated: a management incentive program that applies to all management level employees and depends on the bank's overall profitability; and productivity pay plans based on unit performance.

The organizational level at which pay for performance systems are applied can range from teller to unit manager, depending on the composition of the work team and the mission of the unit. If a manager has received a bonus from the executive program, he or she is not eligible for a productivity plan bonus, or vice versa. The chief business in most of the banks surveyed is the bank's investment program. These programs are selectively tied to the measurement of tangible performance objectives in the areas of cost reduction, profitability, and/or customer service.

If there is one factor that can be pointed to as pervasive throughout the financial service firms surveyed for this study, it is the dependence of their incentive programs on powerful, computer-driven information systems. These systems provide a wide range of potential pay variables that can be linked to the institution's businesses. As might be expected, these pay variables are usually based on financial or cost control objectives. On the positive side, they offer an opportunity to keep the programs flexible and sharply attuned to fluctuations in the market place. On the negative side, they can become so complex that they are understood only by those who develop them, result in objectives that work at cross-purposes to one another, and lose the capacity to do what compensation plans meant to improve performance must do, remain comprehensible to the employee.

Industrial Firms

Four of the industrial firms surveyed that had experience with gain sharing either had or were in the process of installing team-based incentive systems for all or part of their white-collar work force. In firms that have prior experience with gain sharing, the influence of gain sharing principles is dependent on the degree of interaction and cooperation that exists between the developers and administrators of the gain sharing programs and those responsible for developing the white-collar incentive pay systems.

In one large firm with a sophisticated array of gain sharing programs, the company developed a credit service sub-unit which, although initially established to help finance the sale of its products, became a profit center in its own right. The new pay program (established in early 1988) for this unit is designed exclusively for white-collar workers. The manufacturing engineering group, which was responsible for developing most of the company's gain sharing systems, was deeply involved in the development and implementation of the incentive pay program for this unit.

The pay system has two components, one developed to reward individual performance in conformity with job requirements, and one for improvements made in customer service. Individual performance pay can be as high as 20 percent of pay, and customer service bonuses, the team-based component of the program, can be as high as 5 percent of pay. The goals set for improving customer service are determined by the employees themselves.

Any increase in savings resulting from customer service improvements is shared between the employees and the company, with the company receiving 75 percent of the savings and the employees the remaining 25 percent. All employees receive equal shares from a bonus pool. Employees can double their "share" if all customer service goals are met. Thus, the customer service component has the potential to reach 10 percent of pay. Profit sharing in this unit is tied primarily to managerial positions, and increases with pay level. The gain sharing component is associated with those positions, generally occupying the lower pay grades, that have a direct impact on operations identified as affecting the quality of customer service.

A second firm has been exploring incentive compensation programs since 1986 because its management feels that traditional merit pay programs are merely entitlements that offer a guaranteed percentage increase without truly measuring performance. One operation, quite atypical of the environments in which team-based pay systems are usually applied, deals with the development of investment contracts for the sale or lease of timber stands.

The time lines in this business are unusually long, requiring from one to two years to show business results and a much longer time, up to twenty years, to show the impact of a proactive investment strategy. Twenty-five percent of the investment operation is based on public offerings of limited partnerships. Since a limited partner invests for the cash return only, the objective is for the partnerships to earn enough cash to attract investors. Management wished to direct the attention of their investors to increasing cash returns.

The firm's investors include 132 people located in the Southeastern United States, and another 40 in the Northeast. Because of their wide dispersion, the firm's administrative control over these investors is very weak. There is a fundamental clash of objectives that confronts the firm's investment strategy. On the one hand, the sale of the limited partnerships is an important operation that must be encouraged and sustained. On the other hand, management perceives the real value of their investors' contribution as coming when they begin to think like developers.

For this reason, the new incentive program has to be monitored carefully. Too strong an emphasis on producing and conserving cash can discourage the intelligent analysis needed to balance short-term payoffs against long-term investment potential. Management was actively struggling with this dilemma at this writing, but had developed neither training programs nor an incentive strategy that satisfactorily balances short- and long-range objectives.

Team-based pay has proven somewhat disappointing in this application for another reason as well. Under the merit pay system that had previously been used, everyone, according to the manager interviewed, felt fairly treated. Introduction of team-based incentives produced high variability in pay from area to area, not because of performance differences, but because of varying economic and market conditions in different regions. As a result, management has had to reintroduce sufficient homogeneity into the pay program to overcome perceptions among many of the investor-employees that the incentive program is unfair. Thus, in 1987, the incentive opportunity was scaled back from 20 percent to 10 percent of base pay for the incentive component of the pay package because of the impossibility of reconciling these regional differences.

The current pay plan is a hybridized system that offers substantial base earnings, a merit program to recognize individual effort and guide individual development, and a group incentive to encourage meeting productivity goals. Both the merit and incentive pay components of this program are tied to financial measures based on the level of financial success achieved, a financial estimate of the outlook for product(s), forecasts for outcomes, and the nature of the managerial and operational accountabilities of the various plan participants.

Future of Team-based Pay in the White-Collar Sector

Gain sharing systems based on manufacturing and related industrial processes appear to have a future limited primarily to clerical operations in the white-collar sector of the economy because of the requirement for very explicit connections between pay and performance measurement. Difficulty of measurement, the perception among employees in these categories that they may lose security of income, and problems in dealing with questions of equity seem to be the chief obstacles blocking their wider usage in the white-collar sector.

On the other hand, the availability of sophisticated automated information systems capable of defining a wide range of measurable performance variables and the increased emphasis on customer satisfaction in both the service and industrial sectors of the economy favor the development of incentive systems that encourage relatively complex employee involvement in the execution of broad business strategies. The explosive growth of new technologies is having a particularly dramatic effect on both the growth and skill configurations required of the work force in this sector of the economy.

GAIN SHARING RESULTS

Although there has been a significant amount of research on structure, implementation, and perceived results of gain sharing, there are few studies that relate gain sharing statistically to improved firm performance. Where gain sharing has been implemented, the overwhelming response has been positive. One of the most recent and extensive studies found that gain sharing's (Scanlon, Improshare, and Rucker) impact on productivity was reported as "positive" or "very positive" in over 90 percent of the companies surveyed. The impact on costs and quality also exceeded 75 percent with positive or very positive responses.[25]

In 1984, Bullock and Lawler reported on their wide-ranging literature search in the gain sharing area.[26] They found that approximately 75 percent of the gain sharing plans reported some improvement in productivity, quality, cost reduction, or customer service. Two-thirds reported improvements in individual attitudes, morale, and quality of work life. A large proportion reported more ideas,

---

[25] O'Dell and McAdams, *People, Performance, and Pay*, p. 38.
[26] R. J. Bullock and Edward E. Lawler, "Gainsharing: A Few Questions, and Fewer Answers," *Human Resource Management*, Vol. 23, No. 1 (Spring 1984), pp. 23-40.

Gain Sharing

suggestions, and innovations.[27] They also found, as have others, that gain sharing works best when integrated with a participative approach. Unfortunately, there is little evidence about why gain sharing works.

A General Accounting Office (GAO) study in 1981 reported that firms with productivity sharing (gain sharing) plans in operation for over five years averaged almost 29 percent savings in workforce cost for their most recent five-year period. Most firms in the study believed that the benefits anticipated from their plans had been realized.[28] The GAO study, however, concludes that none of these plans should be viewed as a panacea and that they are likely to succeed only where management is willing to devote the time and effort to implement the plans effectively.

INTEGRATING GAIN SHARING AND PROFIT SHARING

Several companies in this study have an array of employee financial participation plans, but it is particularly common for a company to combine profit sharing and gain sharing. These plans should complement or reinforce each other to meet the changing economic needs of the business and to provide appropriate incentives to employees. Unlike gain sharing approaches, profit sharing does not lend itself to the development of measurements that can be readily tied to the performance of the work force. Gain sharing is sometimes perceived as a system that might divert resources away from necessary reinvestment. In this view, gains in productivity should not be paid for if no profits are achieved. Several of the managers interviewed in this study said that they did not feel that a gain sharing program should be installed if the firm is not showing a profit. A widely used approach is to keep gain sharing and profit sharing programs separate but complementary to one another. Many large organizations have adopted this approach in their major plants and subsidiaries. Using profit sharing and gain sharing systems in this manner deals directly with the need to motivate employees to control costs and improve operational efficiency while keeping them aware of the firm's overall performance and viability.[29] Gain sharing plans typically reflect costs and measure productivity at the sub-unit level,

---

[27]*Ibid.*, p. 31.
[28]United States General Accounting Office, *Productivity Sharing Programs: Can They Contribute to Productivity Improvements?* (Gaithersburg, MD: U.S. General Accounting Office, 1981), pp. 15-16.
[29]Lawler, "Paying for Organizational Performance," p. 14.

but do not usually reflect either the operating costs or the earnings of the total business.

Using gain sharing and profit sharing in tandem allows payouts from gain sharing when the organization is losing money but the operating unit is achieving its assigned productivity goals, and payouts from profit sharing when unit goals are not being achieved but the organization is enjoying a profitable year.[30] The company that uses such a system has an opportunity to bring such anomalies to the attention of the workers, to retain a perspective that underscores the value of both types of performance, and to stimulate inquiry into why there might be inconsistency between the two systems.

In this way, both productivity goals and profit outcomes are brought to the attention of the employees and the need to change the system, if it is necessary to do so, can be made more readily apparent. Coordinated in this way, separate but complementary gain sharing and profit sharing programs enable management to use the pay system to educate the work force about the business and as a signalling device for defining what good performance is under a given set of conditions.

---

[30]*Ibid.*

CHAPTER III

Profit Sharing

The United States has proved to be the most fertile soil for the growth of profit sharing. In 1989 there were well over 400,000 companies practicing deferred, cash, or combination profit sharing. Over one-fifth of the American work force was covered by a profit sharing plan. Capital assets in deferred profit sharing plans are estimated to exceed $300 billion.[1]

Significant growth in profit sharing has occurred since 1982. A 1987 survey conducted by the American Productivity Center (APC) and the American Compensation Association found that nearly 30 percent of the profit sharing plans were implemented between 1982 and 1987.[2] At least some of that growth may be attributed to an increase in union-negotiated profit sharing plans for production and maintenance employees. In the early 1980s, profit sharing was often introduced as part of a concession bargaining situation, thus involving more hourly paid collective bargaining unit employees. This growth of collectively bargained profit sharing plans, the increase in federal legislation affecting profit sharing plans, and an increased interest in cash profit sharing as a flexible compensation tool have been the most important developments in the profit sharing field since the first edition of this study was issued in 1979.[3]

THE HISTORY OF PROFIT SHARING

Historians of profit sharing have identified Albert Gallatin, secretary of the treasury under Jefferson and Madison, as the originator of America's first profit sharing plan, established in 1797 at his glass works in New Geneva, Pennsylvania.[4] It was only in the final decades of the nineteenth century, however, that profit sharing

---

[1]This estimate is based on total private pension assets of approximately $1.5 trillion, of which approximately $500 billion are defined contribution plans. It is estimated that 60 percent of defined contribution plans are deferred profit sharing plans.

[2]Carla O'Dell and Jerry McAdams, *People, Performance, and Pay* (Houston: American Productivity Center, 1987), p. 8.

[3]Geoffrey W. Latta, *Profit Sharing, Employee Stock Ownership, Savings, and Asset Formation Plans in the Western World* (Philadelphia: Wharton Industrial Research Unit, 1979).

[4]"Albert Gallatin," *Profit Sharing Trends*, Vol. XIV (March-April, 1959), pp. 2-3.

really began to expand. The origin of some of the early profit sharing proposals was primarily religious. A group of Protestant clergy saw profit sharing as a possible antidote to some of the social problems that accompanied industrialization. A leading member of this group, Nicholas Paine Gilman, was the author of two books on profit sharing[5] and helped form the Association for the Promotion of Profit Sharing in 1892.[6] In 1899 Gilman identified thirty-four profit sharing plans in the United States.[7] By 1896, however, a survey indicated that, of fifty plans, thirty-three had ceased entirely, and only twelve were fully operating.[8]

Much of this early movement was supported by people outside of industry itself. One significant exception was Colonel William Cooper Procter, who was the chief architect of Procter & Gamble's profit sharing plan introduced in 1887. The plan divided net profits between the company and its employees in the same proportion that total wages bore to the total cost of production and marketing. Each employee received a semi-annual cash dividend according to the ratio of his wage to total wages. Procter believed that profit sharing would increase employee involvement in the company and improve efficiency.[9]

The spread of worker unrest created a renewed interest in profit sharing during the early years of the twentieth century. Organizations such as the National Civic Federation saw profit sharing as a means of reducing labor problems.[10] As one supporter wrote, "By making the interests of employer and employee identical, profit sharing will tend to lessen antagonism and friction between owners and employed workers, and to substitute in their stead industrial harmony."[11]

---

[5]Nicholas Paine Gilman, *Profit Sharing Between Employer and Employee* (Boston and New York: Houghton, Mifflin and Company, 1889); Nicholas Paine Gilman, *A Dividend to Labor: A Study of Employees' Welfare Institutions* (Boston and New York: Houghton, Mifflin and Company, 1899).
[6]Kenneth M. Thompson, *Profit Sharing: Democratic Capitalism in American Industry* (New York: Harper and Brothers, 1949), p. 10.
[7]Gilman, *Profit Sharing Between Employer and Employee*, pp. 386-387, 389.
[8]Paul Monroe, "Profit Sharing in the United States," *American Journal of Sociology*, Vol. I (May, 1896), p. 709.
[9]Alfred Lief, *It Floats* (New York: Rhinehart and Company, Inc., 1958), pp. 73-76.
[10]J. J. Jehring, "The Development of the Profit Sharing Idea in the U.S.," in *A New Approach to Collective Bargaining?* (Madison, WI: Center for Productivity Motivation, School of Commerce, University of Wisconsin, 1962), p. 12.
[11]Arthur W. Burritt, et al., *Profit Sharing: Its Principles and Practice* (New York: Harper and Brothers Publishers, 1918), p. 78.

The reaction of the trade union movement was not favorable. In 1916, Samuel Gompers, president of the American Federation of Labor, said of profit sharing:

> This proposition has never been seriously considered by the organizations of labor. I desire to say further that it has come under my observation that some employers who have inaugurated systems of so-called profit sharing have pared down the wages of their employees so that the combined sharing of profits and their wages did not equal the wages of employees in other companies in the same line of industry. What we are especially interested in more than profit sharing is a fair living wage, reasonable hours and fair conditions of employment.[12]

Despite this opposition, the number of profit sharing plans increased between 1910 and 1920. It was in this period that some of the most famous plans that still exist today were established, including those of Eastman Kodak (1912) and Sears Roebuck (1916). Kodak's wage dividend plan was a recognition of the company's faith in its employees. The Sears plan was introduced at the suggestion of a stockholder as a means of creating a better feeling between employee and employer which would also benefit the company.[13]

In the United States during the decade following World War I, emphasis shifted from cash profit sharing to employee stock ownership as a means of interesting employees in the success of companies for which they worked. These plans provided that an employee's share of profits be distributed to him/her in the form of stock or credits on the purchase price of stock. Since stock prices were inflating rapidly, these plans were attractive to employees. Through such stock ownership plans, corporations sought to promote industrial peace and to encourage a sense of proprietorship and loyalty to the firm. Thus, an employee who was a stockholder would be less likely to strike and more likely to take the viewpoint of the owners or managers.[14]

The Great Depression essentially wiped out profit sharing and employee stock ownership as profits disappeared and stock values plummeted. Congressional interest in the subject in the late 1930s led, however, to a new growth of profit sharing plans. In 1939 the report of the Vandenberg Subcommittee of the Senate Finance Committee on profit sharing suggested that such plans were associated

---

[12] The National Civic Federation, *Profit Sharing by American Employers* (New York: E.P. Dutton and Company, 1916), pp. 368-369.
[13] Michael Marrone, "A Brief History of Profit Sharing," *Profit Sharing*, Vol. 36, No. 6 (June, 1988), p. 14.
[14] Burritt, et al., *Profit Sharing*, pp. 85-88.

with labor peace, employee security, and business success.[15] Senator Vandenberg summarized the committee's investigation as follows:

> The committee finds that profit sharing, in one form or another, has been and can be eminently successful, when properly established, in creating employer-employee relations that make for peace, equity, efficiency, and contentment. We believe it to be essential to the ultimate maintenance of the capitalistic system. We have found veritable industrial islands of "peace, equity, efficiency, and contentment," and likewise prosperity, dotting an otherwise...relatively turbulent industrial map, all the way across the continent. This fact is too significant of profit-sharing's possibilities to be ignored or depreciated in our national quest for greater stability and greater democracy in industry.[16]

Tax Advantages

This Senate report created additional public and management interest in profit sharing, particularly as a means of promoting industrial peace. Subsequent to, and partly influenced by, the favorable findings on profit sharing by the Vandenberg Subcommittee, Congress passed legislation that provided tax advantages for qualified, deferred profit sharing plans.

Prior to World War II most profit sharing plans were cash plans which paid cash bonuses to employees annually, or perhaps semiannually. Federal regulations to control wage rates during the war encouraged the use of deferred profit sharing plans. In an effort to stabilize wages and salaries, the government did not permit cash plans to be adopted after October 2, 1942. As long as the wage and salary controls were in force, only deferred profit sharing plans that conformed to the requirements of the Internal Revenue Code were permitted.[17]

During the war years federal tax rates were sufficiently high that the tax advantages of qualified profit sharing plans were a strong incentive to establish profit sharing and pension plans. If a plan met the Internal Revenue Service (IRS) requirements, employers were permitted to deduct, as a wage cost, profit sharing payments up to a maximum of 15 percent of total compensation.[18] Employees found

---

[15]United States Congress, Senate, Subcommittee of the Committee on Finance, *Survey of Experiences in Profit Sharing and Possibilities of Incentive Taxation* (Washington, DC: U.S. Government Printing Office, 1939), pp. 159-160.

[16]*Ibid.*, p. 9.

[17]F. Beatrice Brower, *Sharing Profits with Employees*, Studies in Personnel Policy No. 162 (New York: National Industrial Conference Board, 1957), pp. 8-9. The Internal Revenue Code can be found at 26 *United States Code* (U.S.C.).

[18]Brower, *Sharing Profits with Employees*, p. 9.

the plans attractive because the deferred payments were not currently subject to income taxation and because lump-sum payments made at retirement could be treated as long-term capital gains.

The Rise of Deferred Profit Sharing

Deferred distribution plans also provided a means of attracting and retaining workers during these years. Because wages and salaries were controlled and frozen to a large extent, employers were eager to find a permissible way to provide attractive benefits to hold skilled employees and to attract desirable applicants. Consequently, many profit sharing plans were adopted during the war for this purpose. Included among the other fringe benefits instituted for employees during this time were pension plans designed to supplement public old-age benefits. Retirement income plans financed by a portion of company profits were popular because they allowed the employer to provide benefits without assuming the obligations of fixed contributions as required by an actuarily determined (defined benefit) pension plan. Deferred plans grew rapidly. The IRS approved 2,471 deferred profit sharing plans between January 1, 1940, and August 31, 1946, of which over one-half (1,631) were established during the latter part of the war, September, 1942, through December, 1944.[19] Between 1946 and 1955, an additional 6,000 plans were approved.[20]

Although cash profit sharing preceded deferred profit sharing, the latter has become the dominant type of plan. The 1989 survey by the Profit Sharing Council of America (PSCA) reported that 79 percent of its survey participants had deferred plans, 4 percent had cash plans, and 17 percent had combination plans.[21] Another recent survey by Hewitt Associates found that 16 percent of the surveyed companies (705) had cash profit sharing plans.[22]

---

[19] Stewart and Cooper, *Profit Sharing for Wage Earners and Executives*, p. 56.
[20] Gunnar Engen, "A New Direction and Growth in Profit Sharing," *Monthly Labor Review*, Vol. 90, No. 7 (July, 1967), p. 4.
[21] Profit Sharing Council of America, *1989 Profit Sharing Survey (1988 Experience)* (Chicago: Profit Sharing Council of America, 1989), p. 2.
[22] Hewitt Associates, *Compensation Trends and Practices, 1989* (Lincolnshire, IL: Hewitt Associates, 1989), p. 195.

TYPES OF PLANS

Profit sharing plans are only one of several types[23] of "defined contribution" plans. According to the Internal Revenue Code, a defined contribution plan is one which "provides for an individual account for each participant and for benefits based solely on the amount contributed to the participant's account, and any income, expenses, gains and losses, and any forfeitures of accounts of other participants which may be allocated to such participant's account."[24] A "defined benefit" plan is described as any plan that is not a defined contribution plan.

Treasury regulations describe a profit sharing plan as "primarily a plan of deferred compensation" that is "established and maintained by an employer to provide for the participation in his profits by his employees or their beneficiaries."[25]

Deferred Plans

Deferred profit sharing plans, like savings plans and employee stock ownership plans, provide participating employees with special sums of money placed in trust, in addition to their regular wages or salaries. The primary purpose of most deferred plans, where there is no pension plan in effect, is retirement income. Deferred plans, as well as cash and combination plans, may have other objectives as well: 1) to provide benefits for disability, death, or employment termination (layoff) prior to retirement; 2) to create an incentive for increasing productivity and decreasing costs; 3) to accumulate tax-deferred capital reserves for employees, which may contribute to capital formation and employee stock ownership; and 4) to attract and retain quality personnel by sharing the rewards of the free enterprise system throughout the organization.[26]

Contributions. The annual tax deduction for qualified plans is limited to 15 percent of the compensation of covered participants, and contributions must be "substantial and recurring" in order to maintain tax-exempt status. Other than those broad parameters there is wide discretion left to the employer in determining the company profit sharing contribution. Interestingly, the Tax Reform Act of 1986 completely eliminated the requirement that a company must

---

[23]Other types: stock bonus, money-purchase pension, thrift-savings, employee stock ownership plans.
[24]Internal Revenue Code, Section 414 (i).
[25]Treasury Regulations, Section 1.401-1 (b) (1) (ii).
[26]Profit Sharing Council, *Profit Sharing Philosophy*, p. 5.

have current or accumulated profits in order to make a contribution to a deferred profit sharing plan. It is likely, however, that most companies do relate contributions to profits. The 1989 PSCA survey reported that 35 percent of the 410 plans surveyed utilized a contribution formula related to profits. Another 46 percent of the companies stated that contributions were made on a "discretionary" basis determined by the employer.[27] It is likely that many of those companies also base their contribution on profits in some way. Those companies which do not base contributions on profits utilize measures such as a specific percentage of participant's deposits, a specific percentage of participant's pay, and percentages related to revenues.

The level of employer contribution is probably the most important single aspect of a profit sharing plan. In general, that contribution must be equitable to the owners of the company and must be large enough to be of significance to the employees.[28] After an approximate level of contribution is determined, the profit sharing company must decide more specifically how it will determine and express the amount of its contribution. There are three basic methods: fixed formula plans, discretionary plans, and fixed plus discretionary plans. Fixed formula plans specify a percentage of profits, compensation, or participant's deposits. Discretionary plans provide for an annually determined (by the employer or the directors) contribution. In fixed plus discretionary plans, the plan calls for a stated percentage plus an additional discretionary amount determined by the employer.[29] The PSCA survey for 1989 indicated that 46 percent of the survey plans utilized a discretionary method; 42 percent expressed a specific formula; 7 percent had a combination of a specified percentage plus a discretionary amount; and 4 percent was classified as "other."[30]

Average employer contributions as a percentage of pay have remained relatively stable since the late 1950s at a level of approximately 8 percent. More recently, employer contributions to all types of plans have shown a very narrow spread, ranging from a low of 8.7 percent to a high of 9.5 percent of pay (see Table III-1). Contributions to deferred plans have been more stable than contributions to cash or combination plans, perhaps reflecting the fact that deferred plans are often the only retirement plan in some companies, which

---

[27] Profit Sharing Council, *1989 Profit Sharing Survey*, p. 6.
[28] Raymond H. Giescke, "The Company Contribution," in *Guide to Modern Profit Sharing* (Chicago: Profit Sharing Council of America, 1973), pp. 38-39.
[29] Profit Sharing Council, *Profit Sharing Philosophy*, p. 10.
[30] Profit Sharing Council, *1989 Profit Sharing Survey*, p. 6.

TABLE III-1
Employer Contributions as Percentage of Pay
1980-1988

	Cash Plans	Deferred Plans	Combination Plans	All Plans
1988	5.0	7.9	13.1	8.8
1987	11.1	8.0	12.3	8.7
1986	7.8	8.1	13.5	8.8
1985	9.6	8.4	10.6	8.7
1984	8.7	8.5	10.0	8.8
1983	7.4	8.3	10.8	8.8
1982	8.1	8.5	11.3	8.9
1981	7.6	9.0	10.6	9.2
1980	10.3	8.9	12.4	9.5

Source: Profit Sharing Council of America, Annual Profit Sharing Surveys.

makes it more important to provide a more consistent stream of company contribution.

It might be expected that employer contributions would more nearly approach the 15 percent of payroll which is allowed as an employer tax deduction. There are, however, several factors that tend to hold the contribution at a level under 15 percent. Stock bonus plan contributions are aggregated with profit sharing contributions as part of the 15 percent. Another consideration is that forfeitures are often used to reduce company contributions. Perhaps more importantly, profit sharing plans are only one of many employee benefit plans and must compete for a share of the employer benefit dollar. Employer contributions as a percentage of net profits show a wider fluctuation than employer contributions as a percentage of pay in the 1980s (see Table III-2). Thus, even though there have been substantial year-to-year variations in the percentage of net profits

TABLE III-2
Employer Contributions as Percentage of Net Profits
1980-1988 (All Plans)

1988	19.6
1987	19.5
1986	19.4
1985	25.3
1984	24.1
1983	24.9
1982	24.7
1981	23.2
1980	22.9

Source: Profit Sharing Council of America, Annual Profit Sharing Surveys.

shared, the resulting percentage of payroll has remained relatively stable.

Coverage and Eligibility. Generally, profit sharing plans have broad coverage and include all levels of employees. Recent studies indicate, however, that profit sharing is still significantly more extensive in the nonunion sector.[31] On the other hand, the APC study indicated that few firms reported union resistance to their involvement in group-based reward systems. That study also concluded that successful plans are found in both union and nonunion locations.[32]

The Retirement Equity Act of 1984 requires that nearly all plans allow participation for full-time employees who have reached age twenty-one and who have completed one year of service (or three years of service if the employee is vested immediately upon participation). Most plans use age and/or service as an eligibility requirement.

Allocation of Company Contributions. Treasury regulations require that the terms of the profit sharing plan provide a definite formula for allocating the employer contribution among the accounts of the participating employees. Most plans provide for allocation based on the participant's earnings only.[33] Presumably this reflects, in a rough sort of way, the participant's contribution to the firm's profitability. A few plans provide for allocation related to both compensation and years of service where there is a desire to reward longevity, especially among lower paid participants. The plan must also provide for allocation of investment income, gains or losses, and forfeitures.

Vesting. Regardless of the type of plan, pension, profit sharing, savings, or stock bonus, vesting is defined as a nonforfeitable right to certain benefits which are being held on behalf of a participant in such a plan. The nonvested (forfeited) portion of any account must remain in the trust and cannot be returned to the employer. There are three types of vesting provisions:

1. Immediate, full vesting which vests 100 percent of all account credits at the time the participant joins the plan or at the time of the initial allocation to a participant.

---

[31]*See* Adrienne E. Eaton and Paula B. Voos, "Unions and Contemporary Innovations in Work Organization, Compensation, and Employee Participation," *Queen's Papers in Industrial Relations, 1989-6*, School of Industrial Relations, Queen's University at Kingston (Ont.), 1989, p. 16, and studies cited therein.

[32]O'Dell and McAdams, *People, Performance, and Pay*, p. 89.

[33] United States Department of Labor, Bureau of Labor Statistics, *Employee Benefits in Medium and Large Firms, 1988*, Bulletin 2336, August, 1989, p. 114.

2. Graduated vesting under which an employee's nonforfeitable percentage increases over time and reaches 100 percent after a specified number of years.
3. Cliff vesting which provides full vesting after a stated period of time with no graduated vesting along the way.

Graduated vesting is provided for 73 percent of deferred profit sharing participants in the 1988 BLS survey. Approximately 22 percent of the participants have immediate vesting, and the remainder are covered by cliff vesting.

Since 1974 when the Employee Retirement Income Security Act (ERISA) was passed, the Congress has been heavily involved in establishing minimum vesting provisions in all plans, with a trend toward faster and more uniform vesting. The Tax Reform Act of 1986 established two alternative minimum vesting provisions: (l) five-year cliff vesting, or (2) a graduated seven-year schedule with 20 percent vested after three years and 20 percent each year for four additional years.

Plan Administration and Management. A profit sharing plan must be in writing and must provide for one or more fiduciaries to manage the plan. The plan's assets must be held in trust. A plan administrator in large plans is normally named to carry out the day-to-day administration of the plan, but smaller plans may have a trustee bank perform some of those duties. Fiduciary responsibilities are established by law and are voluminous. There is some tendency for smaller plans to be managed by banks and for larger plans to utilize investment advisors. Employers typically pay for most administration costs.

Investments. Trust assets most commonly include stocks and bonds, some or all of which may be securities of the employer. The PSCA survey showed that 16 percent of the profit sharing plans invest at least a part of the fund in company stock or other employer securities. Forty-four percent of those plans hold 10 percent to 50 percent of their total assets in employer securities.[34] It is not uncommon today for plans to offer several funds for employee investment choice and to permit the transfer of balances among the funds under certain conditions. Examples of types of funds are company stock funds, guaranteed income funds, balanced funds, diversified equity funds, bond funds, and real estate funds.

Distribution. Payment forms vary with the reason for the distribution, with retirement usually offering the widest choice and resignation or discharge the narrowest choice. The most common retire-

---
[34] Profit Sharing Council, *1989 Profit Sharing Survey*, p. 10.

Profit Sharing

ment options are a lump sum, installments over a specified period of time, annuity contracts, deferrable lump sum, and the purchase of additional pension through the employer's retirement plan if one exists and the plans so permit.

Cash Plans

Cash plans typically provide for profits to be shared directly with participants in cash at stated times, usually annually or semi-annually. A primary objective of such plans is to create an employee incentive for increasing productivity and decreasing costs. Amounts distributed are deductible by the employer and taxable to the employee as if they were wages. Such plans do not require IRS approval since there is no tax deferral involved, making them relatively simple to establish and to administer. The 1989 PSCA survey suggests that cash plans are more prevalent in manufacturing and among smaller companies, i.e., firms with fewer than 1,000 participants.[35] The most likely reason is that cash plans are simpler and less costly to establish and to maintain for smaller companies.

Contributions. Most of the same considerations that are involved in deferred plans are also involved in cash plans and need not be repeated here. Employer contributions (as a percentage of employee compensation) to cash plans averaged between 5.0 percent and 11.1 percent from 1980 through 1988 and were more variable than contributions to deferred plans (see Table III-1). The 1989 survey of cash plans was based on a small number (17) of responses, which could affect the variability of the contribution data.

A 1989 Hewitt survey of cash plans found that a specific formula for employer contributions was utilized in 65 percent of the survey companies, and 26 percent had a discretionary figure.[36]

Coverage and Eligibility. The Hewitt survey reported that the cash plans studied typically were extended to all employees. Union employees were eligible in 12 percent of the companies surveyed, not a particularly meaningful number since the number of unionized companies surveyed is not reported.[37]

Allocation of Company Contributions. As with deferred plans, the most prevalent practice is to utilize compensation alone as the basis for allocation of company contributions. Allocation formulas,

---

[35]*Ibid.*, p. 2.
[36]Hewitt Associates, *Compensation Trends*, p. 195.
[37]*Ibid.*

however, need not be limited to pay, and may, for example, allow for service.[38]

Combination Plans

In a combination plan, either a predetermined or an optional portion of shared profits is paid in cash with the balance deposited in trust. Such plans have a dual purpose to create employee incentive and to provide a tax-deferred fund for retirement or other needs. Since combination plans by definition include cash plan aspects and deferred plan aspects, the considerations discussed above are pertinent here also. It is worth noting, however, that average employer contributions, as a percentage of pay, have been consistently higher than those of the other two types of profit sharing plans (see Table III-1). Since employers adopting combination plans have dual objectives of motivating employees as well as providing retirement benefits, it is likely that more money is required to achieve the two objectives. A note of caution regarding Table III-1 is that the sample size for cash plans and combination plans is relatively small so that the statistics could be skewed. Where the employee has an option of amounts to be received in cash or to be deferred, the most common practice, according to an older survey, is to permit the employee to receive up to 50 percent in cash.[39]

LEGISLATIVE DEVELOPMENTS

Prior to 1974 the only significant federal legislation in the areas of pensions and profit sharing were the Internal Revenue Code and the Welfare and Pension Plans Disclosure Act of 1958. Essentially, the purpose of the Internal Revenue Code and the regulations promulgated thereunder was to prevent discrimination in favor of shareholders, officers, supervisors, and highly compensated individuals with respect to coverage, benefits, and financing of private pension plans, and to protect federal revenues against excessive and unjustified tax deductions. The Code was not concerned with the actuarial soundness of pension plans and deferred profit sharing plans; there was no protection of the pension rights of individual participants; and there were no standards of fiduciary conduct for those responsible for handling plan assets. The main thrust of the Welfare and Pension Plans Disclosure Act was the protection of plan assets

---

[38]Profit Sharing Council, *1989 Profit Sharing Survey*, p. 16.
[39]"Cash Allocations Under Combination Plans," *Guide to Modern Profit Sharing* (Chicago: Profit Sharing Council of America, 1973), p. 78.

Profit Sharing

rather than preservation of the rights of individuals in those assets.[40]

ERISA

After over ten years of executive and congressional activity in the pension reform area, the Employee Retirement Income Security Act of 1974 (ERISA) was enacted. This was the first comprehensive pension (the law also covered welfare plans, including profit sharing plans) reform law ever passed by Congress. The major portion of ERISA covered reporting and disclosure, plan participation and vesting, funding, and fiduciary responsibility. Another section (title) of the act established a program of insurance to guarantee the ultimate fulfillment of vested benefit rights of participants. The third major area was concerned with tax matters which amended the Internal Revenue Code. ERISA was an extremely massive and complex piece of legislation, and it required a re-evaluation of all profit sharing plans and the amendment of most. In fact, there was a significant reduction in the number of new profit sharing plans for a few years after 1974 as companies awaited issuance of clarifying regulations.

Since ERISA, the long-term trend has been to enact more federal laws regulating profit sharing plans and other employee benefit plans. Several of these acts have liberalized the minimum standards established by ERISA while others have added new restrictions on the scope and function of profit sharing plans. Unfortunately, the federal government faces conflicting interests with respect to many employee benefit plans. There is a desire to encourage broad and secure coverage for participants and their families. At the same time, there is an interest in eliminating tax breaks for those who are perceived to have an unfair tax advantage over others. With emphasis increasing on the reduction of the federal budget deficit, benefit regulation is also seen as a way of increasing revenues.

Impact of Regulation

Much of the federal legislation has required accounting changes, has increased the cost of administration, and has created substantial regimentation, particularly of defined benefit plans.[41] In order to avoid some of the problems of defined benefit plans, many smaller

---

[40]Dan M. McGill, *Fundamentals of Private Pension Plans*, 5th ed. (Homewood, IL: Richard D. Irwin, Inc., 1984), pp. 30-32.

[41]Defined benefit plans are plans which utilize formulas for calculating retirement benefits and obligate the employer to provide the benefits so determined.

companies have been implementing profit sharing, or other defined contribution plans. By so doing, the small, growing company can provide its employees with retirement benefits without making impractical financial commitments, particularly during the firm's early years.[42] Some larger companies, as well, have added profit sharing or savings plans and then revised their traditional pension plans to reflect the existence of the savings or profit sharing plan.[43] During the early 1980s excess pension plan assets reached relatively high levels, and many companies terminated their pension plans to recover those assets; other companies, squeezed by the recession, froze pension benefit levels.[44] The result has been a slight decline in the proportion of employees participating in defined benefit plans, and a shift toward defined contribution plans.[45]

PROFIT SHARING AND COLLECTIVE BARGAINING

Negotiated profit sharing plans are not a recent development. As early as 1937 the United Steelworkers (USW) had negotiated profit sharing agreements with steel companies. However, unions generally viewed profit sharing with suspicion and distrust. There was a widely held (and perhaps to some extent justified) belief in labor circles that profit sharing had been used as a tactic to defeat union organization in the 1920s and early 1930s or had been used to justify lower wages. Union leaders also saw profit sharing bringing about a deviation from the uniform wage rates which unions sought for industries as a whole. Since unions did not have access to employer financial information or control over accounting procedures, there was room for additional distrust of profit sharing. Whether or not these fears were justified is immaterial. Union uneasiness with profit sharing has existed for many years and has not disappeared completely.

From the 1940s through the 1970s collectively bargained profit sharing plans appeared in scattered locations and industries. Some, such as the plan at American Velvet, were quite successful and are still operating. Other plans, such as that at American Motors, were less successful and have disappeared.

---

[42]Sheryl Cohen, "A Break with Tradition," *Profit Sharing*, Vol. 35, No. 8 (August 1987), p. 5.

[43]Michael I. Lew, "Profit Sharing vs. Pension Plans," *Profit Sharing*, Vol. 35, No. 9 (September, 1987), p. 6.

[44]*Ibid.*, pp. 4-5.

[45]*See* United States Department of Labor, Bureau of Labor Statistics, *Employee Benefits in Medium and Large Firms* (1985-1988), Bulletins 2262, 2281, 2336.

Profit Sharing

At American Velvet, the profit sharing plan was first negotiated with the union, now the Amalgamated Clothing and Textile Workers Union (ACTWU), in 1940. The company has not had a strike since the plan was implemented, and the company remains competitive. Along with profit sharing, American Velvet has been successful with an ambitious employee participation program and an open-book financial policy which gives the union the same information that is available to management. Over the years, profit sharing has paid amounts ranging from zero to thirty-nine cents per dollar earned by employees. There have been union and management disagreements, but the participative climate seems to enable the parties to settle their differences satisfactorily.[46]

The 1961 United Automobile Workers (UAW) profit sharing agreement with American Motors, said to be the first such plan resulting from negotiations between a strong union and a large manufacturing firm, was a precursor of the automobile industry plans of the 1980s. The American Motors plan provided for employees to share 15 percent of profits before taxes but after a deduction from profits of a sum equal to 10 percent of the company's net worth. Two-thirds of the company's contribution each year was used to improve and maintain employee benefits, and the remaining one-third was invested in American Motors stock and credited to individual employee accounts to be held in trust.[47] The plan was designed to meet the differing goals of the parties. The employees received fringe benefit improvements and a portion of company profits while agreeing to a reduction of pay-for-time-not-worked items and a revision of seniority rules and production standards which American Motors had sought. Unfortunately, the plan paid a diminishing amount to employees over the three years of the initial agreement. After 1964, payments lapsed for several years, and the plan never recovered.

The significant profit sharing development of the 1980s is not so much the numbers of plans negotiated but the reason for which those plans were introduced. Traditionally, most profit sharing plans were introduced by prosperous, growing companies which had a management interested in sharing that prosperity with the employees. Many of the more recent collectively bargained plans were included as part of a concession package, a trade-off for wage increases or

---

[46]Rod Willis, "Second-Generation Profit Sharing at American Velvet," *Management Review*, Vol. 77, No. 2 (February, 1988), pp. 39-45.

[47]I.B. Helburn, *Progress Sharing at American Motors* (Madison, WI: Center for Productivity Motivation, School of Commerce, University of Wisconsin, 1964), pp. 12-25.

benefits forgone by the employees, similar to what was done at American Motors in 1961. Thus, it became the economically troubled firm which was interested in profit sharing. In such situations employees often gave up benefits or wage increases in exchange for profit sharing, and in many cases for a greater voice in the affairs of the business which employed them. This came in the form of quality of work life programs, quality circles, employee participation programs, board of directors representation, increased information sharing, rights to audits, and stock ownership. Union leadership has always insisted that a meaningful voice in the business is an essential companion to profit sharing. Employees are beginning to receive that voice, not only with regard to profit sharing plans, but also in a wide range of other concerns that affect them. This development may prove to be the most important result of the profit sharing surge of the 1980s.

In the area of collective bargaining on cash profit sharing[48] there is a continuing philosophical difference between unions and some managements which centers on whether or to what extent basic pay should be put at risk and replaced with variable compensation tied to company performance. The leading theoretical proponent of variable pay, Martin L. Wietzman, argued that fluctuations in aggregate demand have resulted in high unemployment during recessions; whereas, if earnings were tied more closely to profits, economic downturns would produce fluctuations in employee earnings and prices but not in employment.[49] Weitzman proposed to convert a wage system into a share system. The theoretical basis of this view is that a firm will continue to hire workers until the last worker's contribution to revenue equals his wage. If the firm moves from a fixed-wage system to a system under which the workers are paid a lower base (fixed) wage and a supplement tied to profits, then the firm will hire workers until the marginal revenue product equals the base wage. In other words, it will hire additional workers as long as they add more to output than the cost of the base wage. On a more practical level, some employers view this theory as a basis for a system of flexible compensation which allows a firm's wage costs to vary, providing a buffer before layoffs are necessary. When profit levels are good, management would prefer to share profits rather than to increase base wage rates or employment.

---

[48]It should be noted that *cash* profit sharing, not deferred profit sharing, is referred to in the discussion which follows.

[49]Martin L. Weitzman, *The Share Economy: Conquering Stagflation* (Cambridge, MA: Harvard University Press, 1984).

Profit Sharing

Unions and others, on the other hand, argue that profit sharing payments should be treated as benefits with base wages being negotiated at levels competitive with other firms in the industry. If profit sharing constitutes a large portion of a worker's earnings, the argument goes, a drop in profits could have dire results on the employees' personal economic situation. Unlike investors who can spread their risk among various types of investments, employees generally have all of their eggs in one basket. Moreover, profits are affected by factors outside of the organization, by poor management decisions, or by changes in accounting practices or tax laws, none of which can be controlled by the workers. Union leaders argue that the prices workers pay for housing, clothing, automobiles, utilities, and food do not respond rapidly to changes in labor costs. For many workers who spend essentially all (or more) of their income for such items, a precipitous decrease in pay (if a substantial portion of pay is tied to profits) could be disastrous. Of course proponents of a share system point out that unemployment as an alternative might also be disastrous.

In light of the widespread appearance of concession agreements of the early 1980s and the profit sharing that came along with them, what has happened to those plans? To what extent has variable compensation based on performance replaced fixed wage systems in collective bargaining? What types of problems have developed with collectively bargained profit sharing plans? In the analysis of industry and firm experiences which follows, emphasis will be on those plans of major industries or the plans of significant individual companies.

The Automobile Industry Plans

In 1981 Chrysler Corporation and the UAW agreed to negotiate a profit sharing plan as a part of the federal loan guarantee program which Chrysler claimed it needed to survive. The plan which resulted was essentially the same as the 1961 American Motors plan referred to above. In 1982 no payments were made under the plan. Negotiations in 1982 resulted in the workers dropping profit sharing, after the negotiating committee had agreed to continue it, and electing a wage increase instead. The wage increase was intended to restore partially the wage cuts the the employees had accepted earlier to improve the company's financial position. Of course Chrysler rebounded in 1983, and a year after the employees rejected profit sharing it was estimated that they lost approximately $2,000 per employee because of that rejection. In 1985 negotiations Chrysler agreed to make $500 annual payments to employees from 1986 through 1989. In 1988 negotiations profit sharing returned to Chrysler.

In 1982 Ford followed Chrysler with a profit sharing plan as part of an early agreement because of the depressed state of the industry. The major employee concessions were the elimination of nine holidays, a deferral of cost-of-living payments, the elimination of annual improvement factors for 1982 and 1983, and no pension improvements.

General Motors in 1982 adopted a profit sharing plan formula slightly different from that at Ford. In 1987 Ford and General Motors adopted essentially identical plans, and in 1988 the Chrysler plan also followed the same pattern. Table III-3 shows the plan formula in effect at all three companies in 1989.

Table III-4 shows the results of profit sharing at the major automobile companies. Ford and its UAW members are happy with profit sharing. There is something less than joy at General Motors and Chrysler. One of the reasons cited by General Motors for the lower payment in 1984 was that strikes in the United States and Canada reduced the profit sharing pool, and therein lies one of the major

TABLE III-3
Automobile Industry Profit Sharing Plan
(1989)

Profit as Percentage of Sales	Profit Sharing Rate
Between 1.8 and 2.3	7.5%
Between 2.3 and 4.6	10.0
Between 4.6 and 6.9	13.5
Over 6.9	16.0

Source: Ford Motor Company.

TABLE III-4
Average Profit Sharing Payout to Employees of
Chrysler, Ford, and General Motors
1983-1989

| | Average Employee Payout | | |
Plan Year	Chrysler	Ford	General Motors
1983	0	$402	$606
1984	0	1,993	515
1985	0	1,262	329
1986	$500	2,176	0
1987	500	3,700	0
1988	720	2,800	250
1989	0	1,025	50

Source: Chrysler Corporation, Ford Motor Company, General Motors Corporation.

Profit Sharing

dilemmas for union-negotiated profit sharing. The UAW, however, seemed to take it in stride and commented that its members would continue to be militant when required "regardless of the manner in which they are compensated." For 1986 and 1987 General Motors said that unusually high spending for new plants and equipment was the principal reason that earnings were not sufficient for profit sharing payments in those years.[50] Despite continuing problems, General Motors was able to announce late in 1988 that the profit sharing plan would generate payments of approximately $250 per employee for 1988. Ford estimated that its payout would be between $2,000 and $3,000 per employee for 1988.[51] Chrysler's payout exceeded its $500 minimum base. During 1989 all three firms faced greatly reduced payouts.

Partly because it is more vertically integrated, General Motors has a much larger work force over which to spread a profit sharing pool. Even in years during which Ford and General Motors earn equal profit percentages on sales, General Motors must spread those dollars over some 450,000 employees and Ford over perhaps only 160,000. The UAW feels that Ford's greater payout per employee is the price the company must pay for outsourcing of parts and components. On the other side, General Motors has been unsuccessful in attempts to negotiate lower wage rates in parts plants than those in engine, transmission, and assembly plants.

The UAW has been critical of management bonuses at all three automobile companies. Such criticism is not unique to the automobile industry or to collectively bargained plans, but it is likely to receive more publicity in unionized firms with profit sharing, especially when managers receive bonuses and the workers do not receive profit sharing payments. Even at Ford where profit sharing has paid off consistently for UAW members, the union has been highly critical of executive compensation levels. At General Motors some 5,000 top executives received stock bonuses worth approximatley $157 million for 1987 while the profit sharing formula did not trigger a payment for UAW members.[52] The UAW leadership claimed that executive compensation was an "insult to common sense and fairness" and called for management to forgo all increases and supplementary awards in a "spirit of shared sacrifice." The problem is that executive bonuses are based on global business, and

---

[50]"G.M. Plans First Profit-Sharing Payout Since '85," *New York Times*, December 13, 1988, p. D5.
[51]*Ibid.*
[52]"A GM Official Urges Bonus System Be Revised," *Wall Street Journal*, April 15, 1988, p. 3.

profit sharing is limited to United States results. Historically, General Motors did not do as well abroad, but more recently the situation has reversed, hence the disparate situation between bonus and profit sharing plans.

When Chrysler and the UAW returned to profit sharing in 1988, the company made a commitment not to pay cash or stock bonuses to executives in the years when there is no profit sharing for UAW members.[53] Such a move could improve morale, but there is also a risk that managers will ignore long-term planning to boost short-term profits or that Chrysler may have difficulty recruiting top managers because of such restrictions. Obviously, Chrysler's move will place additional pressure on Ford and General Motors to do something similar.

Steel and Aluminum Industry Plans

Bargaining in the steel industry in 1986 was marked by numerous concession agreements as the industry continued to struggle with economic adversity. Most of the concession agreements also contained profit sharing plans designed to recoup wage and benefit sacrifices by the workers.

Although there is some variation in these profit sharing plans, most of them guarantee a minimum payback to employees with provision for additional profit sharing payments possible if profits improve sufficiently. Plans negotiated at Bethlehem Steel and LTV provide for concessions to be returned at a rate of 10 percent of the first $100 million of profits and 20 percent of profits over $100 million, but only equal to the concessions. If profits are insufficient to accomplish the payback, the company is obligated to issue preferred stock to employees.[54] Bethlehem Steel recently (1988) announced that it would distribute $500 in cash and $4,500 in company stock to approximately 5,400 employees at its Burns Harbor, Indiana, plant.

At National Steel the company guaranteed a lump sum profit sharing payment each year equal to $.50 per hour worked regardless of profit level, with a progressive scale up to $1.75 per hour if profits exceed $300 million. The agreement also contained a productivity gainsharing provision which could add additional bonuses for workers.[55]

---

[53]"Analysts Assess Chrysler Agreement's Impact on Industry Competitiveness," *Daily Labor Report*, No. 92 (May 12, 1988), p. A-1.

[54]"Steelworkers Agree to Pay Cuts at LTV in First 1986 Settlement at Major Firms," *Daily Labor Report*, No. 52 (March 18, 1986), p. A-9.

[55]"Steelworkers Settle with National Steel on More Modest Concessions than at LTV," *Daily Labor Report*, No. 69 (April 10, 1986), p. A-9.

Profit Sharing

At USS, Division of USX Corporation, the agreement with the USW contains a unique profit sharing provision in that a minimum profit sharing payment is tied in part to the price of Bethlehem and LTV stock. The rationale behind this provision is to insure that "USX faces the same cost structure for its profit sharing plan as its major competitors face in their stock plans" which now provide for stock payments to union members as noted above. USX workers are seeking to recoup wage and benefit concessions ranging from approximately $2.45 per hour in the first year to $1.95 per hour by the last two years of the four-year agreement.[56] The plan yielded an average of $.90 per hour in 1988 and $1.70 per hour in 1989.

It remains to be seen what the long-term results will be from these profit sharing plans. In 1988, however, several of the major profit sharing plans had begun to make payouts. At LTV a payment in April, 1988, exceeded the wage cuts in the 1986 agreement and some stock has been distributed. The 1988 bonus at National Steel exceeded both the wage and benefit reduction. In 1989 National's employees received an average of $1,835 per eligible employee. Bethlehem Steel's profit sharing payment amounted to $.25 per hour with some stock also being distributed. At Inland Steel the initial payment was only $.05 per hour. The first payment at USX equalled an average of $.90 per hour.[57] In 1989 the plan paid an average of $3,500 per employee based on 1988 performance. Thus, it appears that the goal of the USW to recoup employee sacrifices as the companies return to profitablity is being met, if rather slowly in some cases.

Late in 1988, the Aluminum Company of America and Reynolds Metals Co. negotiated a profit sharing plan with the USW and the Aluminum, Glass, and Brick Workers. In the 1986 negotiations the unions had made concessions to help the companies survive in the face of reduced demand and increased foreign competition. In 1988 negotiations the result was a $1,000 per employee signing bonus with $500 bonus payments in 1990 and 1991 and a $.50 per hour general wage increase in 1989. The profit sharing plan was expected to generate an average payment of $2,500 per employee during the first year. As in steel, the parties in aluminum are using profit sharing and lump sum bonuses in an attempt to maintain a greater degree of wage flexibility as business improves.

---

[56]"Tentative Accord Reached To End Six-Month Work Stoppage at USX," *Daily Labor Report*, No. 13 (January 21, 1987), pp. A-7-A-8.

[57]Bureau of National Affairs, *Changing Pay Practices: New Developments in Employee Compensation* (Washington, DC: Bureau of National Affairs, 1988), pp. 39-40.

Other Industries

In 1986 the western wood products industry was under strong competitive pressure from nonunion, Canadian, and southern lumber and plywood producers. Wage and benefit cuts resulted from negotiations at most of the western wood products operations in 1986. At Weyerhaeuser Company the employees took wage cuts of up to $3.00 per hour, plus cuts in benefits, in exchange for a profit sharing plan in the mills.[58] Employees at other companies took lesser cuts but did not adopt profit sharing. Most of Weyerhaeuser's employees in Washington and Oregon are represented by the International Woodworkers of America, U.S. (IWA); a smaller number are represented by the Western Council of Lumber Production and Industrial Workers (LPIW), a division of the Brotherhood of Carpenters and Joiners. The two unions bargain jointly at firms where they both have members.[59]

Profits at Weyerhaeuser are calculated for profit "units" since the company operates under a decentralized structure. The original profit sharing plan provided for workers to receive one-third of the unit's pre-tax earnings over 5 percent return on sales until $1.20 per hour of the wage cut was restored. After that level was reached it was to be folded into the wage base and not to be removed unless the unit operated without a profit for six months. The workers were to receive 10 percent of the unit's profits above the initial $1.20 with no cap, and payments were to be distributed quarterly.[60]

After two years, management believed the plan was successful, while union leaders insisted that the plan was not working. Total profit sharing payments for the first eighteen months of plan operation were $25 million. Payments for some quarters have been as high as $2.00 to $3.00 per hour but averaged $1.20 per hour. The wide variation in payments arises from the unit-by-unit calculation of profits. Even in a single mill there are separate profit units for different products resulting in workers in the same plant, but on different product lines, receiving different bonus payments, or workers doing the same job on the same product but at different mills receiving differing bonuses. Management claimed the plan not only helped to make Weyerhaeuser more competitive by holding down western labor costs but that it has led to greater cooperation and to plant efficiency improvements.

---

[58]"Woodworkers Vote To End Strike, Accept New Weyerhaeuser Contract," *Daily Labor Report*, No. 145 (July 29, 1988), p. A-11.
[59]Bureau of National Affairs, *Changing Pay Practices*, pp. 169-170.
[60]"Woodworkers Vote," p. A-11.

Profit Sharing

In 1988 negotiations the profit sharing plan was a major issue. The company did not want to give up the unit calculation system as it claimed that would take away from the incentive value by watering down one unit in favor of another one. The union leaders felt that productivity should be taken into account because, as the plan is currently structured, production (over which the workers have some control) can increase substantially and yet profits remain unchanged as a result of many other variables.[61]

The unions also pointed to the apparent success of a different plan in the company's logging operations. There the plan is a "productivity" gain sharing plan in which the system is keyed to the fee a logging contractor would charge to cut and haul the timber to the mill. If the Weyerhaeuser loggers do the job for less than the cost of the outside contractor, the workers split the difference between their cost and the outside bid. If their cost exceeds the outside bid they receive no bonus. The logger's bonuses have run as high as $9.00 per hour.[62]

Negotiations in 1988 resulted in a simplification and a liberalization of the profit sharing plan. Employees were guaranteed a minimum profit sharing payment of $1,400 for the fiscal year ending June 30, 1989. The profit sharing plan now provides for the sharing of pre-tax profits from the first dollar of profits on sales, as opposed to the prior plan which had a 5 percent corridor. There is no cap in the formula, but the profit center concept was retained.[63]

Weyerhaeuser's paper mills also have profit sharing plans negotiated with the Association of Western Pulp and Paper Workers (AWPPW) in 1987. Those plans provide for bonuses ranging from 1.5 percent to 3.75 percent of annual earnings at the company's paper mills. They differ from the wood products plans in that the profit sharing formula is based on a combination of elements—quality, safety, output, and cost. Other paper mills have lump sum bonus plans but not usually based on profits.[64]

In 1986 several of the Regional Bell Operating Companies negotiated "team award" plans with the Communications Workers of America and the International Brotherhood of Electrical Workers. These team award plans extended to all employees the same bonus program that had been in effect for management personnel only.

---

[61]"Weyerhaeuser, Other Western Firms To Begin Contract Talks with Woodcutters April 14," *Daily Labor Report*, No. 71 (April 13, 1988), pp. A-1-A-2.
[62]*Ibid.*, p. A-2.
[63]"Weyerhaeuser, Most Other Wood Firms Reach Settlement with Woodworkers," *Daily Labor Report*, No. 178 (September 14, 1988), p. A-5.
[64]Bureau of National Affairs, *Changing Pay Patterns*, pp. 187-189.

Although there is some degree of regional variation in the team award plans, the common philosophy is to pay a bonus in February based upon the company's previous year's "financial and service" performance. If the financial and service goals are reached, the standard team award would be (for Pacific Telesis, for example) 1.1 percent of pay after the first year; 2.1 percent after the second year; and 3.7 percent after the third year. Payments could be as high as 130 percent of standard or as low as 90 percent of standard depending on the performance results. These payments are not treated like lump sum bonuses but will be a part of base salary for calculating benefits based on salary.

In 1988 DuPont's Fibers Division adopted an innovative pay plan called "Achievement Sharing." This plan calls for a five-year phase-in period, at the end of which participants will be earning 6 percent less than other DuPont employees. If the division meets its annual profit goal, the participants will receive the 6 percent as a bonus. If profits fall below 80 percent of the goal they will receive a 3 percent bonus, and at 150 percent of the goal they could receive 12 percent above the other DuPont employees. The degree of success achieved by the Achievement Sharing program will not be known for several years, of course. Undoubtedly the program will be closely watched by other companies, particularly those which are seriously interested in increasing flexibility in their compensation systems.

PROFIT SHARING RESULTS

As more companies move in the direction of profit-related pay, the inevitable question arises: is there any evidence that profit sharing companies exhibit financial performance superior to those which do not share profits? At least one recent U.S. study attempts to answer that question,[65] and Table III-5 summarizes the results. One interesting aspect of this study is that it shows a positive relationship between return on sales and the rate of employee participation. Clearly, where a larger proportion of employees participate, the return on sales is also higher. The study also indicated that the larger firms tend to share profits with fewer than 25 percent of their employees. The smaller companies were more likely to share profits with 51-100 percent of their employees.

There are some older studies which also indicate that profit sharers enjoy better results than non-profit sharers. A 1969 study of

---

[65]Glen A. Karlov, "Profit Sharing Firms Out-Perform Non-Sharers in '87," *Profit Sharing*, Vol. 36, No. 11 (November, 1988), pp. 17-18.

TABLE III-5
*Performance of Large Profit Sharing
and Non-Profit Sharing Companies
1987*[a]

	Mean Profit/Sales	Number in Group
All 796 Companies	6.57%	796
Non-Sharers	6.52	410
Profit Sharers	6.62	386
0-25% participation	6.53	172
26-50% participation	6.57	112
51-100% participation	6.84	102

Source: Glen A. Karlov, "Profit Sharing Firms Out-Perform Non-Sharers in '87," *Profit Sharing*, Vol. 36, No. 11 (November 1988), p. 17.
[a]Data derived from Forbes 500's Annual Directory and annual reports from these companies.

companies in nine different industries using ten measures of financial performance concluded: "The results of this study show that the financial performance of the profit sharing companies was clearly superior to non-profit sharers for the nine industries as a group."[66] Another study of retail businesses in 1971 found that profit sharing companies outperformed the non-profit sharing companies by substantial percentages on all measures.[67] Table III-6 compares profit sharing and non-profit sharing companies from 1973-1976.

TABLE III-6
*Performance Comparisons, 1973-1976
(Median Percentages)*

	Return on Sales				Return on Equity			
	1973	1974	1975	1976	1973	1974	1975	1976
Industrials[a]								
PSRF	7.0	6.1	5.1	5.9	14.9	14.6	12.1	14.0
Fortune 500	4.5	4.3	3.9	4.6	12.4	13.6	11.6	13.3
Retailers[b]								
PSRF	2.5	1.9	2.2	2.3	13.4	11.0	11.9	12.2
Fortune 41	1.3	1.0	1.4	1.3	9.9	9.1	10.0	11.6

Source: Bruce L. Metzger, *Profit Sharing in 38 Large Companies* (Evanston, IL: Profit Sharing Research Foundation, 1978), p. 17.
[a]Industrials compared are the twenty-three companies in the Profit Sharing Research Foundation study and the Fortune 500 largest U.S. industrials.
[b]Retailers compared are the ten companies in the Profit Sharing Research Foundation study and Fortune's 41 from the top fifty (excluding nine in PSRF study.

[66]Bion B. Howard and Peter O. Dietz, *A Study of the Financial Significance of Profit Sharing* (Chicago: Council of Profit Sharing Industries, 1969), p. 1.
[67]Bruce L. Metzger and Jeromes A. Colletti, *Does Profit Sharing Pay?* (Evanston, IL: Profit Sharing Research Foundation, 1971), p. 72.

Although the author of the Profit Sharing Research Foundation study recognized that these comparisons were not perfect, there was substantial evidence that profit sharing companies tended to outperform the non-profit sharers. There is also a recognition in all of these studies that it is extremely difficult to isolate the effects of one variable (profit sharing in this case) while holding constant all other factors. The companies which have profit sharing may also be the same companies which have an enlightened and progressive management with other appropriate programs to promote employee efficiency. It may well be that profit sharing is often a consequence of the participative style set by top management in a company.

Metzger and Colletti's 1971 study cited above led them to the conclusion that, "profit sharing or any incentive program works best in an incentive-oriented environment, where ancillary programs are initiated to help the company reach specific targets this side of profit. ..."[68] A more recent study also found evidence that any of the nontraditional reward systems (such as profit sharing, gainsharing, small group incentives, individual incentives, and others) work best when used in combination. The author of that study concluded that, "it is no coincidence that firms with group-based pay for performance systems also have more active employee involvement programs, more employment security strategies, and greater information sharing than other organizations."[69]

In addition to studies linking profit sharing to financial performance, there are other studies which have examined profit sharing's effect on productivity, employment stability, and employee commitment in the United States. Kruse's study of 2,976 companies over the period 1971-1985 found that profit sharing firms in manufacturing had smaller employment decreases than other firms during economic downturns. The non-manufacturing profit sharers were found to be no more stable than other firms. Kruse also found that the adoption of profit sharing was associated with a 2.5 to 4.2 percent increase in productivity, with the size of the effect increasing with the number of employees participating.[70] A more recent study found no strong indications that profit sharing plans exert much of effect on job security.[71]

---

[68]*Ibid.*, p. 85.
[69]O'Dell and McAdams, *People, Performance, and Pay*, p. 90.
[70]Douglas Lynn Kruse, "Essays on Profit Sharing and Unemployment" (Ph.D. thesis, Harvard University, 1988).
[71]James Chelius and Robert S. Smith, "Profit Sharing and Employment Stability," *Industrial and Labor Relations Review*, Vol. 43, No. 3 (February 1990, Special Issue), pp. 256-S—273-S.

Profit Sharing

Shepard studied twenty U.S. chemical firms (nine with profit sharing plans) from 1975 to 1982 and found a positive relationship between profit sharing and value-added.[72] On the other hand, a 1987 survey by the American Productivity Center and several supporting organizations, of 1,600 companies (507 with profit sharing plans), concluded that:

> Profit sharing plans are increasing employee commitment and reducing turnover, but do not have as strong an effect on productivity, quality, or cost reduction. Information sharing is somewhat higher than average in profit sharing firms. Profit sharing firms often have formal and informal employment security strategies to increase employee commitment.[73]

After a detailed and exhaustive analysis of studies seeking to relate profit sharing and productivity, Weitzman and Kruse[74] concluded that the connection between profit sharing and productivity is not definitive; yet they also conclude that a variety of sources definitely point toward a positive link.

---

[72]Edward Morse Shepard, "The Effects of Profit Sharing on Productivity" (Ph.D. dissertation, Boston College, 1987).

[73]O'Dell and McAdams, *People, Performance, and Pay*, p. 88.

[74]Martin L. Weitzman and Douglas L. Kruse, "Profit Sharing and Productivity: A Look at the Evidence," Alan S. Blinder (ed.), *Paying for Productivity: A Look at the Evidence* (Washington, D.C.: The Brookings Institution, 1990), pp. 95-140.

CHAPTER IV

Employee Savings Plans

Under modern savings plans employees contribute a predetermined percentage of earnings to an account, all or part of which may or may not be matched by the employer. Contributions are invested in stocks, bonds, money market funds, or other investment choices. Although usually intended as a long-term savings program, plans may allow for withdrawals or loans subject to specified conditions.

Employee savings plans appear under a variety of names. They may be called savings plans, thrift plans, incentive plans, investment plans, or some or all of these or other names in the title of the plan. Surprisingly, neither the Internal Revenue Code nor the Treasury regulations specifically provide for savings or thrift plans. In order to qualify for tax advantages, savings plans must be qualified as, and meet the requirements of, either a profit sharing plan, a stock bonus plan, or a money-purchase pension plan. Usually savings plans are qualified as profit sharing plans because the law and the regulations allow more flexibility to profit sharing plans.[1] Although a savings plan may meet the qualification requirements of a profit sharing plan, there are basic differences between the two types of plans. The typical deferred profit sharing plan does not require employee contributions, and the company contributions are related to profit levels. With savings plans, the company's contribution is basically a function of the employee's contribution. Savings plans are designed to encourage employee thrift and to attract a competent, productive workforce. Profit sharing plans are not ordinarily aimed at encouraging employee thrift, although they may aid in attracting employees to the sponsoring company.

The most important development for savings plans since the first edition of this study[2] was the enactment of Section 401(k) of the Internal Revenue Code in 1978. Section 401(k) permits the establishment of a "qualified cash or deferred arrangement" (CODA), defined

---

[1]Barry I. Cosloy and Jeffrey Perlmuter, "Defined Contribution Plans," in Jeffrey D. Mamorsky (ed.), *Employee Benefits Handbook* (New York and Boston: Warren, Gorham & Lamont, 1987), p. 12-16.

[2]Geoffrey W. Latta, *Profit Sharing, Employee Stock Ownership, Savings, and Asset Formation Plans in the Western World* (Philadelphia: Wharton Industrial Research Unit, 1979).

as part of a qualified profit sharing or stock bonus plan under which an employee may elect to have employer contributions paid to the qualified plan or paid directly to the employee in cash. A 401(k) plan is really an offshoot of a traditional cash profit sharing plan. When Section 401(k) was added to the Internal Revenue Code, it was easier to give employees a choice of receiving a cash distribution or choosing to defer earnings (and taxes). The most attractive feature of such plans is that they provide employees with the opportunity to save for retirement on a "pre-tax" basis.[3] Another advantage is that they provide for tax deferred growth of income on the employee and company contributions. Prior to this, all contributions were on an after tax basis only.

By 1983, as regulations clarifying Section 401(k) became clearer, there was a surge in popularity of these plans. The Bankers Trust survey in 1987 found that two-thirds of the 401(k) plans in that survey were adopted in 1983 and 1984.[4] Approximately 90 percent of companies in the U.S. with 5,000 or more employees now provide 401(k) plans. In 1983 only 39 percent offered such plans. Participation has also increased: in 1983 less than 40 percent of employees who were eligible to make 401(k) contributions did so. Now approximately two-thirds of eligible employees participate.[5]

ADVANTAGES AND DISADVANTAGES OF SAVINGS PLANS

A well designed savings plan can be a popular employee benefit plan with relatively modest cost to the employer. Table IV-1 shows employer payments for some related employee benefit plans as a percentage of payroll. Those percentages indicate that 401(k) plans cost the same as profit sharing plans but substantially less than defined benefit pension plans. From the standpoint of the employee, a savings plan may be preferable because the employer contribution is usually more stable. Profit sharing contributions may be more variable from year to year, and in some years they may be nonexistent. Of course the attractiveness of any plan depends on its features, the most important of which in savings plans are the employer's contribution, the vesting provisions, and the investment choices. Since the employee must contribute to a savings plan, and usually through payroll deduction, the plan is a strong motivator for systematic sav-

---

[3] *Ibid.*, pp. 12-15-12-16.
[4] Bankers Trust Company, *Corporate Defined Contribution Plans* (New York: Bankers Trust Company, 1987), p. 11.
[5] Alexander G. Ross, "Integrating 401 (k) with Profit Sharing," *Profit Sharing*, Vol. 36, No. 6 (June 1988), p. 7.

Employee Savings Plans 59

TABLE IV-1
*Employer[a] payments as a percentage of payroll
for selected employee benefits, 1987*

Type of Benefit	Employer Payments as Percentage of Payroll
Defined benefit pension plans	2.5
Defined contribution plan payments (401(k) type)	0.8
Profit sharing	0.8
Stock bonus and employee stock ownership plans (ESOP)	0.2

Source: United States Chamber of Commerce, *Employee Benefits, 1988 Edition: Survey Data From Benefit Year 1987* (Washington, D.C.: United States Chamber of Commerce, 1988), p. 9.
[a]Based on 910 participating companies.

ings. Although not unique to savings plans, the tax advantages to the employee are significant, particularly if the plan is a 401(k) plan. Not only are taxes on investment income and employer contributions deferred but the employee's contribution is made on a pre-tax basis thus deferring income tax on that portion as well.

Although there are many advantages, there are a few disadvantages of 401(k) savings plans. Since there are significant restrictions on withdrawals from these plans and because there are complex antidiscrimination rules, employers have a heavy educational and administrative burden. Employees must be made aware of the nature of the plan and some of its limitations so that they are not disappointed. The employee participant, of course, bears the investment risk. For the inexperienced investor this can be a substantial responsibility.

SAVINGS PLAN FEATURES AND TRENDS

Although qualified savings plans must meet the requirements of the Internal Revenue Code and a host of other federal laws, considerable discretion remains for employers in designing their plans. The discussion of plan features which follows draws heavily upon the 1987 Bankers Trust survey, *Corporate Defined Contribution Plans*, and the Bureau of Labor Statistics (BLS) study of *Employee Benefits in Medium and Large Firms, 1988*.[6] The Bankers Trust survey covers 242 plans with participant size ranging from 1,000 to 165,000

---

[6]Bankers Trust, see note 3; United States Department of Labor, Bureau of Labor Statistics, *Employee Benefits in Medium and Large Firms, 1988*, Bulletin 2336, August 1989.

in large and medium-sized U.S. corporations. The BLS survey was based on a sample of approximately 2,000 establishments.

Coverage

A majority (67 percent) of companies extend coverage to all or substantially all employees, although a growing proportion of companies cover hourly paid and salaried employees in separate and different plans. The remaining one-third of companies limit coverage to salaried or non-bargaining unit employees. Plans often provide for participation by bargaining unit employees only if the unit accepts the plan. According to the BLS survey, the savings plan participation rate for professional and administrative employees was 37 percent; for technical and clerical employees 32 percent; and for production employees 15 percent, indicating that actual participation, as opposed to eligibility, is more popular among white-collar employees.

Eligibility

Since one purpose of savings plans is to attract, motivate, and retain employees, such plans traditionally have had liberal eligibility requirements. Beginning with the Employee Retirement Income Security Act (ERISA) in 1974, the Congress also has been heavily involved in liberalizing the eligibility provisions. At the present time, a plan may provide that participants be age twenty-one and have at least one year of service (for a 401(k) plan); a non-401(k) plan may specify two years of service only if it provides for full and immediate vesting after two years.

A service-only requirement is most common (73 percent in both the Bankers Trust and the BLS surveys), with one year of service (52 percent) as the most prevalent provision. Plans with no age or service requirement appear to be increasing but make up only 13 percent of the plans in the Bankers Trust survey, reflecting the attitude that it is advantageous to retain some eligibility restrictions in order to reduce administrative costs by excluding employees who have the highest turnover rates.

Employee Contributions

Generally, savings plans allow employees to select from a range of permissible contribution rates. The most common maximum employee contribution is 16 percent of salary or wages according the the BLS survey. The minimum contribution may be as low as 1 or 2 percent. In plans having matching employer contributions, the most

Employee Savings Plans

common maximum employee contribution rate that will be matched by the employer is 6 percent, although there are plans in which the employer matches employee contributions of 10 percent or more.

In addition to the amount of contribution, the employee may also have a choice with regard to the tax status of his or her own contribution. Most plans (68 percent) in the Bankers Trust study allow the employee to choose either pre-tax or post-tax contributions. A pre-tax contribution means that the employee's currently taxable earnings are reduced by the amount of his or her contributions so that income tax is paid only on the reduced earnings figure. For example, if an employee earns $20,000 annually and contributes 5 percent, or $1,000, to the plan, that employee's taxable income for the year would be $19,000. The employee's savings plan account would be credited with $1,000. Of course the tax is not forgiven but is deferred until withdrawal or distribution at some future date. An after-tax contribution means that the employer deducts the $1,000 contribution from the employee's earnings but that does not reduce taxable income so the employee pays tax currently on $20,000 of income. In effect, the pre-tax contribution is treated as though it were an employer contribution on behalf of the employee for tax purposes.

Since the IRS considers a pre-tax employee contribution to be an employer contribution, it devised a unique discrimination test for these plans. Without attempting to explain the details of this discrimination test, the concept is that the top-paid one-third of eligible employees cannot shelter significantly more pre-tax earnings than the lower-paid two-thirds. The concern of the IRS (and Congress as it tightens these provisions) is to protect the lower paid employees from what it considers to be unfair treatment in favor of higher paid employees. Recent legislation also established a ceiling of $7,000 on pre-tax employee contributions, indexed for inflation. In addition, these plans must comply with one of three coverage tests to ensure that the plan covers a wide cross section of employees and does not discriminate in favor of highly compensated employees.

There is a continuing increase in the proportion of plans in which the employee may contribute additional amounts above the basic contribution which are not matched by the employer. Even if these contributions are after-tax contributions, the earnings from the account are sheltered.

Employer Contributions

Typically, employer contributions to savings plans are determined by the amount the employee contributes. Ordinarily, the employer contribution is a specified, uniform percentage of each employee's basic contribution. Some plans establish a range for company matching contributions, with the actual contribution determined by factors such as length of service or profits. Of course there are also plans in which the employer makes no contribution.

The most prevalent employer contribution rate is 50 percent (see Table IV-2). At the same time, there has been a decline in the proportion of plans that match the employee contribution at a rate lower than 50 percent and an increase in the proportion of plans that match at a rate higher than 50 percent. Some plans provide for a basic minimum company contribution and for an additional contribution based on profits. The advantage of such a plan is that when the company is more successful financially the employees share in the prosperity, but the employer also has some flexibility in less profitable years.

As might be expected, there is a positive correlation between the company's contribution and the plan's participation rate. The Bankers Trust study found that plans matching at a rate of 100 percent or higher had a median participation rate of 84 percent, compared with 79 percent for those that match at a rate between 50 percent and 100 percent and 73 percent for plans that match at a rate of 50 percent or lower.

TABLE IV-2
Employer Contribution Rates for Defined Contribution Plans
(as Percentage of Employee Contribution)
1986 and 1977

Matching Employer Contribution Rates	Percent of Plans	
	1986	1977
25% or less	8%	17%
26-40%	7	9
50%	48	46
55-75%	13	4
100%	11	14
Over 100%	a	2
Other Methods[b]	13	8

Source: Bankers Trust Company, *Corporate Defined Contribution Plans*, (New York: Bankers Trust Company, 1987), p. 16.
[a]Less than 0.5 percent.
[b]Includes profit sharing plans.

Employee Savings Plans

The Bankers Trust study computed an approximate cost of the savings plans assuming that all participants contribute at the maximum rate that would be matched by the company and ignoring any "additional" company contributions. The before-tax cost ranged from 1.5 percent to 12 percent of covered payroll with a median cost of 3 percent. It is likely, as the study points out, that the actual cost of a plan will be less depending upon the proportion of participants, the rate at which participants contribute, and the amount of forfeitures applied to reduce the company contributions.

Voluntary Suspensions

Essentially all of the plans in the Bankers Trust study allowed voluntary suspensions of employee contributions, usually for any reason. In general, no company contributions are made to an employee's account during a suspension period. The trend is toward a liberalization of the restrictions on frequency and duration of suspensions. More than one-half of the plans permitted suspension to occur four times or more each year. Three months was found to be the median minimum suspension period, down from six months in the prior study in 1977.

Investment of Contributions

Traditionally, the investment of contributions has been chiefly in employer common stock, and 82 percent of the plans in the Bankers Trust study continue to offer that option. The trend, however, is toward allowing more investment options and more direction from the employees to allocate their own contributions and/or the company contributions. Nine out of ten participants were allowed to choose how they wanted their own contributions invested.

Only 1 percent of the plans required all contributions to be invested in company stock; 50 percent required part of the total contributions (usually the company portion) to be invested in company stock; 31 percent permitted investment in company stock but did not make it mandatory; and 18 percent of the plans excluded the use of company stock.

In addition to allowing more investment direction from the employee there is also a trend toward an increased number of investment funds among which the employee may allocate employee and/or company contributions. The median and the modal number of funds offered is three, and 79 percent offer three or more. Employees have less flexibility in the investment choice for employer contributions. Only one-half of the participants in the BLS survey were permitted to choose how the matching company contributions were to be invested.

There have been some significant changes in the types of investment funds being offered and chosen by employees in these plans (see Table IV-3). Company stock is still the most frequently included. The most dramatic growth, however, has been in guaranteed income contract (GIC) portfolios which increased from 23 percent in 1977 to 63 percent in 1986. Another large increase was found in the use of short term fixed income funds which increased from 5 percent in 1977 to 26 percent in 1986. The funds which have declined in importance are the U.S. government obligation funds. For plans in which it is offered, a GIC portfolio is the fund most frequently elected for current contributions. In addition, the asset value of GIC funds now exceeds that of company stock in those plans in which both are offered.

Investment Transfers

In addition to changes in investment funds for *future* contributions, an overwhelming proportion of plans (95 percent) also permit participants to transfer *accumulated* balances to some degree. The trend is not only toward allowing transfers but also toward offering the choice of more frequent transfers. This liberalization is a recogni-

TABLE IV-3
Prevalence of Investment Funds Offered in Defined Contribution Plans 1986 and 1977

Fund Types	Percent of All Plans	
	1986	1977
Company Stock	82%	85%
Active Equity	49	45
Passive Equity	18	–
GIC	63	23
Fixed Income	31	36
U.S. Government Obligations	18	31
U.S. Series EE Bonds	4	11
Short-Term Fixed Income	26	5
Balanced Income	15	19
Mutual Funds	11	7
Other	6	NA

Source: Bankers Trust Company, *Corporate Defined Contribution Plans*, (New York: Bankers Trust Company, 1987), p. 24.

tion by employers that investment markets are often quite volatile and that individual employee investment objectives are often very diverse and that those objectives may change over time.

The Bankers Trust study found that 31 percent of the plans which permitted transfers specified one transfer per year. Another 62 percent permit transfers more frequently than once per year. Frequently plans specify transfer provisions for accumulated employee contributions different from those for accumulated company contributions, the latter usually being less prevalent and less liberal than the former.

Vesting

All plans provide for fully vested company contributions upon death, retirement, or permanent disability. An employee's own contributions are always 100 percent vested. Therefore, the discussion of vesting provisions which follows relates to the right of an employee to company contributions should the employee leave the company for reasons other than death, retirement, or permanent disability or upon the exercise of withdrawal privileges while still in the service of the employer.

There are three types of vesting provisions: (1) immediate vesting which means employer contributions are 100 percent vested as they are made; (2) graduated vesting under which an employee's nonforfeitable percentage increases over time and reaches 100 percent after a specified number of years; and (3) "cliff vesting" which provides full vesting after a specified number of years. The Tax Reform Act of 1986 specified two minimum vesting alternatives: 100 percent vesting after five years of service or a graduated seven-year schedule (20 percent after three years of service, plus 20 percent for each year thereafter).

The trend in vesting provisions has clearly been toward liberalization, brought on in part by legislation and in part by a desire on the part of plan sponsors to make plans more attractive to employees. The proportion of plans with immediate vesting increased dramatically from 12 percent in 1977 to 25 percent in 1986. The most common vesting requirement found in the Bankers Trust study was five years of plan membership, but 37 percent of the plans provided for full vesting after less than five years of membership, up from 14 percent in the 1977 study.

Some plans also provide for 100 percent vesting upon termination of service under special circumstances such as: layoffs or plant shutdowns; entry into armed forces or government service; involuntary termination without cause; or a combination of the above or other reasons.

Forfeiture Allocation

Forfeitures normally occur when a participant terminates employment without being fully vested. The overwhelming practice (90 percent of the plans) is to apply forfeitures to reduce the company's contributions to the plan. Only 6 percent of the plans allocate forfeitures to participant's accounts.

In-Service Withdrawals

The ability of employees to withdraw their own contributions while remaining in the service of the employer depends upon whether the money withdrawn was contributed pre-tax or post-tax and the terms of the plans themselves.

Post-tax. One-half of the plans in the Bankers Trust study that have a withdrawal provision permit the withdrawal of both employee and company contribution accounts. One-third of the plans exclude the company contribution account and permit the withdrawal of the employee contribution account only. Many of the plans still have penalty provisions for withdrawal of employer contributions and earnings on employee and employer contributions. In the past, penalties were required to avoid assessment of federal income tax liability to the participant. Continuation of penalties for withdrawal is often utilized to discourage withdrawals and to encourage long-term thrift.[7]

Penalties include: suspension of membership for a period of time; suspension of company contributions for a specified period of time; termination of membership; and forfeiture of the company contribution account, subject to ERISA requirements. There was a significant increase (from 2 percent to 27 percent) from 1977 to 1986 in plans that impose no penalty. A large proportion of plans also permit the employee to make a smaller than maximum withdrawal with a less severe penalty.

Pre-tax. Where pre-tax 401(k) contributions or earnings on those contributions are involved, withdrawal becomes more circumscribed. In fact, earnings on pre-tax contributions may no longer be withdrawn nor may employer contributions or earnings thereon. A withdrawal of the employee's own contributions may be made only in cases of "hardship" involving immediate and heavy financial need

---

[7]Dan M. McGill, *Fundamentals of Private Pensions* (Homewood, IL: Richard D. Irwin, Inc., 1984), pp. 661-662.

and then only when the amount needed is not reasonably available from other resources of the employee. The amount of the hardship withdrawal is limited to that which is required to meet the immediate financial need created by the hardship.

The IRS allows hardship withdrawals for four reasons: medical expenses; college tuition; purchase of a primary residence; and prevention of the loss of a home through foreclosure. Requiring the exhaustion of other financial resources includes borrowing (including borrowing from the same plan if it has a loan provision) and/or liquidating assets before making a withdrawal from the savings plan. Of course, a withdrawal of pre-tax contributions is taxable income to the employee and may be subject to a 10 percent penalty tax as well under certain circumstances.

Loans

Loan provisions in savings plans are common. The Bankers Trust study found that 43 percent of the plans had a loan provision. Unlike a withdrawal, a loan is not a taxable distribution. The maximum amount that a participant can borrow is the lesser of: (1) $50,000 less the highest balance on any plan loans during the twelve-month period immediately preceding the date on which the load was made; or (2) the greater of $10,000 and 50 percent of the participant's vested account balance. Interest rates are usually specified in the plan. Repayment must be made within five years unless the loan is used to acquire a principal residence. Loan provisions may be expected to increase in importance since in-service withdrawals of pre-tax contributions are somewhat more circumscribed by recent legislation. The most common source of loan funds is the employee's contributions. Some plans also permit loans from the company contribution account.

Forms of Distribution

Traditionally, distribution of savings plan accounts was made in a lump sum or in company stock if that was an investment choice. The trend is toward providing alternative forms of distribution at the election of the employee or his or her beneficiary. In the 1986 study, 88 percent of the plans permitted optional forms of distribution. The most common choices were installments over a specified period of time, annuity contracts, deferrable lump sums, and purchase of an additional pension through the company pension plan. Recent legislation requires distribution no later than April 1 following the calendar year in which the employee attains age 70-1/2 regardless of whether or not the employee terminates his or her employment.

Trends

Thrift/Savings plans have become a popular employee benefit in the last ten years, encouraged by the rise of 401(k) plans in 1983. Since these plans offered several advantages to employees at reasonable cost to the employer, growth was to be expected. Savings plans should encourage employee thrift at a time when there is a national need to increase personal savings. It may well be the case that 401(k) plans have peaked, however. Recently published IRS regulations seem to discourage relatively lower paid employees from participation in 401(k) plans by imposing more rigorous standards for hardship withdrawals. Lower paid employees may find it too risky to tie up their savings in an investment that is less and less liquid. At best, the employer has a substantial communications burden to educate employees about what the plan cannot do as well as what it can do. The message from the IRS, through its regulations, is that 401(k) plans are meant to be used primarily for retirement purposes. Of course, if a large proportion of lower paid employees do not participate then it is more difficult for the employer to satisfy the discrimination tests because the proportion of higher paid participants increases relative to the lower paid participants.

Although companies which have a 401(k) plan might not drop it because of the new regulation, it is possible that companies considering the adoption of such plans may be less likely to do so. At some point, the administration burden may overcome the advantages that such plans offer. In addition, the Tax Reform Act of 1986 prohibited state and local governments and tax-exempt employers from adopting new 401(k) plans, which will further limit their growth.

CHAPTER V

Employee Stock Ownership

Interest in employee ownership in the United States dates from late in the nineteenth century. It peaked in the 1920s with the establishment of ownership programs in railroads, utilities, and manufacturing firms, but the stock market crash of 1929 destroyed participants' equity value and along with it enthusiasm for employee ownership plans. Early in the post-World War II era, however, interest in employee ownership once again appeared, mainly in the form of stock bonus plans. With the adoption of the Employee Retirement Income Security Act (ERISA) in 1974, the Employee Stock Ownership Plan (ESOP) was given official sanction, and since then has attracted the support of lawmakers, academics, and businessmen who see it as the solution to any number of economic problems, including declining productivity; low employee motivation, job satisfaction and commitment; and industrial conflict.

ESOPs are the principal mechanism by which American workers can attain an ownership stake in their companies. Over the last decade the number of ESOPs has grown significantly, and they are now found in many industries and across public and private and large and small companies. According to the National Center for Employee Ownership, at the end of 1989 there were approximately 10,000 ESOPs covering over 10 million employees.[1] The most well-known cases of ESOP use have been those where workers have bought a plant or company that is scheduled for closure. The use of ESOPs has not been limited to these cases, however, and in fact the ESOP is a very flexible instrument that can be applied in a wide variety of business settings. Although usually designed as an employee benefit meant to supplement more conventional retirement plans, ESOPs are to an increasing extent being viewed as an alternative compensation method.

DEFINITION, TYPES, AND PROVISIONS

An ESOP is a defined contribution employee benefit plan designed to invest primarily (defined as more than 50 percent of a plan's

---

[1] *Benefits Today*, Vol. 6, No. 17 (August 25, 1989), p. 275.

assets)[2] in employer securities[3] with the intention of giving employee participants an ownership stake in the enterprise. To establish an ESOP, a company—only corporations can establish an ESOP, not proprietorships or partnerships—creates a largely separate and tax-exempt entity called an Employee Stock Ownership Trust (ESOT) to which it contributes stock or cash. The ESOT purchases stock of the principal company and is administered and managed by one or more trustees, who are generally appointed by the board of directors. The trustee(s) has the fiduciary responsibility to manage the assets in a prudent manner and for the exclusive benefit of plan participants. Typically an ESOP committee is established to oversee the ESOP and to instruct the trustee(s) on how to vote ESOP shares.

Stock is allocated to participant accounts according to the plan's allocation formula and participants gradually become owners of the stock in their accounts through a vesting process. Because there is no tax on the stock held in individual accounts until it is distributed, ESOPs are a form of tax deferred compensation. In the case of a leveraged ESOP, the trust actually borrows money from a financial

---

[2] The Department of Labor's Advisory Opinion 83-6A states that an ESOP fulfills this requirement if more than 50 percent of its assets are invested in employer securities. Generally, ESOPs will hold cash balances for that proportion of their assets not held in stock. Jared Kaplan, *Fiduciary Concerns in ESOP Leveraged Buyouts*, paper prepared for the ESOP Association's 11th Annual Convention, May 1988.

The ESOP Association's 1988 survey found that 53 percent of all respondent company's ESOPs were invested entirely in their own stock, while 80 percent of all respondent's ESOPs had over 80 percent of their assets in their own stock. ESOP Association, *ESOP Survey: 1988* (Washington, D.C.: ESOP Association of America, 1988), p. 9.

[3] There are a number of aspects to the definition of what constitutes employer securities. Generally speaking, for public companies it refers to common stock that is tradeable in securities markets or to preferred stock that is convertible into common stock. For closely-held firms, the security issued must have voting and dividend rights equal to or surpassing those of any other securities issued by the employer. Section 404 (a) (2) of ERISA exempts employees from the necessity of having to diversify their investment (which generally requires that no more than 10 percent of a plan's investment be in employer securities), as is the case for other deferred compensation plans. ESOPs can be 100 percent invested in employer securities without violating ERISA rules. If an ESOP invests in assets other than employer securities or cash, the diversification requirements of ERISA will apply.

ESOPs are also exempt from Section 406 of ERISA which precludes transactions between a deferred compensation plan and a "party in interest." Without an exemption, this would, in the case of ESOPs, prevent the ESOP from buying stock from major shareholders, officers, or directors. For a detailed examination of these and other legal issues concerning ESOPs, see The Bureau of National Affairs, *Employee Ownership Plans: How 8,000 Companies and 8,000,000 Employees Invest in Their Futures* (Bureau of National Affairs, Inc., 1987), pp. 155-198.

Employee Stock Ownership

institution or the employer in order to purchase employer stock.[4] Thus an ESOP can be used as a method of debt financing, a characteristic which sets it apart from all other deferred compensation plans. If an ESOP complies with the Internal Revenue Code, section 410(a), which requires that it be established for the exclusive benefit of employees and that it meet certain guidelines on vesting, coverage, funding, and contributions, it receives tax qualified[5] treatment, and as a result, employer contributions (either stock or cash to buy stock) to it are tax deductible up to certain limits.

ESOPs are distinct from stock purchase plans, in which employees are allowed to purchase stock from the company at a discount, and other types of stock programs such as stock option and stock appreciation plans. ESOPs are intended to provide plan participants with benefits similar to those of profit sharing plans, with the major difference being that stock bonus plans generally distribute employer stock and not cash. Important distinctions between ESOPs and profit sharing plans are that ESOPs invest almost exclusively in employer securities, allocate stock in a manner not necessarily tied to a company's profit performance, and are not subject to fair return requirements on their investment.

Types of ESOPs

Until recently, there were four different types of ESOPs available: leveraged, non-leveraged, leverageable, and tax credit. As part of the Tax Reform Act of 1986 (TRA-1986), however, the tax credit ESOP was eliminated as of year end 1986 and, therefore, it will not be discussed in this chapter.

Leveraged. As originally conceived, the ESOP program would provide tax incentives to companies to finance their capital expansion or acquisitions with equity rather than debt or retained earnings. The leveraged ESOP, because it can take on debt through a "party in interest" to finance the purchase of employer stock, is arguably the most important type. For companies with closely held stock that are in need of a capital infusion and that are either unable or unwilling to raise capital through a public offering, the leveraged ESOP provides an alternative means. Although there are a variety

---

[4]ESOPs are thus exempt from ERISA Section 406 (a) (1) (B) and I.R.C. Section 4975 (c) (1) (B) both of which prohibit a deferred compensation plan from contracting for debt or any extension of credit with any "party in interest." The exemption allows an ESOP to purchase employer securities with the proceeds of a loan.

[5]Employee benefit plans that are not qualified do not receive favorable tax treatment; frequently plans do not qualify owing to an allocation formula that favors a particular group of employees.

of ways that leveraged ESOP transactions can be structured, the basic leveraged transaction involves:

(1) the company establishes a leveraged ESOP;
(2) the ESOP trust secures a loan from a qualified institutional lender (including commercial banks and insurance companies, but not investment banks) in exchange for a promissory note that may be guaranteed by the company or the company may contract the loan itself and then lend the proceeds to the ESOP;
(3) the ESOP trust uses the proceeds of the loan to purchase stock from the company or from other shareholders;
(4) the company uses the proceeds from the sale of the stock to the ESOP trust to finance capital expansion or acquisitions, to refinance existing debt, or to increase working capital;
(5) the ESOP trust uses the shares acquired as collateral for the loan and places the shares in a suspense account;
(6) the company makes tax deductible (within limits) contributions of cash or payments of dividends to the ESOP trust equivalent to the amount needed to service the loan, and as the loan is paid off the stock held as collateral is allocated to participant accounts.

There are two significant tax advantages for companies using this method of financing. First, company contributions to the ESOP trust to service the loan are deductible for the company, with contributions going to interest payments fully deductible and those to principal payments deductible within certain limits. Second, financial institutions and regulated investment companies are able, in accordance with the incentives provided in the Deficit Reduction Act of 1984 and the TRA-1986, to deduct 50 percent of the interest they receive on loans to ESOPs for the purpose of acquiring employer stock.[6] As a result, financial institutions can lower the interest rate on loans to ESOPs below prevailing market rates. Combined, these two advantages permit companies to reduce their total borrowing costs compared with conventional debt financing. Compared with traditional equity financing, however, the leveraged ESOP does not measure up well in terms of cost.

Leverageable and Non-Leveraged. Leverageable ESOPs are those able to contract debt but which have not yet done so, while non-leveraged ESOPs do not have this capacity. A leverageable ESOP becomes leveraged immediately upon its borrowing money. Both the non-leveraged and leverageable ESOP trusts receive stock solely from free company contributions. Although neither takes advantage

---

[6]The 1989 Budget Reconciliation Act eliminated this tax treatment unless the ESOP owns more than 50 percent of each class of outstanding employer stock or 50 percent of the total value of the corporation and full voting rights are passed through on the stock acquired with a loan under this tax provision.

of the leveraging incentives for equity financing of plant and equipment modernization or debt refinancing, these ESOPs do embody tax incentives that employers have found attractive. Companies can take a tax deduction, within certain limits, equivalent to the current fair market value of the stock, or the money to buy stock, contributed to the ESOP. In the case of a contribution of newly issued stock, the company increases its working capital and cash flow by the amount of the tax deduction. Furthermore, the law allows, within limits, companies to carry forward the unused portion of their allowable tax-deductible contributions to ESOPs.

Provisions

Although there are certain legal requirements governing ESOP provisions, there remain a number of areas in which discretion is permitted. Both required and discretionary provisions are outlined in the following section including eligibility guidelines, allocation and vesting schedules, dividend policy, distribution guidelines, and voting rights.

Eligibility. ESOPs are subject to the Internal Revenue Code's nondiscrimination rules which are designed to provide broad participation in ownership of the sponsoring corporation's stock. There is considerable discretion for the sponsor regarding the categories of employees which can be excluded, among them: foreign nationals; workers who are under twenty-one years old; workers within five years of company retirement age at the time of hiring; and workers with less than one year of service with the company (in the case of workers with more than one year but less than two years service, exclusion is only permitted if the plan allows for immediate 100 percent vesting). It appears that the most prevalent reason for exclusion is membership in bargaining units, but union membership is grounds for exclusion only if the company is willing to bargain with the union over the inclusion of its members and the union refuses.

A 1986 survey by the U.S. General Accounting Office (GAO) reported that the median rate of employee participation for all ESOPs was approximately 70 percent.[7] A study of over 2,000 ESOPs in 1984 found that more than 50 percent of employees were excluded from participating.[8] Of the excluded workers, almost 40

---

[7]U.S. General Accounting Office, *Employee Stock Ownership Plans: Benefits and Costs of ESOP Tax Incentives for Broadening Stock Ownership* (Washington, D.C.: U.S. General Accounting Office, December 1986), p. 35.

[8]Joseph Blasi, *Employee Ownership: Revolution or Ripoff* (Cambridge, MA: Ballinger Publishing Company, 1988), p. 44.

percent were either members of unions or foreign nationals, with the former category undoubtedly accounting for the vast majority of this group. Union membership, therefore, is strongly correlated with exclusion from ESOP participation, but it is unclear why. Without question, management has in some cases deliberately sought to prevent union members from participating in ESOPs, but unions, because of their historical antipathy toward ESOPs, have seldom taken an active role in their formation or in shaping ESOP legislation.

Allocation Formulas, Company Contributions, and Vesting Schedules. As a defined contribution plan, an ESOP must specify a formula for allocating benefits to plan participants. Generally, ESOPs allocate company contributions (normally made annually) of stock, cash, or a combination of the two based on participants' relative compensation levels, with the amount of stock allocated increasing with compensation. Although not frequently used, variables such as years of service or hours of work may be included in the formula, or stock may be allocated equally to each participant. Regardless of the formula, the allocation of stock must be at least equal to that based on relative compensation levels. In the case of a leveraged ESOP, the stock purchased with an ESOP loan must be placed in a suspense account and allocated to individual accounts as principal and interest are repaid. For leverageable and nonleveraged ESOPs, the stock is allocated to participant accounts upon its purchase by the company, or at a later date if the purchase occurs between allocation periods. Allocations to employees' individual accounts and any appreciation in the value of those accounts are not taxable until they are distributed.

There are legal limitations on the amount of deductible stock or cash that a company can contribute annually to an ESOP and on the amount of stock that can be allocated annually to participant accounts. Unless the ESOP is leveraged, companies are not legally obligated to make a contribution, but since the amount and frequency of company contributions affect employee attitudes, it is prudent for companies to make contributions when possible. Ordinarily, contributions to all defined contribution plans (including nonleveraged ESOPs) are deductible by the sponsoring company up to 15 percent of covered payroll. In the case of a leveraged ESOP, contributions to cover loan principal payments are deductible up to 25 percent of covered payroll, with no limit on deductions for interest payments. Deduction for all other defined contribution plans is limited to 15 percent.

At the same time, the annual addition that may be made to each participant's account cannot exceed the lesser of 25 percent of pay or a specified dollar amount, subject to nondiscrimination provisions. Both ESOP companies and the federal government have an interest in the design of allocation formulas: the former because the potential motivational effects of employee ownership might bear some relation to the degree of ownership and the latter because of its need to ensure that the tax benefits accorded ESOP companies are used to distribute stock in a manner that broadens their ownership.

Companies establish vesting schedules to determine when participants actually own the stock that has been allocated to their ESOP accounts. Vesting schedules are based on the length of a participant's membership in the plan in order to provide an incentive for employees to remain with the company. Under the provisions of the Tax Reform Act of 1986, companies can delay the start of vesting for two years, but commencing with the third year, a participant's vesting must accumulate at a rate of at least 20 percent annually. Alternatively, vesting can be delayed until the fifth year of participation, but at this point full vesting is required. Usually, an employee's account vests 100 percent in the case of retirement, death, or permanent disability.

Dividend Payments and Distribution Schedules. One criticism of ESOPs has been the lack of immediate reward (as compared to cash profit sharing plans or gain sharing) for improved performance. By design, an ESOP participant generally does not receive the financial benefit of ownership until leaving the company. ESOP companies can nevertheless provide some immediate reward through the payment of cash dividends on the stock held in individual ESOP accounts, and such payments are tax deductible for the company, but the law does not require ESOPs to make dividend payments. A tax deduction is also allowed, in the case of leveraged ESOPs, for dividend payments used to repay the loan incurred by the trust to purchase the shares. Given the tax advantages for paying dividends, it is somewhat surprising that relatively few ESOP companies make dividend payments. In its 1988 survey, the ESOP Association found that only 11 percent of companies paid dividends directly to employees and only 16 percent to retire ESOP loans.[9]

Although employers have some freedom in the design of allocation formulas and vesting schedules, they have little discretion in regard to the distribution of individual account assets to plan participants.

---

[9]ESOP Association, *ESOP Survey: 1988* (Washington, D.C.: ESOP Association of America, 1988), p. 10.

Distribution to participants may begin as soon as possible after termination of employment or may be deferred for up to six years (or longer if an ESOP loan is outstanding). Where employment terminates because of retirement, disability, or death, distribution must begin in the following year. Unless the participant elects otherwise, the distribution must be in equal annual installments over a period of no longer than five years. Large accounts may be distributed over longer periods of time. An important qualification for leveraged ESOPs is that the portion of participants' accounts that was purchased with the proceeds of an ESOP loan may not be distributed until the entire loan is repaid.

Distribution can be in either employer securities or cash, with the participant able to demand and receive stock unless the terms of the plan restrict stock ownership to employees. If the employer securities are not readily tradable on an established market, the ESOP participant may require the employer (not the ESOP) to repurchase the securities for cash at a fair market value within sixty days after it is distributed. Although this repurchase obligation may represent a significant future liability, the law does not require that companies fund this certain and evolving obligation. A 1988 survey by the National Center for Employee Ownership (NCEO) found that many firms do not have repurchase plans, although those ESOPs with large repurchase liabilities were more likely to have such plans.[10] For publicly traded companies this repurchase obligation does not exist because there is an established market within which employer stock can be sold.

Voting Rights and Worker Control. In a publicly traded company, ESOP participants have voting rights on all shares allocated to their accounts in the ESOP. There is no requirement that voting rights be passed through on stock that is unallocated,[11] and unallocated shares are ordinarily voted by the trustees. In a privately held company, voting rights for shares allocated to participants are required only with respect to matters such as a merger, recapitalization, or liquidation. Most ESOPs (70 percent) hold employer stock with voting rights,[12] but since most ESOP participants are found in large,

---

[10]"How ESOP Companies are Handling Repurchase Liability," *The Employee Ownership Report*, Vol. III, No. 4 (July-August 1988), pp. 1, 6.

[11]When stock is purchased by an ESOP with borrowed funds, all of that stock is unallocated as it is used as collateral for the loan. The stock is allocated to the accounts of participants as the loan is amortized.

[12]U.S. General Accounting Office, *Employee Stock Ownership Plans: Interim Report on a Survey and Related Economic Trends* (Washington, D.C.: U.S. General Accounting Office, 1986), p. 21.

Employee Stock Ownership 77

publicly traded companies and few of those ESOPs own a large portion of the sponsoring company's stock, relatively little effective control is exercised by the participants. Thus it is to closely held firms that one must look in order to ascertain the true nature of voting rights in ESOPs. But the record here does not reveal that closely held firms commonly extend voting rights beyond that called for by law. The 1988 survey by the ESOP Association found that only 17 percent of the companies passed through voting rights on all issues, while 71 percent passed through voting rights on limited issues.[13] In its 1986 survey of majority owned and closely held companies (where one would expect to find a greater willingness to share decision making), the NCEO found that only 15 percent passed through full voting rights.[14] The GAO, however, found that 62 percent of the closely held companies it surveyed passed through stock with voting rights.[15] In summary, although many participants in ESOPs have full voting rights, there are very few ESOP companies in which employees actually have significant influence over areas of decision making beyond those normally addressed in collective bargaining.

HOW ESOPs ARE USED

Most observers would agree that without tax incentives ESOPs would not have grown to anywhere near their present status. During the years that Senator Russell B. Long was on the Finance and Commerce Committee (from the early 1970s to the mid-1980s), no less than nineteen separate pieces of legislation were enacted to enhance the prospects of employee ownership.[16] Congressional legislation has consistently had two chief objectives: (1) to bring about a broader ownership of wealth in the form of corporate stock, and (2) to provide a mechanism of corporate finance for the creation of additional funds for capital formation.[17] An implied objective is improved eco-

---

[13]ESOP Association, *ESOP Survey: 1988*, p. 20.
[14]Cathy Ivancic and Corey Rosen, *Voting and Participation in Employee Ownership Firms* (The National Center for Employee Ownership), September 1986, p. 1.
[15]U.S. General Accounting Office, *Employee Stock Ownership Plans: Interim Report on a Survey and Related Economic Trends*, p. 21.
[16]Bureau of National Affairs, *Employee Ownership Plans: How 8,000 Companies and 8,000,000 Employees Invest in Their Futures* (Washington, D.C.: Bureau of National Affairs, 1987), Introduction by the Honorable Russell B. Long, p. v.
[17]U.S. General Accounting Office, *Employee Stock Ownership Plans: Little Evidence of Effects on Corporate Performance* (Washington, D.C.: U.S. General Accounting Office, 1987), pp. 32-34.

nomic performance of the sponsoring corporations.

At the company level there are a variety of pragmatic reasons for the establishment of ESOPs, the majority of which are in general accordance with the objectives set by the Congress for the ESOP program, or at least support goals to which the Congress certainly is not opposed. In recent years, however, numerous ESOPs have been adopted for reasons that it is unlikely the Congress or some proponents of employee ownership would acknowledge as legitimate. These include ESOPs used as a defense against hostile takeovers or as part of a leveraged buy out (LBO).

The GAO's study found that the three most common reasons cited for establishing an ESOP were to provide an employee benefit, to gain a tax advantage, and to improve productivity.[18] The GAO's data show that a substantial number of companies also established ESOPs in order to buy out a major stock holder, to reduce turnover, or to give employees a majority interest in their company. When companies adopt ESOPs they usually have more than one objective and thus many of the following uses of ESOPs are interrelated.

Provide an Employee Benefit. For companies wishing to provide their employees with a new benefit or for those lacking a retirement plan, ESOPs may represent a comparatively inexpensive means to this end. Like other benefit plans, ESOPs have initial and ongoing administrative and legal costs, but their funding is not as burdensome. When a company contributes newly issued stock to an ESOP, it does not have a major outlay of cash, although current stockholders do suffer a dilution in the value of their shares. At the same time, the company is allowed to deduct the value of the stock contributed and in effect to improve its working capital position and cash flow. Thus, used as an alternative compensation device, ESOPs allow companies (even those with tight budget constraints) to offer employees another reward for their services.

Another potential advantage from a company standpoint is the use of an ESOP as a replacement for other benefit plans. Although not widespread, some companies have terminated pension plans and established an ESOP as employees' sole retirement benefit.[19] This, of course, drastically increases the risk employees must bear and is

---

[18]U.S. General Accounting Office, *Employee Stock Ownership Plans: Benefits and Costs*, p. 20.

[19]Prior to 1989, companies could terminate a defined benefit or contribution plan, and use the excess assets to establish an ESOP without having to pay a 10 percent excise tax.

not looked upon with favor among ESOP proponents.[20] Recently, a number of companies, including Boise Cascade, Whitman, and Ralston Purina, have begun phasing out post-retirement medical coverage and have instead instructed employees to tap their ESOP accounts to cover such expenses.[21] While saving money, this also increases the stake that employees have in the success of the company and as such may naturally lead to demands for participation in those decisions that vitally affect company viability.

Tax Advantages. In leveraged ESOPs, company contributions to service both interest and principal loan payments are deductible, and the 50 percent deduction that lenders receive (somewhat limited by 1989 legislation) on interest payments by ESOPs has lowered companies' borrowing costs. For leverageable and nonleveraged ESOPs, company contributions to the ESOP of stock or cash to buy stock are deductible up to certain limits, while regardless of the type, ESOP dividend payments passed through to participants are deductible. There are also numerous tax advantages for owners who wish to sell their company to its employees. Although the tendency of Congress in the past has been to add more tax incentives for ESOPs, recently Congress has begun to look more critically at these tax breaks.

Enhance Company Performance and Employee Motivation. The improvement of company performance was one of the primary objectives of Congress in enacting ESOP legislation, and many companies have established ESOPs in the hope that they will have a positive effect on productivity, and thus on profitability and competitiveness. Theoretically, the principal channel through which this improvement will be achieved is the effect on employees of having an ownership stake in the enterprise in which they work. Another spur to company performance would also be the generous tax breaks and the resulting increase in working capital.

The evidence to date is inconclusive on the question of improved company performance, although there is some support for this occurring when employee ownership is combined with worker participation. There has not been extensive empirical research into the effect on employees of an ownership stake, and thus there "is no

---

[20]When pension plans are terminated, participants generally receive an annuity contract equal to the amount in the account at the time. But whereas defined benefit (and not defined contribution) plans are guaranteed by the government's Pension Benefit Guarantee Corporation, annuities are not and thus represent a far greater risk. Furthermore, annuities are not indexed to inflation so retirees will probably not receive cost-of-living increases.

[21]"ESOPs: Are They Good for You?" *Business Week*, May 15, 1989, p. 122.

evidence supporting the hypothesis that a stock account existing as a deferred benefit will influence worker behavior and attitudes."[22] It appears that the amount of stock held in the account of a typical ESOP participant is not large enough to generate increased motivation, commitment, and work effort, especially since actual ownership of the stock is not realized until after the employee leaves the company. One major study found that the positive psychological effects of ownership occur when the ownership stake is reinforced with financial benefits (the company makes large contributions to participant's ESOP accounts) and participation opportunities.[23]

Buyout Owner(s). ESOPs can be used to effect buyouts of a departing owner in a closely held firm and buying a company/subsidiary/division that is scheduled for closure or sale because of financial problems or for reasons unrelated to its financial performance. Providing a market for the stock of a departing owner has been one of the most frequent uses of leveraged ESOPs by closely held companies.

Although the number of cases is relatively small, the most publicized and, to some critics, controversial use of ESOPs has been to allow workers to buy companies/subsidiaries/divisions that are facing the threat of closure because of poor financial results. Generally, the transaction involves the formation of a new company which in turn establishes a leveraged ESOP. Through the leveraged ESOP a loan is contracted and the proceeds are used to purchase the stock of the new company. The new company then purchases the assets of the selling company. Some of the more noteworthy companies that have been through this process are Wierton Steel, Rath Packing, and Hyatt-Clark Industries, the last two of which did not survive. The majority of such buyouts have been successful, however. To proponents, these efforts have (at least temporarily) saved jobs and prevented the destruction of the economic base of entire communities. It is also felt that if these companies institute new labor-management relations and instill greater motivation in the work force, they can actually be profitable operations. To critics, however, providing tax breaks to keep unprofitable plants in operation represents a severe distortion of the efficient allocation of capital resources and a creation of undue competitive pressure which can negatively affect healthy companies in the same industry.

---

[22]Tove Helland Hammer, "New Developments in Profit Sharing, Gainsharing, and Employee Ownership," *ILR Reprints* (New York State School of Industrial and Labor Relations, 1988), p. 356.

[23]Katherine J. Klein, "Employee Stock Ownership and Employee Attitudes: A Test of Three Models," *Journal of Applied Psychology*, 1987, Vol. 72, No. 2, pp. 319-332.

Finally, a corporation may be interested in selling a subsidiary because it does not fit into its long-term strategic plans or is not achieving the required return on investment. In turn, the employees of this subsidiary may fear the consequences of being sold to a new owner and thus desire to purchase the subsidiary themselves. This can be accomplished through a leveraged ESOP.

General Financing Needs. A company in need of capital infusion can potentially lower its cost of funds by borrowing money through a leveraged ESOP and repaying the loan with pre-tax dollars. Companies can also use ESOPs to finance stock repurchases and to refinance debt. Since the passage of the 1984 and 1986 tax bills, which embodied new incentives for leveraged ESOPs, companies have made greater use of this financing mechanism partly because many of their previous tax breaks were eliminated at the same time. During the first five months of 1989, an estimated $8 billion was borrowed through leveraged ESOPs,[24] while $6.5 billion was borrowed in 1988, $5.5 billion in 1987, and $1.2 billion in 1986.[25] Although in 1989 Congress restricted the tax deduction available to institutions which lend to ESOPs, the leveraged ESOP remains a viable debt financing tool.

Hostile Takeover Defense. ESOPs employed as a means to prevent hostile takeovers have drawn criticism for their role in entrenching management. In recent years numerous large corporations have taken this approach, including Polaroid,[26] Texaco, Procter & Gamble, General Mills, Lockheed Corporation, and J. C. Penney. By placing a substantial portion of shares at the discretion of an ESOP trustee or in the hands of employees, both of which are more likely to remain loyal to current management, ESOPs present a substantial hindrance to would-be raiders. Further, the ESOP itself may also discourage bidders. But because an ESOP is meant for the exclusive benefit of plan participants and not to protect the jobs of manage-

---

[24] Anise C. Wallace, "Rostenkowski Seeking ESOP-Loan Benefit Cut," *New York Times*, June 8, 1989, p. C7.

[25] "Leveraged ESOP Transactions Reach $6.5 billion in 1988," *The Employee Ownership Report*, Volume IX, No. 1 (January/February 1989) pp. 1, 9.

[26] The case of Polaroid has received much attention from not only the media but also the Department of Labor. Polaroid, just prior to a hostile takeover attempt by Shamrock Holdings Inc., decided to expand the stake of an effectively blocked Shamrock's bid for Polaroid because in the state of Delaware, where Polaroid is incorporated, a prospective buyer must acquire at least 85 percent of a company's shares or be forced to wait three years before taking control of the target company. Shamrock tried but failed to have Polaroid's ESOP nullified on the grounds that it was meant solely as a defensive measure and that Polaroid's board breached its fiduciary duty.

ment, the potential exists that a court might overturn an ESOP established in the face of a takeover threat.[27]

Leveraged Buyouts (LBOs). The use of ESOPs to effect LBOs[28] has been quite popular with financiers since the early 1980s, while at the same time criticism of many such deals has been intense. The desire to finance LBOs with ESOPs is understandable given the large debt load such transactions impose on a company and the ability of an ESOP to considerably lower overall borrowing costs. Although there are many examples of ESOP-financed LBOs structured so as to distribute both risk and reward equitably between investors (employees and management and/or outside institutions or individuals), there are also cases, including Dan River Mills Inc. and Raymond International Inc., where pension plans have been terminated and the excess funding used to finance part of the LBO.

Those who defend ESOP-financed LBOs argue that the LBO will occur whether or not the ESOP is involved, and thus employees might as well have the opportunity to share in the potential financial gain. Detractors feel that the ESOP is used simply as a means of receiving tax-favored treatment, and as such their use in such deals represents a severe distortion of Congress' original intent in establishing the ESOP program.

DISADVANTAGES OF ESOPs

Not surprisingly, ESOPs also have disadvantages for both publicly traded and closely held companies although these appear to be far less important than their advantages. In the GAO's study almost 60 percent of respondent companies indicated that ESOPs had no disadvantages, while companies reporting disadvantages most commonly cited the repurchase liability and the dilution of stock value. For companies which find that the disadvantages of ESOPs outweigh the advantages there are other ways to make employees into shareholders, including stock bonus or purchase plans, profit sharing plans, and stock option plans.

---

[27]For example, in Danaher Corp. v. Chicago Pneumatic Tool Co., 635 F. Supp. 246 (S.D.N.Y. 1986), a court ruled against Chicago Pneumatic Tool Co. which had established an ESOP following the initiation of a takeover attempt.

[28]One of the most common types of LBOs occurs when management arranges for a loan to buy the company's stock using the company's assets as collateral. When an ESOP is involved, it becomes the mechanism through which the loan is contracted with which to buy all or part of the company's stock; in some notable cases companies' pension plans have been terminated and the excess funding used to buy stock, with the ESOP taking the place of the pension plans as the employees' only retirement plan.

Setup and Operating Costs. The cost to companies of the initial design, implementation, legal, and perhaps, negotiating costs, and the ongoing costs for administrative personnel (needed to allocate stock to participant accounts, to comply with the demands of ERISA, etc.) and communication programs are not inconsiderable. Also, for closely held firms there is the additional expense associated with the need to have an annual appraisal by an outside expert of the company's value. Generally speaking, unless a company is mid-sized or larger with an annual payroll of at least $500,000, these costs will probably outweigh any ESOP tax advantages.

Repurchase Liability. Closely held ESOP companies are required to purchase the shares of departing plan participants because of the absence of a public market for their stock. This repurchase liability generally increases over time if the company is successful and the appraised value of the company's stock rises. If a company does not adequately plan to meet this liability, it may be forced to make a public offering of its stock and in this way eliminate the repurchase obligation. Of course, this solution is not ideal since public offerings are very expensive and also involve a loss of control and independence.

Risk. An ESOP entails a higher degree of risk than other investment options because to a significant extent it is undiversified. This problem was reduced by the Department of Labor's ruling that only 51 percent of a plan's assets need be invested in company securities and by the 1986-TRA which mandates that companies offer participants nearing retirement the opportunity to diversify a portion of their ESOP accounts. Nevertheless, ESOPs are not a diversified investment portfolio, and the risk to participants is greatly magnified if they are relying on the ESOP as their principal retirement benefit. (This is not, however, very common among medium- and large-sized ESOPs.)[29] An example of this risk occurred in the wake of the October 1987 stock market crash when the portfolio values of most publicly traded ESOPs suffered heavy losses; FMC's declined by $247 million (39 percent) and Lowe's by $143 million (43 percent).[30]

---

[29]U.S. Department of Labor, Bureau of Labor Statistics, *Employee Benefits in Medium and Large Firms, 1988* (Washington, D.C.: Government Printing Office, 1989), p. 107. The BLS found that of full-time employees in medium- and large-sized companies, only 1 percent of those participating in capital accumulation and retirement plans relied on ESOPs as their sole retirement benefit.

[30]Randall Smith, "Popular ESOPs Have Been Hit by the Crash Just as Hard as Other Large Stockholders," *The Wall Street Journal*, November 16, 1987, p. 63.

Another aspect of risk relates only to leveraged ESOPs. Whereas profit sharing plans represent a variable financial burden, leveraged ESOPs require fixed loan amortization payments regardless of the company's financial performance. In this sense a leveraged ESOP is similar to taking on debt. In fact, an ESOP loan is treated as a liability if the company guarantees the loan or commits to future contributions to service it. (For publicly traded companies this can cause problems since the stock purchased with an ESOP loan is treated as a reduction in stockholder equity.) Thus, if a company is not growing and is unprofitable, the need to service the loan can threaten its ability to survive.

Dilution of Shareholder Stock. When a company contributes newly issued stock to an ESOP, the current stockholders suffer a dilution in equity per share. Theoretically, this dilution can be compensated for if the company increases its productivity and profitability as a result of higher employee motivation and increased working capital, and in the process raises the value of its stock.

Reduction in Management Control. In the vast majority of ESOPs, there has not been any significant transfer of decision making authority from management to employees. Depending on the structure of the plan, however, it is possible that management could lose some control as employees gradually become more substantial stakeholders. With the exception of distress buyout situations where unions have at times taken an active role in establishing ESOPs, it is almost always management that initiates and implements ESOPs.

Failure to Meet Expectations. If a company's management establishes an ESOP in the belief that the employee ownership plan alone will lead to higher productivity and profitability, it will undoubtedly be disappointed in the results. The research to date fails to establish any link between stock ownership and greater employee motivation and commitment. When ownership has been accompanied by worker participation programs, however, it does appear that employees react in a positive manner and that firm performance improves. But it is not clear whether or not employee ownership is a necessary element in such improvement. It may be that through a willingness to cede some control, management can achieve its desired objectives with or without an ESOP.

Viewed from the perspective of the employee, an ESOP can create the expectation of a greater role in decision making as a natural accompaniment to the ownership stake. Employee frustration and discontent could arise if these expectations are not met, and thus the ESOP potentially could have a negative effect on productivity and

Employee Stock Ownership

profitability. In fact, the "wide gap between workers' expectations and reality" has been cited as one of the many problems that plagued the Rath Packing Company ESOP.[31] Another potential employee disincentive could occur if the value of the sponsoring company's stock falls for reasons perceived by employees as unrelated to their own or the company's performance. This has historically been a cause of the termination of several plans, including Sears.

PERFORMANCE OF ESOP COMPANIES

An evaluation of the performance of ESOP companies must begin with an analysis of whether the explicit congressional objectives of broadening the ownership of capital and facilitating the use of equity financing and the implicit objective of improving corporate performance have been met. Because numerous studies have found that the economic performance of ESOP companies is related to the degree that employees participate in management decision making, this section will also examine the extent to which ESOP companies embody worker participation and labor-management cooperation characteristics. No aspect of ESOP law, however, was intended to foster the development of either of these characteristics. Finally, it is important to note that there appears to be some dispute, as well as confusion, concerning the appropriate variables to be used when evaluating the performance of ESOP companies.[32]

Ownership of Capital

The primary justification for the ESOP legislative program was to expand the ownership of capital assets, in particular corporate stock, and thus to rectify what was (and most economists would agree still is) a very uneven distribution of stock ownership. The Joint Economic Committee of the U.S. Congress estimated that in

---

[31]Tove H. Hammer and Robert N. Stern, "A Yo-Yo Model of Cooperation: Union Participation in Management at the Rath Packing Company, *Industrial and Labor Relations Review*, Vol. 39, No. 3 (April 1986), p. 344.

[32]For example, in Corey Rosen and Michael Quarrey, "How well is employee ownership working?," *Harvard Business Review*, September-October 1987, the authors state that "the ultimate test of employee ownership is how well ESOPs affect corporate performance" (p. 1). On the other hand, in Corey Rosen and Jonathan Feldman, "How well do ESOPs reward employees?" *Pension World*, February 1986, the authors state, "the principal evaluation of how well ESOPs are working should not focus on corporate profitability, on how well ESOPs fit into corporate planning, or whether ESOPs create more democratic corporations. All of these are ancillary issues. The key question about ESOPs is ... how much they put in the pockets of employees" (p. 1).

1983, excluding stock in pension trusts, the wealthiest 10 percent of American households owned 90 percent of corporate stock.[33] Although the assets held in pension funds are enormous and thus their inclusion in the statistics would certainly change the percentages, it nevertheless remains that significant stock ownership is not widespread in America.

One can examine the effect ESOPs have had on broadening stock ownership from either a macro or micro perspective. In a macro sense, the GAO has found that ESOPs have not materially expanded the ownership of stock; in 1983, ESOP accounts held assets valued at almost $19 billion and this represented just under 2 percent of total corporate stock owned by households.[34] Accounting for this result are a number of factors, including the relatively small number of companies and employees involved with ESOPs and the characteristics of the type of ESOPs used. With respect to the latter point, nearly 80 percent, or $14.8 billion, of total ESOP assets were held in tax-credit ESOPs which generally provided lower median account balances—for example, one-third the amount held in leveraged ESOPs—although spread over a larger number of participants, than other types of ESOPs.[35] Also, tax-credit ESOPs tended to exclude a large proportion of employees from participating in the ESOP. Because of the high cost to the U.S. Treasury ($11.8 billion), in the form of foregone tax revenues, relative to the benefits derived from the tax-credit program, Congress eliminated the tax-credit ESOP in 1986. Although the elimination of tax-credit ESOPs will probably reduce the total amount of assets held in ESOP accounts, the significant incentives for forming leveraged ESOPs contained in the 1984 and 1986 tax bills has in part led to a vast expansion of ESOP leveraged financing. In 1987, 1988, and through May 1989, approximately $20 billion was contracted through leveraged ESOPs.[36]

Although ESOPs have had little effect on the macro-level distribution of stock ownership, at the level of ESOP firms it is possible to argue that stock ownership has been broadened. Because ESOPs are bound by the nondiscrimination rules contained in the Internal Revenue Code and ERISA, the distribution of stock within ESOP companies cannot favor highly compensated employees, or within

---

[33]*See* U.S. General Accounting Office, *Employee Stock Ownership Plans: Benefits and Costs of ESOP Tax Incentives for Broadening Stock Ownership*, Table 4.1.
[34]*Ibid.*, p. 36.
[35]*Ibid.*, p. 19.
[36]*See*, Anise C. Wallace, "Rostenkowski Seeking ESOP-Loan Benefit Cut," *The New York Times*, June 8, 1989, p. C7, and "The Employee Ownership Report," *The National Center for Employee Ownership*, Vol. IX, No. 1 (January-February 1989), pp. 1 and 9.

restraints, exclude certain categories of employees. Combining this with the fact that the median participation rate in all ESOPs is approximately 70 percent, it is logical to conclude that stock is more equally distributed in an ESOP company than in the economy as a whole. But countering this is the argument that most ESOP companies base their allocation formulas on relative compensation and tend to exclude a fair proportion of their work force (generally the lowest paid employees) from participating in the ESOP, and thus do not materially broaden the internal ownership of stock.

While recognizing the limited effect of ESOPs on broadening the ownership of stock, it is important to note that participants in ESOPs can realize a large increase in the level of their accumulated wealth. According to a 1987 study of ESOPs by the NCEO,[37] the average company contribution to participant accounts was 10.1 percent of payroll from 1980 through 1984, and the average appreciation of the value of stock held in such accounts was approximately 11 percent. The NCEO calculates that if these levels of contribution and appreciation were to continue for a ten-year period, then the ESOP account of a worker at the median wage level of $18,058 in 1983 would total over $31,000 by 1992.[38] Lending support to these estimates is the 1988 survey of the ESOP Association; it is reported that the average account balance of participants in responding companies was $19,000, a significant amount when considering that 46 percent of the surveyed companies had had ESOPs for five years or less.[39] ESOPs are thus able to augment the wealth of participants substantially.

In terms of public policy, the questions before Congress and state legislators are: is it important as an objective to create a more equal distribution of stock ownership, and are ESOPs the appropriate vehicle for attaining that goal? The latter question is particularly relevant today—and received much attention in the early debates on ESOPs—because of the suspect equitability of using tax incentives (which all Americans eventually must finance) to encourage employee ownership for what has turned out to be a narrow segment of the national work force. However, if the answer to both questions is yes, then it is evident that either incentives more generous than those currently existing will have to be offered, or some of the

---

[37]Jonathan Feldman and Corey Rosen, *Employee Benefits in Employee Stock Ownership Plans: How Does the Average Worker Fare?* (Oakland, CA: National Center for Employee Ownership, 1987), p. 8.

[38]*Ibid.*, p. 9.

[39]ESOP Association, *ESOP Survey: 1988* (Washington, D.C.: ESOP Association of America, 1988), p. 29.

administrative burden and restrictions on the design of ESOPs eliminated, in order to encourage corporations to adopt ESOPs.

Equity Financing

There were a number of interrelated factors that compelled the Congress to set as an objective the increased use of equity financing by corporations. First, it was believed that corporations should not only increase their use of external sources to fund capital investment, but also increase equity as opposed to debt financing.[40] Second, for political and economic reasons the basis upon which to broaden the ownership of stock had to be an increase in newly issued equity rather than either a redistribution, or reduction in the value, of existing stock portfolios. Thus increased equity financing was a necessary objective, and the mechanism created for its realization was the leveraged ESOP. Through leveraged ESOPs, broadened stock ownership would take place at least partly by redirecting the traditional distribution pattern (i.e., to current owners of stock) of the benefits of new capital formation. Of course, in order to accomplish its objectives the leveraged ESOP would have to be at least as attractive a financing mechanism as traditional equity or debt financing.

Companies either have engaged in a form of equity financing if they have a leveraged ESOP, or can do so in the future through a leverageable ESOP. This is accomplished by the company issuing new or existing shares to an ESOP trust in exchange for the proceeds of a loan which the trust has secured from a financial institution. Where ESOP and traditional methods of equity financing differ is that in the former companies have a fixed repayment obligation (the company guarantees that it will make contributions to the ESOP trust in an amount equal to the loan amortization) while in the latter the company is not legally required to pay dividends. Equity

---

[40] Since 1955, corporations have used internal sources of funds (capital-consumption allowance, retained earnings, and others) to finance the majority of their investment requirements. Corporations' use of equity financing has not increased since the ESOP program began, and in fact has declined significantly in recent years. For example, in 1984 and 1985 the use of equity financing declined 16 percent and 18.9 percent, respectively, as corporations bought back more stock than they issued. This was, of course, largely in response to the mergers and acquisitions boom on Wall Street and the accompanying threat of unfriendly takeovers.

financing through a leveraged ESOP is thus a hybrid of traditional equity and debt financing techniques.[41]

It is not easy to measure the extent to which ESOPs have promoted the use of equity financing by corporations primarily because it is difficult to determine whether a company that uses a leveraged ESOP to raise capital would have used traditional equity financing if the leveraged ESOP option had not been available. The original intent was for leveraged ESOPs to finance new capital formation but contemporary leveraged ESOPs are not necessarily employed for this purpose. For example, when the financing for an LBO is provided through a leveraged ESOP, there is no net creation of capital assets but only a change in their ownership. Even from a historical perspective, however, leveraged ESOPs have not led to significant new capital formation. The majority of leveraged ESOPs have been used to transfer ownership, and as such have bought existing shares rather than newly issued stock.[42]

It does not appear that the ESOPs have increased the use of equity financing by corporations. At the macro-level, the use of equity funding by nonfinancial and nonagricultural corporations has not increased relative to other external and internal sources of funding since 1975; in 1981, 1984, and 1985, the use of equity financing actually fell relative to the previous year as corporations purchased more stock than they issued. Given the dramatic changes that have taken place in the United States financial markets during the 1980s, however, macro-level measurements do not present a fair picture of the effect of equity financing through ESOPs.

Examining the absolute value of ESOP equity financing (using as a proxy the asset value of leveraged ESOPs) does not lead one to conclude that the ESOP program has increased the use of equity financing even by ESOP companies themselves. As of 1983, the GAO reported that the value of assets held in leveraged ESOPs was only 8 percent of total assets held in ESOP accounts.[43] (Prior to the Deficit Reduction Act of 1984 and the Tax Reform Act of 1986, con-

---

[41] In a leveraged ESOP transaction, if the company either guarantees the debt or makes a commitment to contribute funds to the ESOP sufficient to service the debt, then the company must carry the loan on its balance sheet as a liability. Thus the transaction has both equity and debt features from a company's standpoint.

[42] In the ESOP Association's 1988 survey, only 25 percent of leveraged ESOPs reported acquiring newly issued stock. *See*, ESOP Association, *ESOP Survey: 1988*, p. 7. The GAO found that only 12 percent of leveraged ESOPs purchased newly issued stock, and that even these firms did not necessarily invest the funds in new plant and equipment. *See*, U.S. General Accounting Office, *Employee Stock Ownership Plans: Benefits and Costs of ESOP Tax Incentives for Broadening Stock Ownership*, p. 51.

[43] U.S. General Accounting Office, *Employee Stock Ownership Plans: Benefits and Costs of ESOP Tax Incentives for Broadening Stock Ownership*, p. 19.

trary to the claims of ESOP proponents, the leveraged ESOP was not a particularly beneficial way for companies to raise capital when compared to conventional debt or equity financing.[44]) This percentage has undoubtedly increased substantially since 1983 owing to the elimination of tax-credit ESOPs and the incentives for leveraged ESOPs found in the 1984 and 1986 tax bills.[45] The use of leveraged ESOPs has grown rapidly since 1986, but nonetheless it is doubtful that this will have a significant long-term impact on corporations' use of equity financing. In particular, leveraged ESOPs are still at a disadvantage compared to conventional debt or equity financing, and the tremendous increase in the number and size of leveraged ESOPs during the last three years, is attributable to factors largely divorced from the leveraged ESOP itself.

Economic Results

Though not explicit, an important congressional rationale for the ESOP program was the belief that employee ownership would enhance employee motivation, organizational commitment, and productivity, and thereby increase the competitiveness and profitability of American private enterprise. A second avenue through which ESOPs could improve the economic performance of sponsoring companies would be to finance the acquisition of new capital. Shareholders theoretically could also be more than compensated for the dilution in the value of their stock upon the issuance of new stock[46] by

---

[44]There are numerous analyses comparing the use of a leveraged ESOP to that of traditional debt and equity financing. Prior to the 1984 and 1986 tax bills, the use of a leveraged ESOP was not a cost effective means to raise money. Leveraged ESOPs now compare more favorably with traditional debt financing, but still are at a disadvantage vis-a-vis conventional equity financing. For examples, see U.S. Congress, Joint Economic Committee, *Broadening the Ownership of New Capital: ESOPs and Other Alternatives* (Washington, D.C.: U.S. Government Printing Office, 1976), and Michael A. Conte and Jan Svenjnar, "The Performance Effects of Employee Ownership Plans," (Alan S. Blinder, ed.), *Paying for Productivity: A Look at the Evidence* (Washington, D.C.: The Brookings Institution, 1990), pp. 143-172; and Joseph Blasi, *Employee Ownership: Revolution or Ripoff* (Cambridge, MA: Ballinger Publishing Company, 1988), pp. 68-72.

[45]The ESOP Association found that the proportion of respondents to its survey that had leveraged ESOPs increased from 34 percent in 1986 to 53 percent in 1988. See, ESOP Association, *ESOP Survey: 1988*, p. 9, and *ESOP Survey: 1987*, p. 12.

[46]The value of current shareholders' stock is diluted when new shares are issued and corporate assets (plant and equipment, etc.) are not increased. This happens in the case of nonleveraged ESOPs, because newly issued stock is by definition not accompanied by an increase in corporate assets, and thus there are a larger number of shareholders owning the same amount of corporate assets. In the case of leveraged ESOPs, newly issued stock is in theory accompanied by an increase in corporate assets, and there is not necessarily a reduction in the value of current shareholder's stock.

the expected long-term improvement in corporate profitability. The acknowledgement of the expected benefits to be derived by the private sector and by current shareholders from employee ownership and the tax benefits bestowed thereon was an important element in the political process that resulted in the passage of the ESOP legislation.

Thus it is not surprising that today ESOP advocates insist both that continued congressional support is in part dependent on the successful performance of ESOP firms and that ESOP firms have indeed manifested excellent economic results. Since the mid-1970s, there have been numerous studies evaluating the economic performance of ESOP companies, based on measures of profitability, productivity, employment generation, technological adaptiveness, and sales growth. Because many of these studies fail to control for factors other than employee ownership that may affect corporate performance, and in some cases report contradictory findings, it is not possible to draw any general conclusions from them. Although there is no conclusive evidence supporting the claim that ESOPs improve company performance, it should be noted that the research does not suggest that companies with ESOPs are at a competitive disadvantage compared with non-ESOP companies.

The most well-known and comprehensive study to date of the performance of ESOP firms is that done by the GAO.[47] After examining a relatively large number of ESOP firms across a broad section of industries, company sizes, and types and sizes of ESOPs, the GAO concluded that companies with ESOPs did not show measurable improvement in terms of profitability or productivity following the establishment of an ESOP. The GAO study did find, however, that productivity increased substantially in those ESOP firms with, as compared to those without, decision-making structures allowing for nonmanagerial employees to participate in company decisions. Although a similar finding has been made by other researchers, it has not been determined if employee ownership was a contributing factor in the rise in productivity or if the productivity improvement was attributable to employee participation alone.

There are at least a dozen other published studies cited in the GAO study which attempt to relate employee ownership and the performance of firms. These studies generally have not found a strong link between the adoption of an ESOP and improved company perfor-

---

[47]U.S. General Accounting Office, *Employee Stock Ownership Plans: Little Evidence of Effects on Corporate Performance* (Washington, D.C.: U.S. General Accounting Office, October 1987).

mance. Each study has limitations, but each offers something of value to our overall understanding of ESOPs.[48]

Worker Participation and Labor-Management Cooperation

The ESOP legislation does not require or encourage ESOP companies to establish any form of worker participation or other aspects of labor-management cooperation, but the research suggests that, absent some type of informal or formal participatory programs to operationalize the ownership stake, ownership alone has not provided enough incentive to entice greater employee motivation and

---

[48]The studies listed here are selected as being representative of the general types of studies found in the literature. No judgment is made on their conclusions or methodology.

Michael Conte and Arnold S. Tannenbaum, "Employee-Owned Companies: Is the Difference Measurable?" *Monthly Labor Review*, Vol. 101, No. 7 (July 1978), pp. 23-28 (tentative finding that nonmanagerial employee ownership increases profitability, with the amount of equity owned by the workers being most often associated with profitability).

T. Marsh and D. McAllister, "ESOPs Tables: A Survey of Companies with Employee Stock Ownership Plans," *Journal of Corporation Law*, Vol. 6 (Spring 1981), pp. 521-623. (ESOPs outperformed the national average increase in productivity in six major industries, equalled it in one, and lagged behind in three.)

Corey Rosen and Katherine Klein, "Job-Creating Performance of Employee-Owned Firms," *Monthly Labor Review*, Vol. 106, No. 8 (August 1983), pp. 15-19. (Employee-owned firms, not all ESOPs, averaged an annual employment growth rate 2.78 percent higher than that of comparable conventional firms.)

Arnold S. Tannenbaum, Harold Cook, and Jack Lohmann, "The Relationship of Employee Ownership to the Technological Adaptiveness and Performance of Companies," prepared for the National Science Foundation, Ann Arbor, MI, University of Michigan Institute for Social Research, 1984. (Companies with employee ownership did not demonstrate higher levels of technological adaptiveness or improved firm performance in growth or profit to sales ratios when compared with non-ESOP companies.)

Steven M. Bloom, "Employee Ownership and Firm Performance," Ph.D. Dissertation, Department of Economics, Harvard University, Cambridge, MA, 1985. (No strong evidence found for positive productivity effects for ESOPs; no ESOP effect on employment growth; little or no positive ESOP effect on profitability.)

Michael Quarrey and Corey Rosen, *Employee Ownership and Corporate Performance* (Oakland, CA: National Center for Employee Ownership, 1986). (Significant improvement by ESOP companies in employment, sales growth, and ratio of sales to employment; extent of employee participation programs important as a determinant of firm performance.)

Michael A. Conte and Jan Svejnar, "Productivity Effects of Worker Participation in Management, Profit Sharing, Worker Ownership of Assets and Unionization in U.S. Firms," *International Journal of Industrial Organization*, Vol. 6 (March 1988), pp. 139-151. (Study suggests that the productivity effect of ESOPs is positive at low and moderate levels of ownership but diminishes at high levels.)

productivity. Numerous authors have noted the importance of employee participation,[49] including Blasi who says:

> The only way employee ownership will improve a company's productivity is if it serves as a basis for practical labor-management problem solving of questions that have a strategic relationship to that company's productivity.[50]

It is, therefore, somewhat surprising that ESOP companies are not significantly more likely to establish these programs than are non-ESOP companies,[51] and only rarely were programs established with the intent of changing the structure of the organization and design of the workplace. This remains true even given the notable examples of ESOP firms that have established progressive worker participation programs. In its 1988 survey, the ESOP Association found that in 24 percent of ESOP companies' employees had direct input on decisions affecting job-related matters, but that on decisions concerning corporate policy this participation fell to only 13 percent.[52] The GAO study similarly concluded that on job-related issues—specifically, safety (42 percent), working conditions (34 percent), management-employee relations (33 percent), and reducing costs (30 percent)—workers in a larger number of ESOP companies

---

[49]For example, Long notes that "the beneficial consequences [of employee ownership] appeared to vary with the degree of ownership and the extent to which traditional patterns of employee influence and participation in decision making changed subsequent to employee purchase." Richard J. Long, "Job Attitudes and Organized Performance Under Employee Ownership," *Academy of Management Journal*, 1980, Vol. 23, No. 4, p. 736. *See also*, Tove Holland Hammer, Robert N. Stern, and Michael A. Gurdon, "Workers' Ownership and Attitude towards Participation," in *Workplace Democracy and Social Change*, ed. Frank Lindenfeld and Joyce Rothschild-Whitt (Boston: Porter Sargent, 1982), chapter 3, and John Logue and Cassandra Rogers, *Employee Stock Ownership Plans in Ohio: Impact on Company Performance and Employment*. Some authors have noted the importance of other factors, along with participation, that contribute to positive employee attitudes that should, in turn, increase employee motivation and job satisfaction. These include the amount and frequency of company contributions and management's communications program. Corey Rosen, Katherine Klein, and Karen Young, *Employee Ownership in America: The Equity Solution* (Lexington, Mass.: Lexington Books, 1986); and Katherine Klein, "Employee Stock Ownership and Employee Attitudes: A Test of Three Models," *Journal of Applied Psychology*, 1987, Vol. 72, No. 2, pp. 319-332. Klein found no support for the notion that employee ownership has an intrinsic effect of employee commitment and satisfaction.

[50]Blasi, *Employee Ownership: Revolution or Ripoff?*, p. 219.

[51]There are numerous studies which do not find that ESOP companies are significantly more likely to have participation programs than non-ESOP companies. These include, Donna Sockell, "Attitudes, Behavior, and Employee Ownership: Some Preliminary Data," *Industrial Relations* 24 (Winter): 130-38; and Douglas Kruse, *Employee Ownership and Employee Attitudes: Two Case Studies* (Norwood, PA.: Norwood Edition, 1984).

[52]The ESOP Association, *ESOP Survey 1988*, p. 19.

had input into decision making than on more strategic matters, such as finance (11 percent), planning (13 percent), or new product development (14 percent). The GAO also found that on average only 15 percent of the ESOP companies (though 27 percent of leveraged ESOPs) had established formal mechanisms for channelling workers' participation in decision making.[53]

Another study based on the GAO's data found that formal nonmanagerial participation in decision making was not significant in firms that were identified as having established ESOPs in part in order to transfer ownership to their employees.[54] In a survey including majority- or near majority-owned ESOP firms, Rooney found little evidence of worker participation in decision making, although he did find that employee participation was more likely to occur in firms with employee ownership than those without.[55] It should be noted that this finding is not universally accepted.[56] Although not directly comparable, support for the latter conclusion was provided by a New York Stock Exchange study wherein ESOP firms were found to be four times more likely to have quality of work life programs than non-ESOP companies.[57]

Both the ESOP Association and the GAO have found that the vast majority of closely held ESOP firms do not pass through full voting rights to plan participants.[58] (ESOP firms with publicly traded stock are required by law to pass through voting rights on all issues, but the generally low proportion of stock held in ESOP trusts of publicly traded firms when compared to total stock outstanding militates against their having meaningful participation in management decisions.) Although many ESOP experts do not believe that the extent of voting rights is an appropriate measure of employee partic-

---

[53] U.S. General Accounting Office, *Employee Stock Ownership Plans: Benefits and Costs of ESOP Tax Incentives for Broadening Stock Ownership*, p. 42.

[54] Terry J. Hanford and Patrick G. Grasso, *Employee Ownership through ESOPs: The Ultimate Participation?*. The authors, employees of the Program Evaluation and Methodology Division, U.S. General Accounting Office, presented this paper at the Conference on Participative and Gainsharing Systems held in 1986. The authors did conclude that worker participation was more likely to be found in the ESOPs they studied than in the average non-ESOP American corporation.

[55] Patrick Michael Rooney, "Worker Participation in Employee-Owned Firms," *Journal of Economic Issues*, Vol. XXII, No. 2, June 1988.

[56] Katherine Klein, *Employee Stock Ownership and Employee Attitudes: A Test of Three Models*, p. 321.

[57] New York Stock Exchange, "People and Productivity: A Challenge to Corporate America" (New York Stock Exchange Office of Economic Research, 1982).

[58] ESOP Association, *ESOP Survey 1988*, p. 20, and U.S. General Accounting Office, *Employee Stock Ownership Plans: Benefits and Costs of ESOP Tax Incentives for Broadening Stock Ownership*, p. 39.

ipation,⁵⁹ it nevertheless is one channel through which employee stockholders could affect management decisions and does reflect a company's commitment to employee ownership. Of the ESOP firms surveyed by the GAO that had boards of directors, only 4 percent (10 percent in the 1988 ESOP Association survey) had nonmanagerial employees (union or otherwise) as members.

There are a number of explanations why ESOP companies generally have organizational structures (hierarchical) and labor-management practices (adversarial) similar to those existing in much of American business. One is the unwillingness or inability of both labor and management to break with the roles they have traditionally played in the corporation. This is not solely the result of union intransigence. Unionized ESOPs are a small proportion of total ESOPs but account for a large proportion of the innovative labor-management structures found in ESOPs.⁶⁰ This latter point is largely explained, however, by the fact that unions have been heavily involved in buyouts of failing firms which have inevitably required significant wage and benefit concessions in exchange for greater worker participation in company decision making.

Although ESOP companies have a slightly greater tendency to incorporate some aspects of worker participation and labor-management cooperation in their management philosophies than the average American firm,⁶¹ the failure of this to occur in a widespread fashion has certainly harmed the performance of ESOP companies generally and disappointed many advocates of employee ownership. The potential of employee ownership to recast labor-management relations in a more cooperative, and many would argue productivity and profitability enhancing, way has yet to be realized.

Evaluation

The evidence currently available supports the view that the original objectives set by the Congress for ESOPs have not been achieved. The results of the GAO's study clearly show that the costs of ESOPs in terms of foregone tax revenues have outweighed the

---

⁵⁹Corey Rosen, Katherine Klein, and Karen Young, *Employee Ownership in America: The Equity Solution* (Lexington, MA: Lexington Books, 1986), chapter 4.

⁶⁰Raymond Russell, *Sharing Ownership in the Workplace* (Albany, NY: State University of New York Press, 1985), p. 217.

⁶¹Corey Rosen, Katherine Klein, and Karen Young, *Employee Ownership in America: The Equity Solution*, p. 37. This finding was not based on empirical research. In Rooney, *Worker Participation in Employee-Owned Firms*, however, it is noted, based on direct research, that although firms with employee ownership do not have significant levels of employee participation, they do in fact have more than non-ESOP firms. *See also* study by the New York Stock Exchange, note 58.

benefits generated.[62] But this does not necessarily mean that the ESOP program has been a failure or that employee ownership is not a viable organizational structure for business in America. To a large degree it reflects the unrealistic nature of these goals, and in turn indicts the political process through which they were set, and the overly optimistic assessments by ESOP proponents as to their potential for benefiting American enterprise.[63] To broaden the ownership of stock in American society and increase corporate equity financing were goals far too ambitious given the scope and characteristics of the ESOP program. In terms of firm performance, it was not only the incongruity between objectives and means, but the fact that many firms adopted ESOPs solely as a means to reduce their tax burden or to provide another benefit to employees.

Economists have found fault with the reasoning that firms' productivity would be enhanced by employee ownership's effect on employee commitment and motivation.[64] Most economists would argue that improvements in productivity have historically occurred as the result of the introduction of new technology and greater investment in human capital. Furthermore,

> The psychological processes that translate conditions of employment and work experience into behaviors and attitudes are complex, and the contingent relationships between the programs, worker effort, and financial gains are not always clear.[65]

Additional questions concern the underlying presumption that there exists a reservoir of untapped productivity within the American corporation and that the incentives built into the ESOP would allow for its exploitation. It has been suggested that in a free market such opportunities would already have been exploited without the entice-

---

[62]*See*, U.S. General Accounting Office, *Employee Stock Ownership Plans: Benefits and Costs of ESOP Tax Incentives for Broadening Stock Ownership*.

[63]For example, former Senator Russell B. Long, a staunch proponent of ESOPs, has recently said that "Employee-owners typically become more motivated and more dedicated. Work quality and workplace creativity increase; productivity and competitiveness improve; absenteeism and turnover decline." The author knows of no reliable studies that support these contentions. *See* The Bureau of National Affairs, *Employee Ownership Plans: How 8,000 Companies and 8,000,000 Employees Invest in their Future* (Bureau of National Affairs, Inc., 1987), p. v.

[64]In the record of the congressional hearings concerning employee stock ownership legislation there are statements by economists questioning the notion that an ownership stake for employees will boost motivation commitment, and productivity. *See*, U.S. Congress, Joint Economic Committee, *Hearings on Employee Stock Ownership Plans* (Washington, D.C.: U.S. Government Printing Office, 1976). More recent criticisms have been made by economists including Paul Samuelson.

[65]Tove Holland Hammer, "New Developments in Profit Sharing, Gainsharing, and Employee Ownership," *ILR Reprints* (New York State School of Industrial and Labor Relations, 1988), p. 333.

ment of reduced taxes.[66] While this is undoubtedly true in many cases, there are recent examples of dramatic increases in productivity and profitability at American manufacturing facilities (e.g., Motorola and Wierton) resulting from changes in the organization of work, decision making structures, and incentive systems. The scope therefore exists for improving firm productivity and profitability through nontraditional means.

Although it cannot be argued that ESOPs are incompatible with these goals, there is dispute as to what are the best vehicle(s) to attain them. Some combination of employee ownership, profit sharing, gain sharing, employee participation, reorganization of work, and investment in new technology may be needed to increase a firm's productivity. The combining of employee ownership with profit sharing or gain sharing is important as this provides a closer connection between performance and reward. Especially in large firms, the free rider problem[67] can present particular difficulties where a performance-reward contingency is not well-established. The research clearly shows that employee ownership alone is not sufficient to enhance the performance of companies, while at the same time it has not been found to harm company results.[68] If the spread of ESOPs is to continue in the future, then it appears that the legal framework which governs ESOPs will have to be adapted to encourage some form of labor-management cooperation. Since the government is not likely to provide more tax incentives toward this end and the business community would strongly object to any mandatory requirements (although this is advocated by some as a quid pro quo for the tax incentives provided to ESOPs),[69] adjustments to the

---

[66]Bloom, *Employee Ownership Plans and Firm Performance*, p. 248.

[67]In this case, a free rider problem occurs when an individual feels that the reward associated with employee ownership will be forthcoming whether or not he or she changes work practices or behavior patterns to reflect the establishment of employee ownership.

[68]A few studies have suggested that ownership does have an influence on commitment, job satisfaction, and organizational performance, but these do not have wide applicability. *See*, for example, Richard Long, "The Effects of Employee Ownership on Organizational Identification, Employee Job Attitudes and Organizational Performance: A Tentative Framework and Empirical Findings," *Human Relations*, 31 (1), 1978, and S.G. Goldstein, "Employee Share-Ownership and Motivation," *The Journal of Industrial Relations*, September 1978.

[69]There is a considerable debate within the community of ESOP advocates as to the appropriateness of linking employee ownership to worker participation through legislation. Generally speaking, this battle is being waged by those who see ESOPs as primarily a means to widen stock ownership and those who view it as a means to transform the American workplace. *See*, "ESOPs: Are They Good for You?" *Business Week*, May 15, 1989, p. 122. *See also*, Patrick Michael Rooney, *Worker Participation and Employee-Owned Firms*, p. 456.

UNIONS AND EMPLOYEE STOCK OWNERSHIP

Historically, the American labor movement's attitude toward employee stock ownership has generally been characterized either by indifference or open hostility.[70] Except for the sponsorship of worker cooperatives in the decades following the Civil War and during the 1920s, organized labor has mostly focused its attention on the traditional and economic aspects of its relationship with management and has shied away from any programs that had the potential to blur the distinction between labor and management. Notwithstanding the tacit support of some labor leaders for the concept of employee ownership in the post-World War II era, including the United Auto Workers' Walter Reuther and the National Maritime Union's Joseph Curran,[71] the trade union movement's distrust of and lack of interest in employee stock ownership continued essentially unchanged until the 1980s.

Contemporary Views of Organized Labor

Today much of organized labor still retains a sense of caution about employee stock ownership plans. But because of a host of factors including the concessionary bargaining climate that resulted in the exchange of wages for stock, organized labor has been forced to adopt a more pragmatic and receptive stance toward employee stock ownership. Growing involvement by unions in the establishment and operation of ESOPs has served to alleviate some of organized labor's fears of employee ownership.[72]

Organized labor's changing view of employee ownership is reflected in the positions now taken by a number of prominent national unions. The Steelworkers (USWA), the United Auto Workers (UAW), the Communications Workers of America, and the National Maritime Union have all endorsed and bargained for

ESOP program would have to be made in aspects such as allocation formulas.

---

[70]*See*, for example, Robert Stern and Philip Comstock, *Employee Stock Ownership Plans: Benefits for Whom?* (Ithaca, NY: ILR Press, 1978).

[71]Mary H. Cooper, "Employee Ownership," *Editorial Research Reports*, Vol. 1, No. 23, June 17, 1983, p. 458.

[72]Joyce Rothchild-Whitt, "Who Will Benefit from ESOPs?" *Labor Research Review*, No. 6, Spring 1985. Cited in this article are two surveys of national union leaders: the first, conducted in 1977, found that 75 percent of the union leaders questioned had negative feelings toward employee ownership; the second, conducted in 1980, found that only 29 percent had such feelings.

ESOPs, while the International Brotherhood of Teamsters has participated in numerous employee ownership plans.[73] Rather than addressing ESOP proposals on a case by case basis (a practice that is still generally adhered to), these national unions have also developed guidelines to be followed and services to be consulted when analyzing an ESOP proposal and have at times initiated discussion of ESOPs with management.[74] In contrast, the United Electrical Workers[75] and the International Association of Machinists (IAM) have severely criticized employee stock ownership plans. The IAM's opposition was fueled by its experience at Eastern Airlines,[76] but it has reconsidered its policy and has participated in ESOPs.[77] Perhaps the strongest support for ESOPs has come from local unions as they have felt, more directly than their regional or national organizations, the hardships associated with plant closures. Although it is now common for local unions to receive support (financial and/ or advisory) from their international parents, this was rarely the case in the late 1970s and early 1980s. For example, in the celebrated worker buyouts at South Bend Lathe and Hyatt-Clark Industries, the local

---

[73]Corey M. Rosen, Katherine J. Klein, and Karen M. Young, *Employee Ownership in America: The Equity Solution* (Lexington, MA: Lexington Books, 1986), p. 38. This book notes the involvement of the Communications Workers and the National Maritime Union. For the USWA's views on and participation in ESOPs, see various issues of the union's publication *Steelabor*, and the AFL-CIO's *Labor and Investments*. As for the Teamsters, they have not officially endorsed ESOPs, but nonetheless have had considerable experience in negotiating ESOPs and appear to have set informal guidelines as to what must be included in them. For example, all ESOPs in which the Teamsters have been involved in the trucking industry have contained full voting rights for plan participants and board representation for the union, and disclosure of the firm's financial condition. See, Michael Friedman, "The Bumpy Road of Trucking ESOPs," *The Employee Ownership Report*, Vol. VIII, No. 3, May-June 1988, and "Changing Pay Practices: New Developments in Employee Compensation" (Bureau of National Affairs, Inc., 1988), p. 41.

[74]Norman Eiger, "Changing Views of U.S. Labor Unions Toward Worker Ownership and Control of Capital," *Labor Studies Journal*, Vol. 10, No. 2, Fall 1985. This article reviews the policies of the UAW, IAM, and USWA concerning employee ownership.

[75]Bureau of National Affairs, *Employee Ownership Plans: How 8,000 Companies and 8,000,000 Employees Invest in Their Future*, p. 13.

[76]Following the exchange of wage concessions for a significant degree of stock ownership, Eastern's management unilaterally extended wage concessions, and later Eastern's employee owners were unable to prevent the sale of the airline to Frank Lorenzo.

[77]Norman Eiger, *Changing Views of U.S. Labor Unions Toward Worker Ownership and Control of Capital*, pp. 114-117.

unions' efforts to secure employee ownership were actively opposed by their Internationals.[78]

The AFL-CIO has refused to take a policy stance either for or against ESOPs. In 1987, the AFL-CIO Executive Council adopted a resolution that urged prudence when evaluating an ESOP proposal and specifically did not endorse the establishment of ESOPs. A recent statement by an AFL-CIO economist underscores the ambivalence of the AFL-CIO's position:

> Within the labor movement, there is no consensus that there is a moral or ethical advantage in worker ownership, cooperatives, or stock ownership. In over a hundred years, it has never been a major goal or affected a significant number of labor agreements or workers.[79]

As a result of this attitude, organized labor did not vigorously take part in the political or academic debates concerning ESOP legislation, except at times to raise objections to the preferential tax treatment accorded to ESOPs by the lawmakers.[80] Only recently has the trade union movement begun to lay down its own rules and guidelines concerning participation in ESOPs. The USWA, one of the unions most actively involved with ESOPs,[81] has established its own guidelines which do not deviate substantially from those of the AFL-CIO. In part, these require that ESOPs not replace pension plans and that members have full voting rights and immediate vesting, and suggest that ESOPs should preferably be negotiated as part of a collective bargaining agreement.[82]

---

[78]There are other examples of national unions refusing to assist locals to establish ESOPs, including that of the Bunker Hill Company. *See*, Michael A. Gurdon, "Is employee ownership the answer to our economic woes?" *Management Review*, May 1982.

[79]John L. Zalusky, "A Trade Union Overview of Negotiated Worker Ownership," *The Employee Stock Ownership Association: Proceedings of Eleventh Annual Convention*, May 1988, pp. 27-31.

[80]U.S. Congress, Joint Economic Committee, Staff Study, *Broadening the Ownership of New Capital: ESOPs and Other Alternatives* (Washington, D.C.: Joint Economic Committee, 1976), p. 38, and Blasi, *Employee Ownership: Revolution or Ripoff?*, p. 24.

[81]The USWA has participated in the establishment of over ten ESOPs, the majority of which have occurred in distress situations where the choice was between closure or employees' taking a significant ownership position in the company. According to the USWA, in all of these cases a substantial degree of employee control was negotiated. The one non-distress ESOP that the author is aware of was the purchase of Republic Storage Systems from LTV.

[82]"USWA Workers Become Owners," *Steelabor*, July 1988, p. 7, and "Participant-Run ESOP Buys Out McLouth Steel Products," *Labor & Investments*, July-August 1988, p. 3.

Organized Labor's Criticisms of ESOPs

Behind organized labor's cautious, or in some cases hostile, view regarding ESOPs are a number of beliefs or concerns about employee ownership. These are: (1) that ESOPs could be used to eliminate important employee benefit plans, such as pensions; (2) that ESOPs could result in workers identifying more closely with the firm's interest; (3) that ESOPs could subvert the collective bargaining process; (4) that ESOPs could allow owners to unload financially and operationally weak firms on unsuspecting employees; (5) that ESOPs could create relationships between unions and management that violate the National Labor Relations Act and Landrum-Griffin Act. The unions' suspicions have been exacerbated by some prominent advocates of employee ownership concerning the role of unions in ESOPs.[83]

Pension Plans. One of organized labor's major fears of employee ownership is that the formation of ESOPs will have a deleterious effect on pension plans. As previously noted, both the AFL-CIO and USWA do not approve of replacing a pension plan with an ESOP. ESOPs can take the place of pension plans in one of two ways: (1) they can replace existing secure pension plans; or (2) they can be established instead of pension plans. In either case, there would be an increase in risk to employees as their financial assets would largely be concentrated in an undiversified portfolio. Furthermore, with respect to the termination of pension plans, not only would there be an increase in risk, but those employees who are not fully vested in the pension plan upon its termination would also suffer high costs in the form of foregone benefits and security.

Although there are cases, most notably Dan River Inc. and Raymond International, where pension plans were terminated and the excess funding used to finance part of the ESOPs' purchase of employer stock, this has not been a common feature in the establishment of ESOPs.[84] The 1988 ESOP Association survey found that only 13 percent of companies established ESOPs as part of a conver-

---

[83]For example, in Louis Kelso and Mortimer Adler, *The Capitalist Manifesto* (New York, Random House, 1958), unions are not thought to be a necessary ingredient in companies with employee ownership. Another example is a comment by a representative of the ESOP Association that "There is no legitimate reason for their [organized labor's] opposition to ESOPs except for the fact that employee ownership dilutes the power and influence of the union leaders." Mary H. Cooper, "Employee Ownership," *Editorial Research Reports*, p. 461.

[84]There are potentially adverse financial consequences for a company that terminates a covered pension plan. If such a plan is not fully funded when terminated, the Pension Benefit Guarantee Corporation can place a lien on the company's assets in order to make up for the plan's funding deficit.

sion of a pension plan, and that this appeared even less likely to occur in unionized companies. The survey results indicate that many companies with ESOPs also have defined benefit pension plans to augment their ESOPs and thus to reduce the financial risk.[85] Another study of ESOPs in Ohio reported that only a small portion of ESOPs were begun as the result of the conversion of a pension plan.[86] Regarding whether or not ESOPs are commonly established instead of pension plans, the NCEO believes that this has occurred in approximately 10 to 15 percent of the companies that have established ESOPs.[87] The magnitude of these figures, though not great, indicates that organized labor's concern is legitimate and it provides an excellent reason for trade unions, where applicable, to involve themselves in setting the terms of a proposed ESOP.

Organizing Workers and Retaining Membership. It is conceivable that ESOPs could be used by management to adversely affect the ability of unions to organize workers. Some unions[88] claim that management has employed ESOPs in such a manner as to deter organizing drives, and probably this has occurred. Proponents of ESOPs have gone to great lengths, however, to assure organized labor that ESOPs are not incompatible with unions, and in fact there are numerous ESOP companies that have unions. Although organized labor has been increasingly willing to participate in ESOPs, management still has the legal right to exclude union members from employee ownership plans as long as the union is able to bargain for inclusion. Union members do in fact account for a large proportion of the employees who are excluded from participating in ESOPs. In the ESOP Association's 1988 survey, 94 percent of ESOP companies with 1-49 employees excluded union members, 83 percent with 50-99 employees, 89 percent with 100-249 employees, 83 percent with 250-499, and 96 percent with over 500 employees.[89]

In terms of retaining membership, there have been few instances of unionized companies establishing ESOPs and then subsequently having unions decertified. A collaborative study by the National

---

[85] ESOP Association, *ESOP Survey: 1988*, p. 24.

[86] John Logue and Cassandra Rogers, "Employee Stock Ownership Plans in Ohio: Impact on Company Performance and Employment." Paper prepared for the WCEO's Sixth Annual Conference on Employee Ownership and Participation, March 1987.

[87] *The Employee Ownership Union Handbook* (National Center for Employee Ownership, 1987), p. 41.

[88] *AFL-CIO News*, December 5, 1987, p. 3, and June 4, 1988, p. 6. For a discussion of the attempted use of an ESOP to break the USWA International at South Bend Lathe, see Deborah Groban Olsen, "Union Experiences with Worker Ownership: Legal and Practical Issues Raised by ESOPs, TRASOPs, Stock Purchases and Cooperatives," *Wisconsin Law Review*, 1982, No. 5.

[89] The ESOP Association, *ESOP Survey 1988*, p. 8.

Center for Employee Ownership and the AFL-CIO's Industrial Union Department found that of twenty-nine majority-employee owned and unionized companies, only one had had a decertification election (the union was decertified).[90] Although the sample size of this survey is small, it does not appear that ESOPs have been used by management as a means to get rid of existing unions.

The Need for Unions. The evidence concerning the use of ESOPs to hinder organizing efforts or to remove unions is not very revealing. The far more important question for organized labor is to what extent employee ownership creates—or could create—attitudes and institutional frameworks that reduce or eliminate the need for independent representation. Some union representatives and most proponents of employee ownership adamantly espouse that even in a well-structured and successfully functioning ESOP, union representation will be necessary in order to promote the demands and protect the interests of workers. Among those factors cited by unions as calling for continued union representation are the need for a grievance system in which workers retain independent representatives and for an organization to prevent the subversion of industry collective bargaining as a result of workers in ESOP firms having different and conflicting economic interests from those in non-ESOP firms. Lynn Williams, president of the USWA, has said that:

> The worker-owner has two sets of interests arising out of his separate roles of worker and investor. Business managers, even if the worker helps select them through stock-voting processes, cannot effectively represent workers' interests as workers. The need for unions will therefore continue.[91]

The NCEO believes that unions will still be needed in the realm of grievance procedures and to keep management abreast of developments on the shop floor. Its research has led it to conclude that even in democratically structured ESOPs, unions will play a role as representative of workers in bargaining with management and as an organizer of joint action when employees vote their shares of stock. A number of other researchers have concluded that employee ownership has little effect on workers' perception of the need for a union, although these studies have been limited in scope and suggest that the role of unions may change if the organization becomes more par-

---

[90]Samuel Wessinger, Corey Rosen, and Alex Dreier, *The Employee Ownership Union Handbook* (National Center for Employee Ownership, 1987), p. 44.
[91]"Steelabor," *United Steel Workers of America*, July 1988, p. 7.

ticipative.[92] One can anticipate then that the role of unions in companies with progressive organizational structures will change in numerous ways, including a move away from legalism and contract enforcement as job descriptions broaden and a decentralization of responsibility as control over the production process is pushed down to the shop floor level.[93]

It has not been found that companies with ESOPs are any more likely to have participative management structures than non-ESOP companies, and in fact relatively few of them do.[94] Ownership has not transformed labor-management relations toward employee control or participation in decision making in most companies with ESOPs. Ownership has only rarely been accompanied by control, and thus the union remains the only reliable form of independent representation for workers since ownership interests fail to outweigh traditional occupational group interests.

Subverting Collective Bargaining. In theory, ESOPs could subvert the collective bargaining process above the plant level and hamper efforts to foster solidarity among workers in an industry through their potential to bond employees more closely to companies. This argument centers on the notion that workers whose compensation is partly dependent on the success of their companies will be quite willing to accept lower wage increases or reduced benefits if this will improve company performance. For other companies in the same industry or line of business, this competition would probably require similar sacrifices from their workers but without the corresponding benefits flowing to those workers. Thus workers at ESOP companies or plants could conceivably lower (or apply pressure towards that end) the wage and benefit packages of their fellow union workers at non-ESOP firms or at non-ESOP plants within the same firm operating under the same master contract. An example is

---

[92]*See*, David J. Toscano, "Employee Ownership and Its Effects on Attitudes Toward Trade Unions, *Labor Studies Journal*, Spring 1984; Donna Sockell, *The Union's Role under Employee Ownership: Stability or Change?* (Ann Arbor, MI: University Microfilms International, 1982); Richard J. Long, "Employee Ownership and Attitudes Toward the Union: An Empirical Study," *Relations Industrielles*, Vol. 33, No. 2, 1978; Ben Fischer, "A Skeptic Looks at Employee Buyouts," *ILR Report*, Vol. XXII, No. 2, Spring 1985; and Douglas Kruse, *Employee Ownership and Employee Attitudes: Two Case Studies* (Norwood, PA: Norwood Editions, 1984), pp. 111-118.

[93]For an excellent account of the changes facing the trade union movement, *see* Charles C. Heckscher, *The New Unionism* (New York: Basic Books, Inc., 1988).

[94]*See*, U.S. General Accounting Office, *Employee Stock Ownership Plans: Interim Report on a Survey and Related Economic Trends* (Washington, D.C.: U.S. General Accounting Office, February 1986), and Patrick Michael Rooney, "Worker Participation in Employee-Owned Firms," *Journal of Economic Issues*, Vol. XXII, No. 2, June 1988.

the UAW's refusal to support its local's buyout of Hyatt-Clark in part because of the potential for undermining industrywide agreements.[95] This could also occur because of the positive effect on the profitability of ESOP firms flowing from the tax advantages that they enjoy, and as a consequence, unions have not favored granting special tax treatment to ESOPs.

There have been instances where the adoption of employee ownership has led to the acceptance of wage and benefit standards below those contained in a national agreement,[96] but these have been in crisis situations and thus represent special cases with little applicability to the general population of ESOPs. Furthermore, studies have shown that ESOP companies tend to have wage and benefit packages at least equal to industry levels, and in some cases surpassing the industry standard.[97] In any case, unions concerned with the damaging effect of ESOPs on industry wage and benefit standards could make whatever concessions are given so expensive in terms of increasing worker participation in decision making or ownership control that other unions would be able to resist similar concessionary demands barring similar benefits in exchange. Additionally, guidelines could be established at the industry level in order to regulate the terms and conditions under which unions will support the establishment of an ESOP.

Unloading Unprofitable Companies. Organized labor has expressed a general concern that in employee buyouts of financially distressed firms the creation of an ESOP may simply serve to provide a buyer for a plant or firm with little hope of operating at a sustainable level of profits. Some of the most highly acclaimed and publicized instances of ESOP formation have come in the guise of worker buyouts, and the NCEO has found that a disproportionate number of worker buyouts involve unions.[98] While many of these buyouts have been very successful, including Wierton Steel, there have been those that have ended in failure, the most noteworthy being Rath Packing Company, South Bend Lathe, and Hyatt-Clark

---

[95] A number of factors worked against the UAW cooperating with its local. First, the UAW was close to entering renegotiations with GM and Ford, and thus it did not want to unfavorably bias its position. Second, the UAW had not formulated a policy for dealing with a local's request for funding an ESOP buyout, and was concerned that precedent might not substitute for policy.

[96] For example, in the early 1980s, the Teamsters approved the reduction of wages and benefits in numerous companies below the standards set in the National Master Freight Agreement in exchange for the establishment of ESOPs.

[97] For example, Corey Rosen, Katherine Klein, and Karen Young, *Employee Ownership in America The Equity Solution* (Lexington, MA: Lexington Books, 1986).

[98] *The Employee Ownership Union Handbook* (National Center for Employee Ownership, 1987), p. 4.

Industries. Union fears are not unfounded, but it is recognized that employee ownership has never been the sole cause of the success or failure of employee buyouts using ESOPs. According to statistics compiled by the NCEO, there have been over 100 worker buyouts since 1975, accounting for around 2 percent of all ESOPs formed during this period. Of the approximately 50 such cases for which it has specific information, the NCEO has found that 32 are still operating.[99] If one assumes that the remaining cases for which NCEO does not have information had a similar failure rate, then 40 percent of all worker buyouts have eventually been forced to close. In terms of employment maintenance, the NCEO estimates that successful buyouts have saved approximately 50,000 jobs.[100]

Where wage concessions have been exchanged for the establishment of an ESOP, however, the outcome has not been so clear. During the 1980s, many such arrangements were made in, for example, the steel, airline, and trucking industries, in some cases with the ESOP owning a majority of the stock. With respect to the trucking industry ESOPs, it appears that the overwhelming number of ESOPs ended in either the failure of the company or the abandonment of the ESOP.[101] Similarly, some of the ESOPs in the airline industry, including those at TWA, PanAm, and Eastern, were beset by problems.

Conflicts with Labor Law. There exists the possibility that union participation in an ESOP will lead to conflicts under American labor law.[102] Some of the questions that could arise concern: the status of employee-stockholders under the National Labor Relations Act; the implications, including those deriving from antitrust law and the Landrum-Griffin Act when union representatives sit on company boards of directors; and duty of fair representation issues arising from union representation of employee owners.

Perhaps the most basic legal question that could arise for unions in companies with employee ownership is related to the status of employee-stockholders, i.e., are they to be considered employees or

---

[99] Using Employee Ownership to Save Jobs: The Record to Date, *The Employee Ownership Report*, Vol. VIII, No. 4, July-August 1988, p. 5.

[100] *Legislative Guide to Employee Ownership* (National Center for Employee Ownership, 1986), p. 11.

[101] Of the approximately twenty ESOPs established in the trucking industry, only three were in existence in 1988. See, *Changing Pay and Practices: New Developments in Employee Compensation* (Bureau of National Affairs, Inc., 1988), p. 41.

[102] Although somewhat dated, the most complete article concerning this matter and the source of most of the arguments contained in this section, is Deborah Groban Olsen, "Union Experiences with Worker Ownership: Legal and Practical Issues Raised by ESOPs, TRASOPs, Stock Purchases and Co-operatives," *Wisconsin Law Review*, 1982, No. 5.

owners, and how does this affect the union's representation function? Generally, the National Labor Relations Board has ruled that employee-stockholders are covered by the Act except in those cases where they exercise a powerful and decisive influence on a company's policy-making apparatus. The status of employee-stockholder, however, does not prevent employees from pursuing their interests through participation in collective bodies.

When a union member(s) sits on a company's board of directors,[103] there exists an obligation to represent and promote the interests of the union membership and a fiduciary responsibility to represent the interests of all shareholders. The dual nature of these responsibilities does not necessarily lead to conflicts of interest, but the possibility does exist. For example, when a board is considering investment decisions or collective bargaining strategies, the interests of union and other shareholders could conceivably diverge and create a conflict for the union board member(s). Something along these lines did occur at Hyatt-Clark Industries when the nonunion majority on the board decided to plow anticipated profits into new capital investment rather than distributing it through a profit sharing plan as was desired by the union board members.[104] Unfortunately, no guiding principle has yet developed in the case law concerning union board membership,[105] and this perhaps reflects the fact that unions have generally approached board membership with a good deal of caution. The USWA and the Teamsters both have policies of appointing persons independent of their unions to their board seats—albeit persons with philosophies not dissimilar to those of organized labor—thus avoiding conflict of interest.[106]

Board representation on different companies in the same industry could lead to a violation of the antitrust laws if the access to confidential information thus created were used to restrain trade through price fixing. But barring an actual finding to this effect, there is no legal prohibition on such an arrangement. Unions can limit the potential for antitrust problems by taking certain actions, including

---

[103] Among the larger companies with union board representation are Chrysler, CF&I Steel, Kaiser Aluminum, Transcon, and Wheeling-Pittsburgh.

[104] *See*, "Labor's Voice on Corporate Boards: Good or Bad?, *Business Week*, May 7, 1984, p. 153. The situation of Hyatt-Clark Industries is not completely analagous because the company was 100 percent employee-owned. Nevertheless, it illustrates well that conflicts of interest can arise.

[105] "Union Input is Viable Tool in Mergers, Acquisitions, Banker Says," *Daily Labor Report*, No. 110, June 8, 1988, p. A-3.

[106] John Hoerr, "Blue Collars in the Boardroom: Putting Business First," *Business Week*, December 14, 1987, pp. 126-27. Neither the USWA nor the Teamsters directs the voting of their board appointees, but they do receive reports concerning board meetings.

ensuring that the respective board members do not have an occasion to meet on a regular basis and not giving advice concerning voting. The legal issues that could arise under the Landrum-Griffin Act include employer payments to union officers (in this case, union officers on the board of directors), the investment of union funds in employer stock, and the holding of stock by union officers.

There is a lack of judicial precedent with respect to duty of fair representation cases in unionized companies that have employee ownership plans. To avoid duty of fair representation cases, unions must ensure that in the process of establishing an employee ownership plan they do not discriminate against union members in the local, or locals within the international, that are not participating in the ESOP. Additionally, unions should not

> become a guarantor of the business proposition involved. A union may give its members the information and assistance they seek, but needs to protect itself from making any guarantees about the feasibility of a project.[107]

Potential Uses of Employee Ownership for Organized Labor

In the future, it is likely that unions will expand on what has been their traditional role of simply "structuring fairly the distribution of economic resources and legal rights"[108] by taking a more strategic view of the opportunities presented by employee ownership. This more aggressive posture, which to a certain extent has already manifested itself, will in some cases involve unions seeking to improve their position in ways not altogether incompatible with the interests of management. For example, employee ownership might be established as a means to thwart a hostile takeover, to provide an additional employee benefit when employer resources are stretched too thin to increase other deferred benefits, or to maintain jobs. But pursuit of employee ownership in other instances might involve motives that are potentially not so innocuous to management interests. These include using employee ownership to take over successful companies, to restrict the mobility of capital, to organize workers, to create union jobs in nonunion environments, and to increase the scope of collective bargaining. Employee ownership could serve to help unions regain a portion of the power which they lost during the

---

[107]Deborah Groban Olsen, "Union Experiences with Worker Ownership: Legal and Practical Issues Raised by ESOPs, TRASOPs, Stock Purchases and Co-operatives," p. 799.

[108]Joseph Blasi, "Employee Ownership: Revolution or Ripoff?," p. 205.

1980s, and thus to redress what in labor's view has been an adverse change in the relationship between capital and labor.

Using an ESOP as a means to take over a company has normally occurred in crisis situations where the option has been between employee ownership or closure. Only rarely have ESOPs been employed in an attempt to gain control of financially sound firms, among the most noteworthy examples being the ALPA's effort to buy United Airlines,[109] the joint effort of the USWA and UAW to buy Robertshaw Controls, Co., and the effort by rail unions to buy Southern Pacific. Partly fueling these union takeover attempts was displeasure with management practices that were felt to threaten jobs and the firm's long-term viability. The use of ESOPs by unions, or unions and outside investors, in future takeover attempts could increase significantly because of their financial attractiveness.

Employee ownership also can be used to restrict the ability of management to redirect capital resources toward ends not favored by the union(s). Through participation in decision-making structures, or at a minimum greater to information and oversight of management decisions, unions would be in a better position to either control or exert considerable pressure on management. Although unions are legally restricted by the NLRA on the subjects that can be collectively bargained, by coordinating workers' stock voting a union could affect a wider range of corporate decision making since stockholders are allowed to raise any issue at stockholder meetings. Some combination of these measures would reverse unions' traditional role of simply negotiating to minimize the damage and maximize the benefits flowing from already taken management decisions. Supporting this notion is the comment by an AFL-CIO economist that ESOPs can be looked upon as providing "damage control in an era of plant shutdowns, takeovers, and wholesale export of U.S. manufacturing jobs."[110]

---

[109]The ALPA was concerned that the attempt to make United into an integrated travel company was not a sound financial or operational strategy.
[110]"Stock Plans Approached Cautiously," *AFL-CIO News*, June 4, 1988, p. 6.

CHAPTER VI

Canada and Mexico

CANADA

The Canadian business community's interest in programs aimed at improving productivity closely parallels similar trends in the United States.[1] Concern over lagging productivity and its relationship to stagflation has been particularly pronounced in Canada since the early 1980s. One illustration of this concern is reflected in the business literature. The *Canadian Business Periodical Index* of 1976 carried only one entry under the heading of productivity, compared to fifty-one entries under the same heading in 1985.[2]

Annual average productivity growth slumped from 4.5 percent between 1960 and 1973 to 2.1 percent between 1973 and 1984.[3] A recent survey of 322 organizations selected from the country's top 300 firms and its major governmental bodies indicated that 95 percent of the respondents felt that they were doing more to counteract lagging productivity in the five-year period extending from 1982 to 1986 than they had been doing in the previous five-year period (1977 to 1981).[4] When asked what factors contributed most to convincing them that it was critical for their firms to improve productivity, over 90 percent of the respondents cited cost pressures, a need to improve management decision making, and the need to cope more effectively with both domestic and international competition as their chief motivation.[5]

The stagflation that marked the early 1980s in the United States continued to persist well into the 1980s in Canada. Wage settlements have not been tempered by a sustained high level of unemployment, nor have they slowed sufficiently to even approximate the

---

[1] Gary Spraakman, Sandra Kogawa, and Wanda Kogawa, "A Survey of Productivity Improvement Practices of Canadian Organizations," *Optimum*, Vol. 18, No. 1 (1987), p. 85; also, Patricia L. Booth, "Employee Involvement and Corporate Performance," *Canadian Business Review*, Vol. 15, No. 1 (Spring 1988), pp. 14-16.
[2] Spraakman et. al., p. 85.
[3] *Ibid.*
[4] *Ibid.*, p. 91.
[5] *Ibid.*, p. 93.

average annual increase in productivity.[6] As a result, both private enterprise and the federal government have become seriously interested in promoting concepts like gain sharing.[7]

Gain sharing in Canada has been defined generically as any arrangement that links employee compensation to the performance of the firm.[8] Thus, the Canadian view of gain sharing embraces not only the productivity improvement systems to which gain sharing refers in the United States (i.e., Scanlon, Rucker, Improshare) but also profit sharing and equity sharing systems. The productivity improvement programs that are used in Canada are patterned largely after those found in the United States, and no further reference need be made to those programs here. Since the Canadian definition of gain sharing also includes profit sharing and equity sharing plans, the basic features of such plans in the Canadian environment are outlined in this section.

Profit Sharing Plans

Three types of profit sharing plans are utilized in Canada as in the United States. Current distribution or "cash" programs pay a share of company profits to employees in cash or company shares, deferred payout plans place a designated share of company profits into an employee trust fund for distribution at a later date, and combination plans offer both cash and deferred payouts to employees. Combination plans may either combine current distribution and deferred distribution features into a single plan or consist of separate but coordinated programs that offer flexibility to employees to elect current distribution or deferred payment according to their individual needs.[9] Most firms make a current distribution (cash or shares) on an annual basis, but some make awards at more frequent intervals. Both cash and shares are taxed as ordinary income in the year received.[10]

---

[6]Frank R. Anton, *Gain Sharing: Is It the Solution to Stagflation in Canada?* Discussion Papers Series No. 107 (Calgary, Alberta: The University of Calgary, Department of Economics, May 1987), p. 4. This paper is a comprehensive analysis of the feasibility of applying the principles of a share economy, as advocated by Martin Weitzman, in Canada. For a concise discussion on the same issue, see Christopher Beckman, "Will Profit Sharing Reduce Unemployment?" *Canadian Business Review*, Vol. 13, No. 2 (Summer 1986), pp. 50-52.

[7]Anton, p. 4.

[8]Donald V. Nightingale and Richard J. Long, *Gain and Equity Sharing*, Quality of Working Life Case Study Series (Ottawa, Ontario: Labour Canada, 1984), p. 5.

[9]Nightingale and Long, *Gain and Equity Sharing*, p. 7; Donald V. Nightingale, "Profit Sharing: New Nectar for the Worker Bees," *Canadian Business Review*, Vol. 11, No. 1 (Spring 1984), pp. 11-14.

[10]Nightingale and Long, *Gain and Equity Sharing*, pp. 7-8.

There are two types of deferred payout plans, the Deferred Profit Sharing Plan (DPSP), and the Employee Profit Sharing Plan (EPSP). The DPSP is a tax-deferred program in which both employer contributions and annual earnings of the trust established for employees are exempted from an employee's taxable income until he or she receives the benefit. Employer contributions to the DPSP are tax deductible for the employer to an annual maximum payment established by the federal government, less the lower of any contributions to a regular pension plan or 20 percent of the employee's annual wages.[11] Because of its tax deductible status, the DPSP must be registered with the Department of Revenue.

The EPSP is not a tax-deferred plan. Taxes are paid by the employee on the company's contribution and other trust income when these amounts are allocated to the employee's account. Both employer and employee contributions to an EPSP trust can be unlimited. Employee contributions, however, are not tax deductible. The employee must pay income tax on interest, dividends, and capital gains earned by the trust in the year of allocation.[12]

Equity Sharing

Two recent Canadian surveys suggest that over 60 percent of companies with publicly traded stock offered at least one form of employee share ownership plan to their employees by 1987, compared with only 27 percent of large publicly-owned firms offering such programs in 1981, as reported in an earlier survey.[13] Nevertheless, since the great majority of these programs cover only the top management, most Canadian employees are not covered by them and are not likely to be in the future unless government incentives are offered to encourage their further development,[14] as happened with ESOPs in the United States.

Recently, the federal government has been advocating employee equity programs as a means of achieving public policy objectives. One use of employee plans that has recently received considerable attention has been the use of stock ownership as a vehicle for "Canadianizing" foreign-owned subsidiaries.[15] Both the federal and provincial governments appear to be exploring other uses of employee own-

---

[11] Nightingale, "Profit Sharing, New Nectar for the Worker Bees," p. 12.
[12] *Ibid.*
[13] Booth, "Employee Involvement . . . ," pp. 14-16; Nightingale and Long, *Gain and Equity Sharing*, p. 23; *The Worklife Report*, "Employee Share Ownership in Canada," Vol. 5, No. 5 (1987), pp. 8-10.
[14] Nightingale and Long, *Gain and Equity Sharing*, p. 23; *The Worklife Report*, p. 9.
[15] Nightingale and Long, *Gain and Equity Sharing*, p. 22.

ership as alternatives to government takeover of private enterprise where foreign ownership might be considered to be against the public interest, or where the government was contemplating taking over a failing firm in order to save jobs.[16]

There are four types of employee equity plans in use in Canada, and some companies may use more than one of these variations.

Stock option plans are the most common form of equity participation. These plans give an employee the right to purchase company stock in the future at or near today's price. They are usually restricted to key personnel as a long-term incentive.

Stock purchase plans allow employees to obtain company stock voluntarily with their own funds, sometimes with an employer subsidy.

Employee stock ownership plans, which are relatively uncommon, enable the employer to contribute stock to a trust on behalf of individual employee (similar to Employee Stock Ownership Plans in the U.S. but without significant tax benefits).

Profit sharing plans pay a portion of company profits and sometimes distribute stock as well as cash to employees.[17]

Although there has been substantial growth in employee share ownership in Canada in recent years, broad-based stock plans remain much less common in Canada than in the United States. A 1986 study by the Toronto Stock Exchange concluded that government incentives to encourage share ownership plans are essential to ensure broad exposure to employee share ownership across the country.[18]

Other than legislation governing DPSPs, few laws have been passed in Canada governing employee ownership programs. Quebec is the only province with specific legislation governing employee ownership. In 1979, Quebec passed legislation permitting existing shareholders or company employees to claim a tax deduction of up to 20 percent of income at a maximum of $15,000 per year, if the deduction is used to purchase new issues of stock in Quebec-based companies approved by the Quebec Securities Commission.[19] A program that could conceivably have an impact on employee ownership plans in Ontario is the Foreign Subsidiary Buyback Program established in 1980. Under this program, a Canadian manager, employee, or

---

[16] *Ibid.*
[17] Ian Allaby, "Sharing the Wealth," *Canadian Business*, Vol. 58, No. 9 (September 1985), p. 44.
[18] "Employee Share Ownership in Canada," *The Worklife Report*, Vol. 5. No. 5 (1987), p. 9.
[19] Nightingale and Long, *Gain and Equity Sharing*, p. 33.

investment group may receive financial assistance from the provincial government for buying out subsidiaries of foreign-owned corporations operating in Ontario. Most provinces have agencies offering financial assistance to employees wishing to purchase their companies, but they must compete for these funds on an equal footing with other businesses operating in those provinces.[20]

The Union Reaction to Gain Sharing

Whatever the specific form of gain sharing, whether it be productivity improvement, equity sharing, or profit sharing, its spread has been inhibited in Canada, as in the United States, by trade union opposition and middle management fear. The result has been perpetuation of an adversarial system of industrial relations in both countries. At the international level, the Canadian Auto Workers' leadership has rejected gain sharing. Nevertheless, despite indifference and opposition on the part of Canadian trade union leaders at the international level, many trade union locals have actively participated in gain sharing plans and strongly supported them. Locals of the Canadian Auto Workers, United Steel Workers, Electrical Workers, and the Energy and Chemical Workers are examples of the breadth of support that has manifested itself at the local level.

Union opposition to gain sharing takes form in one or more of the following objections:

1. Gain sharing provides an income that fluctuates with the prosperity and competitive position of the firm. Most trade unionists prefer to bargain for fixed wages and benefits rather than have their members face the uncertainties of what they see as an erratic and insecure flow of income.

2. Because unions feel that workers are not allowed to participate in making decisions that truly affect company profitability, they argue that there is little point in encouraging what they deem to be "pseudo-participation" in a gain sharing plan. Implicit in this argument is a fear that surfaces constantly in union-management relations in the United States, i.e., will the worker be made the scapegoat for management's mistakes?

3. Unionists frequently charge that unions are rarely allowed any voice in the administration of gain sharing plans. Specifically, they contend that without access to company books they cannot be assured that gain sharing allocations reflect real gains in productivity or profits. Under these conditions, there is little chance for

---

[20]*Ibid.*

mutual trust to develop between union and management representatives.

4. Many trade unionists oppose gain sharing programs because they represent a form of labor-management cooperation. These unionists contend that gain sharing is merely a tool designed to undermine the collective bargaining process by persuading workers that they can achieve financial gains without the union. This argument reflects a problem that appears to be the foundation of a growing schism in the United States labor movement, as well as the Canadian, over whether there is any basis at all for labor-management cooperation.

MEXICO

Profit Sharing Legislation

Profit sharing has been a constitutional right in Mexico since 1917 but was not formally implemented until 1963, during the Lopez Mateos administration (1958-64). In December 1963, a National Profit Sharing Commission, composed of representatives from the government, organized labor, and the private sector, adopted profit sharing regulations which entitled employees to 20 percent of employers' profits. In practice, however, this percentage was reduced to an average of 6 percent after employer deductions for "reasonable return on interest" and capital investment. Many employers also exploited loopholes in the system, such as reclassifying managers who were not entitled to profit sharing payments as "confidential employees" who could participate, which further reduced the employees' share. These and other problems were addressed in the 1970 revision of the Federal Labor Law and then further clarified by a second commission, formed in October 1974, and additional profit sharing legislation in 1975. The following provisions were adopted:

Employees are entitled to 10 percent of an employer's taxable income, excluding only pension fund earnings, dividends received from Mexican companies, and gains from the sale or exchange of corporate securities.[21] This served to increase the percentage of profits distributed to employees while presumably leaving companies sufficient profits to reinvest. The employees are not entitled to intervene in any way in the administration of their companies.

---

[21]Robert E. Looney, *Economic Policymaking in Mexico* (Durham, N.C.: Duke University Press, 1985), p. 143.

Each employee's share is divided into two parts: one-half of the share is distributed according to the number of days worked by each employee, and one-half is distributed based on the salary or wages earned during the year.

The exact amount of each employee's share is determined by a tripartite committee composed of one labor, one employer, and one government representative. In practice, the government often supports labor's position.

Confidential employees (*empleados de confianza*), those employees who exercise the functions of management or supervision of a "general nature" (a term deliberately kept vague), can participate in the profit sharing system; but if the salary they receive is greater than the salary of the highest paid worker in the plant, the latter's salary plus 20 percent will be the maximum salary of the confidential employee.[22] This provision was included as part of the government's attempt to address the loophole mentioned above by making the reclassification of managers less attractive. It also served to appease labor without alienating employers outright.

An employer must distribute profits within five months after the end of the fiscal year and "must supply a copy of the income tax declaration to the workers' representative within ten days of filing, and ... must make available a copy of any annexes submitted to the Secretariat of Finance and Public Credit for a period of thirty days."[23] This provision was included in response to a labor union campaign which sought employee access to employer records when an employer is suspected to evading the law.

"Any objections of the employees to the tax return must be communicated to the Revenue authorities ... and employees may not contest the final decision."[24] This provision, in turn, takes back some of the authority granted to organized labor in the above provision. Failure by an employer to comply with profit sharing regulations is considered legitimate grounds for declaring a strike.[25] Profit sharing regulations do not apply to newly established companies during the first year, mining and similar companies during the exploration period, newly established firms that manufacture a new product during the first two years, public and private welfare institutions, or

---

[22]Susan Kaufman Purcell, *The Mexican Profit-Sharing Decision* (Berkeley: University of California Press, 1975), p. 128.

[23]*Regulations made under sections 121 and 122 of the Federal Labour Act*, dated 1 May 1975 (Diario Official, 2 May 1975, No. 1, p. 24), cited in International Labour Office, "Mexico 1," *Legislative Series*, 1975 (Geneva: ILO, 1977), pp. 1-2.

[24]Price Waterhouse & Co., *Doing Business in Mexico* (1981), p. 65.

[25]Purcell, *Profit-Sharing Decision*, p. 128.

companies whose capital and gross income are less than a certain minimum established by the Labor Department.[26]

The Role of Organized Labor

Organized labor played a very minor role in the establishment of a viable profit sharing system in Mexico. In the 1930s the labor movement actually opposed profit sharing for two reasons: first, because profit sharing promoted labor-management cooperation and this might "weaken the workers' class consciousness and undermine their revolutionary spirit";[27] and second, because profit sharing allowance would be at the expense of other labor demands. By the 1950s industrial production had greatly expanded, profits were increasing, and less revolutionary labor leaders began to see the benefits to be reaped from profit sharing. The Confederacion de Trabajadores de Mexico (CTM) led the campaign to institute compulsory profit sharing, because its efforts were stifled by factionalism within the labor movement and a general disinterest among the rank-and-file members—an attitude which prevailed throughout most of Lopez Mateos' profit sharing crusade.

Obligatory profit sharing, therefore, was not a labor initiative. In fact, the labor movement's greatest show of unity behind the profit sharing decision did not come until after the system was in place, when it protested private sector attempts to circumvent the profit sharing regulations. Labor's action eventually led to the revision of the Federal Labor Law as mentioned above, but for the most part profit sharing was promulgated by Lopez Mateos out of concern both for improving labor's lot and for enhancing his own image.[28]

---

[26]Price Waterhouse & Co., *Doing Business*, pp. 65-66.
[27]Purcell, *Profit-Sharing Decision*, p. 50.
[28]*Ibid.*, p. 65.

CHAPTER VII

United Kingdom

British economic growth fell behind that of other European countries in the 1950s and continued to do so through the 1960s and 1970s. A series of governments, Conservative and Labor, failed to reverse the country's economic slide until the Thatcher government came to power in 1979. Since that time, the Conservative government has differed sharply from those of the past by following policies designed to encourage a free market economy, to promote competition, and to control trade union power. In addition, this government has also made it clear that it supports performance related pay schemes by offering tax incentives to firms that link pay to profits. That policy actually began in 1978 under the preceding Labor government which established a profit-related share system. The Conservative government followed with profit sharing legislation in the 1980s.

COMPANY PROFIT SHARING

Prior to 1978, individual company profit sharing plans were limited in number. Most of the plans were cash profit sharing plans or share bonus plans, but there were no tax incentives to encourage the adoption of such plans. Some of the companies sponsoring those plans were foreign companies with facilities in Britain to which company-wide profit sharing was extended (e.g., Hewlett-Packard and Kodak). There were also a few share-option and share purchase plans in existence prior to 1978. When shares were distributed under these plans there usually were no conditions attached to prevent employees from disposing of the shares as soon as they were received. Since an important objective of a share bonus plan is to increase employee identification with the employer by making employees shareowners, the rapid conversion of shares to cash thwarts that objective.

The Finance Act of 1978 and Amendments

The Finance Act of 1978 was a commitment by the government to promote profit sharing but only through the medium of share ownership. Politically, most of the support for passage of the Act came from the Liberal Party. The objective of the profit sharing provisions of the Finance Act of 1978 was to encourage employees to retain shares received as a profit sharing bonus thereby making them owners as well as employees. The plans, which are called Approved Deferred Share Trusts (ADST), provide income tax concessions to employee participants, and must be approved by Inland Revenue. The original Act established a ceiling of £500 (U.S.$817)[1] on the market value of shares which could be transferred to any one employee in a tax year. This limit has been raised over the years to £2000 (U.S.$3267) or 10 percent of an employee's earnings, whichever is greater, subject to a ceiling of £6000 (U.S.$9804). Allocation is made from pre-tax profits, and all employees with at least five years of service must be allowed to participate.

The amounts allocated are placed in a trust which purchases shares in the company on behalf of the individual participants. Employees may request cash distribution which is taxable in the normal way. If shares are purchased, the employee agrees to leave the shares in the trust for at least two years. If the shares are held for over five years (originally seven years) there is no tax liability for the employee. If the shares are sold after two years but before four years, they are fully taxable, and shares held from four to five years are 75 percent taxable. An employee may be liable for capital gains tax when the shares are sold if the sale proceeds exceed the value of the shares at the time they were set aside for the employee. No tax is payable if an employee dies, irrespective of how long the shares were held. Employees who retire, become disabled, or are laid off, may sell their shares immediately regardless of the length of time they were held, but if they were held less than five years tax is paid on 50 percent of the original value. Employer contributions to the trust are tax deductible.

The growth of ADST plans from 1979 to 1987 was steady but not spectacular, as Table VII-1 indicates. Initially, many companies which already had profit sharing plans switched to ADST plans to take advantage of the tax concessions offered after 1978 for Inland Revenue approved trusts. After the initial rapid growth of approved plans, the growth rate has since settled down to approximately 15 percent per year.

Despite the growth of deferred (ADST) plans, cash profit sharing plans are apparently the most common type in the United Kingdom. A 1987 survey by the Glasgow University Centre for Research into

---

[1]Exchange rate used in this chapter is the 1987 average, £0.612 = US$1.

Table VII-1
Growth of ADST Profit Sharing Plans, 1979–1987

Year[a]	Cumulative Totals for ADST Plans		
	Plans Submitted	Plans Dropped	Plans Approved
1979	96	—	3
1980	228	—	117
1981	327	—	210
1982	400	—	278
1983	476	89	344
1984	552	107	392
1985	635	116	462
1986	733	135	532
1987	845	144	634

Source: Incomes Data Services, Ltd., *IDS Study, PRP and Profit Sharing*, No. 397 (November 1987), p. 12.
[a]Up to March.

Industrial Democracy and Participation found that, of 396 profit sharing plans surveyed, 31 percent were cash plans and only 6.6 percent were ADST plans. That study also found that larger companies were more likely to have a share-based plan than were smaller organizations. The assumption here is that the larger companies are better equipped to develop and administer the more complex share-based plans.[2] Although until recently there were no tax advantages involved in cash plans, the relative ease of administration and the possibility of enhancing employee motivation, particularly where there is a close relationship between employee effort and the profit share payout, make cash plans quite attractive.

Profit-Related Pay (PRP)

In May 1986, the British government set in motion its ideas for revamping profit sharing in the United Kingdom when it presented a discussion paper to the National Economic Development Council on ways to link pay more closely to profits. The government's initial proposal (which drew heavily on the profit sharing theories of Martin Weitzman[3] of Harvard University) would have taken profit sharing well beyond the share-based concept of the Finance Act of 1978. The theory behind the new proposal was that tax relief would be

---

[2]Incomes Data Services, Ltd., *IDS Study, PRP & Profit Sharing*, Study 397 (November 1987), pp. 11-12.

[3]*See* Martin L. Weitzman, *The Share Economy: Conquering Stagflation*, (Cambridge, MA: Harvard University Press, 1984).

given to employees who agreed to take a "significant proportion" (originally 20 percent) of their income from a profit sharing plan. Tax relief was to be temporary for an initial period to encourage participation and would have amounted to 50 percent of the profit-related income received by an employee. Decisions concerning the adoption of such agreements were left entirely as a matter for employers and employees to settle voluntarily.

It is important to understand the difference between profit-related pay and traditional profit sharing. The latter ordinarily has been introduced as an additional bonus over and above the basic wage or salary but related to the profits of the employer. If the business is profitable, the employees would share in that success according to some formula previously announced. If the business failed to enjoy profits at a level sufficient to generate a bonus to the employees, these employees would still have the same income from their basic wage or salary. Profit-related pay, on the other hand, was designed to shift some of the risk of an economic downturn to the employees' pay. A portion of the employees' base pay would consist of a profit-related payment with the result that if profits fell the employees' pay would fall also.

The benefits from PRP were not seen as a "quick fix" but as a way of improving the performance of the economy over time. Chancellor Nigel Lawson allowed that profit sharing would give the work force a direct personal interest in and identification with the employer's success and would make employees more alert to the importance of profits. Profit sharing in the form of PRP was also seen as making pay more responsive to business conditions which could reduce the pressure for layoffs in a downturn. Employers would have more confidence to invest and to hire additional employees. PRP would operate more widely because, unlike ADST plans, it would not depend on the issue of shares but on linking a portion of pay to profits.[4]

Response to the British government's original proposals was very cautious. Probably the most controversial provision was that of placing 20 percent of pay at risk. Critics contended that 20 percent was too high and would be unworkable even with the tax incentive. After initial talks with employers and the unions, the government's final proposals were substantially watered down from the original proposal. The minimum amount of pay at risk was reduced, the tax relief was reduced, and the concept of a profit sharing bonus pool was introduced.

---

[4]Edward Townsend, "Lawson sets profit-share ball rolling," *The Times*, May 13, 1986, p. 1.

United Kingdom

The major features of the PRP legislation ultimately enacted in 1987 are as follows:

1. Plans must be registered and approved by Inland Revenue from three to six months prior to the effective date.
2. The unit to which the plan relates must be identifiable and clearly stated. It need not be a single company and may be a part of a business, such as a department or division.
3. A plan may cover all employees except those with a substantial "material interest" (such as controlling directors). It may exclude part-time employees and those employees having less than three years of service. At least 80 percent of the remaining employees in the unit must be included.
4. A plan must be adopted for a minimum of one year.
5. The profit measure is ordinary profit after taxes with several adjustments permitted as defined in the legislation.
6. One-half of any PRP payments are exempt from tax subject to the lower of two limits. The amount which can be paid under an approved plan is unlimited, but the amount calculated for tax relief purposes is limited to 20 percent of an employee's initial pay, or £4,000 (U.S.$6,480), whichever is lower. The net result is that up to 10 percent of an employee's total pay, or £2,000 (U.S.$3,240), whichever is lower, could be exempt from tax in any one year.
7. Originally, the amount of profits to be distributed in the first year of plan operation had to be equal to at least 5 percent of the total payroll for eligible employees if profits remain unchanged from the previous (or base) year. This provision was abolished in 1989.
8. A distributable "pool" is the total amount of PRP that must be paid to employees for a profit period. One of two methods may be used to determine the amount of the distributable pool:

   Method A: The employer simply states a fixed percentage of profits which will be paid out for the profit period.

   Method B: The employer specifies an amount which will be the size of the PRP pool if profits in the profit period are the same as in the previous year.

What is actually paid out will be that amount adjusted up or down in line with the change in profits. Either method must produce a pool which equals at least 5 percent of the total pay of the eligible employees if profits remain unchanged. Plans may specify that if the pool created by Method A or Method B would be less than 5 percent of total pay then no pool need be created for distribution.

9. Individual PRP payments may be related to length of service or to pay levels as long as the criteria are clearly specified and consistently applied.

10. Payments to participants may be weekly, monthly, quarterly, semi-annually, or annually, but timing must be specified in the plan.

Evaluation

The government estimated the cost of PRP to the Inland Revenue to be £50 million (U.S.$81.7 million) and set a goal of more than a million people on profit sharing by March 1989. Since the first plans were not effective until 1988, the tax consequences have not yet been reported and analyzed. There was evidence that some of the initial pressure to change over existing plans to PRP came from managers and the higher paid employees who would benefit more from the tax breaks.[5] Employers with existing cash plans may feel that they have no choice but to apply for registration of their plans simply to give their employees the benefit of tax relief.

By June 1989, 902 companies had registered plans, covering 129,000 employees, with Inland Revenue.[6] The largest group covered, 9,500, is at Nationwide Anglia, the third largest building society in the United Kingdom. Reportedly, Nationwide Anglia is attempting to move away from across-the-board pay increases to a more performance-related pay structure. Other performance-related plans include increased use of individual merit pay and team bonuses.[7]

With an average of 143 employees per plan, it appears that PRP plans are more common among small employers. Incomes Data Services, which regularly surveys its subscribers, concluded that the majority of PRP plans involve better paid employees and employers who do not have collective bargaining agreements.[8] It is not yet entirely clear why small firms are adopting PRP plans more rapidly than larger firms. The tax advantages, of course, are more significant in companies with a relatively small number of highly paid employees. It is also likely that many larger, unionized companies would have delays in implementing PRP because of a need to discuss the plan with the union, or in some cases to negotiate it.

---

[5] *See IDS Report*, No. 501 (July 1987), p. 25.

[6] "Mixed Picture on Profit-Related Pay," *IDS Report*, No. 538 (February 1989), p. 6.

[7] "Nationwide Anglia Agrees to 6.5 Per Cent Plus Profit-Related Pay Scheme," *IDS Report*, No. 520 (May 1988), p. 2.

[8] "Profit-Sharing Payouts and the Extent of PRP in 1988," *IDS Report*, No. 524 (July 1988), p. 25.

The requirement, eliminated in 1989, that the minimum payout will be 5 percent if profits remain the same in the first year of plan operation may have discouraged some employers. Most payouts under cash profit sharing plans or ADST plans have been within a range of 3 percent to 9 percent of payroll. The high is probably the 24 percent paid by John Lewis Partnership in 1987. Under many existing plans, profit sharing payments have been made solely at the discretion of the directors of the company. Obviously, those companies would lose some flexibility by adopting a PRP plan.

Another common and related criticism is that the PRP program is too restrictive. Pure profit (rather than return on investment or some other factor) may not be the best measure of performance. Guidelines revised in 1988 now permit the limited use of total turnover or the return on net assets. Profit may also be rather remote from actual employee performance and can be easily manipulated. The first payment to employees in many cases could be as long as six months after the end of the profit period, making it difficult for employees to relate efforts with results. These are not unique criticisms but represent some of the same profit sharing pitfalls that exist anywhere.

Although the original plan to link 20 percent of pay to profits was abandoned, the government guidelines for PRP suggest that it could be introduced (or increased in amount) in place of a conventional pay increase and this might be coupled with a conversion of some part of existing pay to PRP. The wording is sufficiently ambiguous, it seems, to allow employers to comply with the criteria but place little, or nothing, of employees' pay at risk. The risk, of course, is that PRP becomes an efficiency bonus over regular pay, which is what the unions feel it should be, but not what it was intended to be.

The official union stance is one of opposition. At least one union, the General, Municipal, Boilermakers and Allied Trades Union (GMB), has issued guidelines on PRP to negotiators. GMB urges resistance to any PRP proposal as an unattractive proposition and a poor use of public money for tax concessions. GMB's detailed objections to PRP are probably typical of those being raised by other unions:

- Employees have no control over levels of profitability;
- Wages become the only element of cost that varies with profitability;
- Profits can vary for a number of reasons unrelated to employee effort;
- New recruits and part-timers may be excluded from the plan;

- Employees retiring in years when profits fell may lose some pension entitlement;
- PRP institutionalizes uncertainty about pay levels;
- PRP undermines collective power as a part of earnings becomes non-negotiable.[9]

GMB suggests resistance to any attempts by employers to convert existing pay to PRP, and it claims that the legislation allows PRP as an addition to regular pay rates.[10]

No data have been published concerning the number of plans which have made PRP payments supplementary to existing pay and the number of those which involve placing some proportion of existing or base pay at risk. There are various ways PRP can be introduced. First, PRP can be made a part of basic pay either by reducing existing pay or by introducing PRP in lieu of a wage increase. If it is introduced and base pay is reduced, a decline in profits means that the employees will lose money. Second, PRP may be introduced as a new version of an existing bonus or profit sharing plan. In this case, employees should gain because of the tax relief afforded by PRP. Third, PRP may be introduced as an entirely new payment over and above base pay. This is likely to be the most expensive option for employers since it involves paying out "new" money.

The first alternative is the one which the government hopes will be followed by substantial numbers of employers. The third alternative is the least desirable from the standpoint of creating a more flexible wage system. At least initially, it seems likely that the most common move to PRP will be the second alternative, as existing plans are converted to PRP plans in order to offer the tax advantages to employees. However, PRP is aimed directly at companies which do not have profit sharing rather than those which do have it. Employers who take the conversion route may, of course, eventually make PRP a supplement to base pay, but that is not certain. The second alternative also raises the issue of compatibility of ADST (share) plans and PRP plans.

The Department of Employment has stated that, "Share schemes and PRP are not in any way competitors, rather they can play a complementary role."[11] The accumulation of shares presumably reinforces the employee's long-term commitment to the company while PRP could provide a short-term motivation for employees and rein-

---

[9] Incomes Data Services, *IDS Study, PRP & Profit Sharing*, p. 6.
[10] *Ibid.*
[11] "Profit related pay: a new challenge—and a new opportunity," *Employment Gazette*, Vol. 95, No. 9 (September 1987), p. 457.

forcement of the long-term commitment which share ownership engenders.

Employers and employees in the United Kingdom now have a choice of three types of profit sharing or profit-related pay plans: (1) cash plans which provide for periodic cash payments to employees at either a specified amount or at management's discretion with no tax incentives; (2) deferred ADST (share) plans with tax incentives; and (3) PRP plans with cash payments and tax incentives. Theoretically, an employer could have all three types, but tax relief would be available only once for any individual employee. Although there are no statistics on the number of these plans operating, Bell and Hanson in 1987 estimated that in the United Kingdom there were approximately 700 companies with cash plans or ADST plans covering more than two million participants.[12] Bell and Hanson's estimates were made before passage of the PRP legislation, and PRP plans are consequently not included. Approximately 900 PRP plans had been approved by 1989, but some of those 900 were undoubtedly converted from either cash or ADST plans, so the two numbers cannot be simply added to obtain a total.

Perhaps a more important question than the number of plans is how does the performance of profit sharing companies compare with that of non-profit sharing companies? Bell and Hanson have attempted to answer that question in their study. They studied 113 profit sharing companies and 301 non-profit sharers in the United Kingdom from 1977/1978 to 1984/1985, using the financial ratios shown in Table VII-2. They concluded that the economic performance of profit sharing companies as a group was superior to that of non-profit sharers as a group in terms of profitability, growth, and investor returns. The authors are quick to point out, however, that their findings on performance do not prove there is a causal link between profit sharing and economic performance. Rather, they suggest other management characteristics which also contribute to greater success. These characteristics include a recognition that employees are the most important resource of a business and must be treated differently from other resources; a view of employees as co-partners and an attempt to eliminate the "them and us" barriers between management and employees; the promotion and development of a free flow of information to tap the full employee potential available to the company; and an ability to generate employee com-

---

[12]D. Wallace Bell and Charles G. Hanson, *Profit Sharing and Profitability: How Profit Sharing Promotes Business Success* (London: Kogan Page, Ltd., 1987), p. 18.

TABLE VII-2
*Comparative Performance of Profit Sharing and
Non-Profit Sharing Companies, 1977–1985*

	Profit Sharing Companies	Non-Profit Sharing Companies
Profitability Ratios:		
Return on equity (%)	25.1	19.1
Return on capital employed (%)	20.6	15.5
Earnings per share (pence)	16.3	12.8
Return on sales (%)	8.4	5.6
Growth Ratios:		
Annual sales growth (%)	15.5	13.7
Annual equity growth (%)	17.6	16.0
Annual profit growth (%)	13.6	9.7
Investor Returns:		
Dividends per share (pence)	5.2	4.9
Total annual returns (%)	24.8	18.0

Source: D. Wallace Bell and Carles G. Hanson, *Profit Sharing and Profitability: How Profit Sharing Promotes Business Success*, (London: Kogan Page Ltd., 1987), p. 58.

mitment by sharing information and by linking the financial interest of employees with the financial interest of the company.[13]

Bell and Hanson argue rightly that a company should not attempt to introduce profit sharing until it has a management style that approximates most of the employee participation philosophy outlined above. For that reason they have reservations about tax incentives which may induce some companies to introduce profit sharing before they are ready for it. They believe that profit sharing should stand on its own merits.

SAVINGS-RELATED SHARE OPTION PLANS

Savings-related share ownership plans are regulated by the Finance Act of 1980 and are not dependent upon profits of the employer. These plans are similar to savings plans in the United States and are often referred to as Save-As-You-Earn (SAYE) share option plans. Although employers may have different reasons for instituting such plans, the most common reason seems to be to make employees feel they are a part of the company and to create a feeling of involvement and interest in the company's fortune.[14] One per-

---

[13]*Ibid.*, pp. 60-67.
[14]*See* results of the 1985 Department of Employment survey reported in Gillian R. Smith, "Profit sharing and employee share ownership in Britain," *Employment Gazette*, Vol. 94, No. 8 (September 1986), pp. 380-385.

ceived advantage that the SAYE plans have over other types of plans is that they require a greater commitment from the employees and are seen as more likely to result in a higher degree of personal interest in the well-being of the employer.

Features of SAYE Plans

In order to realize tax benefits, plans must first be approved by Inland Revenue and must be open to all full-time employees with five years or more of service. Employees choose to save a monthly or weekly amount (minimum of £10, maximum of £100, or U.S.$16 to U.S.$163) for sixty months or 240 weeks with the Department for National Savings (DNS) or with a building society. At the time the savings agreement is concluded, the employee is given an "option" to buy company shares at a fixed price which may not be less than 90 percent of the market value of the shares at that time. At the end of five or seven years, the employee will have saved enough to produce the funds to pay for the shares. If the date of the option is five years, the employees have a choice of: (1) buying the shares (if the price at that time is higher than option price); (2) taking their savings and any accumulated bonus (equivalent to interest); or (3) allowing the SAYE contract to continue for an additional two years to earn a greater bonus. If the date of the option is seven years then only the first two choices are available. Even if the price of the stock at the time the option date is reached is lower than the option price, the employees still have their savings plus bonuses earned. There are, of course, provisions to cover the disposition of funds in the event of retirement, death, or termination of employment.

Tax Aspects

Employees are not liable for income tax on any gain realized through the exercise of their option and acquiring shares at less than market value. If the option is not exercised, the employees may simply take the proceeds of their savings plus bonuses tax free in the usual way.

Evaluation

The 1985 survey by the Department of Employment concluded that both profit sharing and share-option plans were regarded as generally successful by employers. The profit sharing plans consistently received a higher rating than the SAYE arrangements, however. In both cases, success was rated much higher for the more general objectives, such as improving employee identification with the company and improved employee understanding of financial issues, than the more measurable factors such as improved productivity. From the employer's point of view, the SAYE plans are less costly and do not depend upon profits. Actually, the deferred profit sharing (ADST) plans do not require that a profit be made each year since funds are allocated to the trust on the basis of an employee's earnings, and they are not required to be related to any given level of profits. There is some evidence that employees do not sell shares quickly but tend to hold them unless the share price has risen substantially or the employee has left the company. At least there appears to be no rush by employees to sell shares as soon as they become available. A 1986 survey of 192 companies showed that only 10 percent of employees sell their profit sharing shares within three years and only 20 percent within twelve months from the end of the five-year holding period.[15]

Share-based plans are still relatively few among small, privately owned companies. The Department of Employment survey of 1985 found that most of those companies had never seriously considered adopting approved profit sharing or share plans. Reasons often cited were that share-based arrangements are not appropriate to the way these firms operate or that the management knew very little about share-based plans. Cash plans without tax benefits remain the most common form of profit sharing in the smaller private companies.[16]

EMPLOYEE STOCK OWNERSHIP PLANS (ESOP)

Although ESOPs have flourished in the United States and number in the thousands, they are a relatively new development in the United Kingdom. The first ESOP in the United Kingdom was established in 1987, and as of 1989, there were only approximately one dozen in the country, covering perhaps 12,000 employees.[17] Of course, ESOPs are not the only method of transferring ownership to employees in Great Britain. The Department of Employment in 1986 estimated that 37 percent of publicly quoted firms had an approved share ownership plan, either an ADST plan or an SAYE plan.[18] Yet, the Department of Employment acknowledged that the extent of employee ownership is very small, reaching over 10 percent in only 6

---

[15]Shares for the workers," *Investors Chronicle*, Vol. 78 (October 17, 1986), p. 41.
[16]Smith, "Profit sharing and employee share ownership in Britain," p. 384.
[17]"ESOPs—a new share ownership option," *European Industrial Relations Review*, No. 181 (February 1989), p. 17.
[18]Smith, "Profit sharing and employee share ownership in Britain," p. 381.

United Kingdom

percent of large firms and 1 percent of small firms.[19] ESOPs offer a vehicle for increasing employee shareholding, and the relative success of ESOPs in the United States appears to have aroused considerable interest in the United Kingdom.

Although there are significant differences between the United Kingdom ESOP and the United States ESOP, there are also important similarities. One of the most fundamental differences is that in the United Kingdom, the ESOP is designed to place actual shares of stock into the hands of individual employees before termination of service. Another difference is that United Kingdom ESOPs enjoy few special tax incentives; for example, there is no special tax treatment for ESOP lenders. A basic similarity is the right of the ESOP to borrow money with financial support from the sponsoring company with the consequent possibility of acquiring substantial equity percentages on behalf of employees. The uses for ESOPs are also much the same in the United Kingdom: purchase of ownership from a proprietor, the raising of new capital on a tax efficient basis, and participation in leveraged buyouts and takeover defense applications.[20]

Nearly one-half of the ESOPs in the United Kingdom were initiated as part of a management-led employee buyout. There has also been a strong connection between ESOPs and the government's privatization program. With the spread of privatization in the United Kingdom, there exists a unique opportunity for employee ownership to flourish. One of the most successful employee ownership efforts is that of the National Freight Consortium (NFC), where 10,300 employees subscribed for 82.5 percent of the company when it was privatized in 1982. At the same time the government is moving ahead with privatization, it is encouraging wider share ownership, and is particularly supportive of the ESOP concept. There is also abundant evidence, acknowledged by trade union leadership, that workers want shares. Officially, the trade union leadership is opposed to privatization, but also recognize that it is inevitable. With the realization that privatization appears to be unstoppable, the union leadership is pressured to obtain the best deal possible for an industry's employees. In fact, most of the ESOPs have been planned and developed with assistance from Unity Trust, a trade union backed financial institution organized to provide an oppor-

---

[19]"ESOPs—a new share ownership option," p. 17.
[20]John Cahillane and Clifford Chance, "Transatlantic ESOPs," paper delivered at the ESOP Association, 12th Annual Convention, May 24-26, 1989, at Washington, D.C.

tunity for union members to benefit from equity participation in British firms.

A major initiative in the ESOP area is expected as the electricity supply industry moves toward privatization. The eight unions in the Electricity Supply Trade Union Council (ESTUC) are looking for a 10 percent share of the post-privatization companies for the employees in the form of free and preferential shares. The unions hope to set up ESOPs to create an internal market for shares of the privatized electricity companies. In early 1989, the Department of Energy was considering the unions' proposals and had assured the employees that there would be attractive provisions to enable them to acquire shares.[21]

Several other companies due to be privatized, or which are being considered for privatization, are candidates for ESOP treatment. British Coal, the Scottish Transport Group, and Girobank, the banking subsidiary of the Post Office, are all possibilities for ESOP utilization. In addition, some forty-two municipality owned bus companies are likely to be privatized in 1989, and these should result in several new ESOPs. The United Kingdom's largest ESOP was formed when the Yorkshire Rider bus company was privatized late in 1988. It was heavily leveraged with a debt of thirty-six times the equity. Yet, the banks who loaned the money to the trust expect to recoup their investment in ten years. In 1987, the People's Provincial Bus Company was successfully privatized with an ESOP taking 80 percent of the equity and the employees buying the remainder as individuals.[22]

Management buyouts of private companies also offer increasing possibilities for the use of ESOPs by managements which have an interest in involving employees in the enterprise. In these cases the trust is established to buy shares which are set aside for employees and then offered to the employees after the buyout is completed. An example, and one of the first ESOPs in the United Kingdom, is the management buyout of KTM, one of the United Kingdom's leading machine tool manufacturers, from Vickers. Initially, the work force will acquire 19 percent of the company's equity capital. The purchase of the employer shares was funded by Unity Trust, the trade union bank. As the ESOP borrowings are repaid, the ESOP will give

---

[21]Michael Smith, "Electricity workers go for share ownership," *Financial Times*, October 31, 1988, p. 9.
[22]"Many more fares please," *The Economist*, Vol. 309, No. 7576 (November 12, 1988), pp. 90-91.

away some of its shares to all eligible employees. Eventually, the employees could receive more than 19 percent of employer shares.[23]

Although it is too early to fully evaluate the success of employee share ownership schemes, some effort has been made in that direction. Because of increased interest in employee share ownership in the United Kingdom, the Department of Employment funded a study in 1988 to examine the problems and performance of firms with a "significant"[24] degree of employee share ownership. Twenty firms with a significant degree of employee share ownership were studied, and the results were published in the *Employment Gazette*.[25]

The study found that the most important reason for the introduction of employee share ownership was to motivate employees. This tends to confirm the earlier findings of Smith in the 1985 Department of Employment survey cited above. These employers appear to be attempting to create a relationship with their employees that goes beyond their pay envelopes and to promote a source of employee income in addition to the basic wage. The study also confirms what the experts in profit sharing and employee ownership have concluded: any of these programs must be seen as part of other changes in management style and should be designed to work in conjunction with other employee participation schemes.[26] In addition, it is important that sufficient time and effort be given to explaining the share ownership plan to the employees. In one company in the Department of Employment study, the introduction of share ownership without fully communicating the plan to employees resulted in only 2 percent subscription by employees. Usually, participation rates are 30 to 50 percent or higher.

Another relatively recent study by Blanchflower and Oswald, involving 637 manufacturing plants, concluded that employee share ownership makes no difference in the level of employment and capital investment behavior of the firms.[27] The authors conclude, how-

---

[23]David Waller, "A big stake for the workers," *Financial Times*, October 13, 1988, p. 6.
[24]Defined as a firm where 10 percent or more of the equity is held individually or collectively by 10 or 10 percent (whichever is greater) of the employees of the company, and where decision-making is not by one person, one vote.
[25]*See* Vicky Price and Chris Nicholson, "The problems and performance of employee ownership firms," *Employment Gazette*, Vol. 96, No. 2 (June 1988), pp. 346-350.
[26]*See* Chapter II where U.S. studies are cited which reach this same conclusion.
[27]D. G. Blanchflower and A. J. Oswald, "Shares for Employees: A Test of Their Effects," Discussion Paper No. 273, London School of Economics, Center for Labour Economics, 1987.

ever, that despite their findings employee share ownership may produce other beneficial results.

The authors of the Department of Employment study did not attempt to determine whether employee share ownership resulted in improved profitability, turnover, or productivity. The conclusion was drawn, however, that most of the firms in the study felt that share ownership had a positive effect on results. There was a strong caveat that it is difficult to isolate the effect of share ownership per se and that other forms of incentive may have had as much influence as share ownership. One area where employee share ownership does appear to influence behavior is in businesses in which employees have frequent contact with customers. In those cases, a substantial improvement in customer relations was perceived.

Similar conclusions were reached from a survey reported by the *European Industrial Relations Review*. The survey included all ten companies which had ESOPs at the time. All of the companies cited three broad areas of improved performance: (1) assistance in the creation of a better industrial relations climate; (2) increased receptiveness to change; and (3) greater commitment to company objectives.[28] Although tax advantages in Great Britain are not as great as those in the United States, the survey cited above found that the companies perceived ESOPs as having the following advantages over other employee share plans:

- they treat all employees equally;
- they allow a significant employee share stake and thus enhance a feeling of involvement;
- they allow companies time to create an internal market in their shares;
- they are a method of raising new capital without having to resort to short-term payback requirements of many venture capital institutions, and without the risk of letting in potential predators; and
- they are flexible and relatively tax efficient.[29]

The most significant disadvantages were found to be the tax and legal complexities surrounding ESOPs in Great Britain which are time-consuming and costly for companies who wish to adopt ESOPs. Future growth of ESOPs may depend largely on government initiatives to increase tax incentives.

---

[28]"ESOPs—a new share ownership option," p. 19.
[29]*Ibid.*

GAIN SHARING

In the United Kingdom there exists an important payment system known as "payment by results" (PBR), under which pay is related to effort and/or output. One of the most widely known PBR systems is piecework, but there is a variety of group-based plans as well which fall under the broad heading of gain sharing. Traditionally, the aim of PBR was to encourage greater output.[30] Increasingly, however, new systems have been designed to be used as instruments of management strategy to meet a variety of business needs. Male manual workers are the most likely to have a PBR system. Table VII-3, which shows Department of Employment data, indicates that 42.8 percent of male manual workers received such payments. The trend over the four years shows a smaller percentage of employees receiving PBR pay in all categories. For those employees who receive PBR payments, the percentage of gross earnings attributable to PBR has been increasing in virtually all categories, as shown in Table VII-4. The data in Tables VII-3 and VII-4 indicate that PBR as a payment system has declined somewhat for the population as a whole, but for those who are still receiving PBR payments, those payments represent an increasing proportion of their gross average earnings.

TABLE VII-3
Percentage of Employees Receiving Payment by Results Payments

	1983	1984	1985	1986
Males				
All non-manual occupations	18.8	19.1	16.7	16.7
All manual occupations	46.9	46.5	43.2	42.8
All occupations	33.8	33.8	30.8	30.5
Females				
All non-manual ocupations	13.8	13.4	11.7	11.4
All manual occupations	34.0	35.3	33.3	32.3
All occupations	18.4	18.4	16.6	16.0

Source: Incomes Data Services, Ltd., *IDS Study: Incentive Bonuses*, No. 389 (July 1987), p. 2.

---

[30]Bob Hepple and Sandra Fredman (R. Blanpain, ed.), "Great Britain," *International Encyclopaedia for Labour Law and Industrial Relations*, Vol. 5 (The Netherlands: Kluwer Law and Taxation Publishers, 1986), p. 23.

TABLE VII-4

*Payment by Results Payments as a Percent of
Gross Average Earnings for Those Receiving such Payments*

	1983	1984	1985	1986
Males				
All non-manual occupations	14.6	17.3	19.1	19.2
All manual occupations	18.5	19.8	19.4	19.5
All occupations	17.2	18.9	19.3	19.4
Females				
All non-manual ocupations	8.1	9.2	9.9	10.2
All manual occupations	22.4	26.7	25.3	25.2
All occupations	13.4	15.7	15.9	15.8

Source: Incomes Data Services, Ltd., *IDS Study: Incentive Bonuses*, No. 389 (July 1987), p. 3.

CHAPTER VIII

France

BACKGROUND OF FINANCIAL PARTICIPATION

According to the late Bert Metzger, a widely known student and proponent of profit sharing, it was a French house painter, Jean Le Claire, who was the father of modern profit sharing. In 1843, Le Claire began sharing profits with his forty-four employees and found that the system worked to everyone's advantage.[1] In spite of this colorful beginning, individual profit sharing plans developed slowly in France for over 100 years until the de Gaulle era.

General Charles de Gaulle's view of the social order relied heavily upon the concept of financial participation by employees. His objectives were, on the one hand, to draw together the interests of employers and employees, and, on the other hand, to increase the level of investment in the economy and of personal savings. The de Gaulle government, therefore, promoted financial participation legislation as a positive response to bolster the French economy.

1959 Profit Sharing Law (Voluntary)

The first Gaullist law in 1959 was an attempt to encourage companies to establish voluntary cash profit sharing schemes based on company trading profits or productivity improvements. Such payments were exempt from corporate income tax, social security contributions, and other payroll taxes, but allocations received by employees were taxable. The legislation also had the disadvantage of tying companies into agreements with a minimum duration of three years, and which also required the official approval of a commission set up by the local labor authorities. As a result, few companies took advantage of these voluntary profit sharing schemes. By 1978, it was estimated that only 300 firms with 140,000 employees were covered by these voluntary plans.[2]

---

[1]Bert L. Metzger, *Profit Sharing as a Motivator* (Evanston, IL: Profit Sharing Research Foundation, 1984), p. 9.
[2]"France: An A to Z of employee shareholding and profit sharing," European Industrial Relations Review, No. 53 (May 1978), p. 8.

1967 Profit Sharing Law (Compulsory)

Voluntary profit sharing schemes never really became popular in France, and in 1967, compulsory *deferred* profit sharing was introduced for all companies with more than 100 employees. Companies having fewer than 100 employees could adopt a plan voluntarily, and all employees, regardless of status or remuneration were covered. The law was intended to develop more harmonious industrial relations, to increase the level of investment in the economy, and to increase the level of personal savings. When a company's net profits exceeded 5 percent of its capital, a proportion (calculated by a standard formula) of those profits was paid into a special profit sharing reserve (RSP). This reserve was tax deductible for the company and was exempt from both employers' and employees' social security contributions, provided it was frozen for five years (reduced by later legislation to three years if done by company agreement). The employee paid no income tax on his or her allocation. The RSP could be used in one or more of five specified ways: (1) the issue of company shares to employees; (2) the issue of company debentures; (3) the opening of a current account by the company, with a fixed interest system; (4) the investment of the money in a mutual fund; and (5) the investment of the money in a special mutual fund set up specifically for the company concerned. In addition, the employer could set up a reserve for investment equal to the RSP amount, which, if used within one year to finance the acquisition of assets, was also deductible. The amount allocated to individual employees was proportional to the annual salary up to a specified maximum. Funds were subject to a five-year holding period with exceptions for cases of dismissal, retirement, layoff, or death.

The 1967 legislation apparently did not have the impact that was intended. In December 1975, 4.73 million workers, or 22.5 percent of the country's labor force, were covered by profit sharing agreements.[3] In December 1984, not only was there no increase in the number of workers covered, but only 52.2 percent of those covered actually received any benefits from such agreements, since many companies affected by the economic downturn were not sufficiently profitable. By 1985, the number of workers covered by a profit shar-

---

[3]France, Ministry of Labor, "La Participation: Situation des Accords au 31 Decembre 1975." France has a relatively high proportion of small employers.

ing agreement had declined to 4.5 million, but 67.6 percent of those covered by an agreement actually received a payment.[4]

By the 1980s, employee financial participation had become a complex array of fiscal and legal regulations which included several share ownership and capital accumulation schemes as well as profit sharing plans.

THE 1986 LEGISLATION

With the arrival of the conservative Chirac government (1986-1988) came the implementation of an ambitious privatization program which included goals to quintuple the number of individual share owners and to spread the ownership of state companies to such a degree that they could never be renationalized. The mood of the country was receptive; the interventionist stance of the Socialist government and its resulting economic problems had convinced the French that the government could not provide for everything.

At the company level, differentiation of earnings had become one trend of a broader pattern of participative management that also included employee involvement. The individualization of the employees' relations with management and the abolition of wage indexation in France favored the expansion of profit sharing plans. Companies were seeking ways to make the organization of work more flexible as well as ways to make pay more flexible.

On the initiative of the Minister for Economy, Finance and Privatization, Edouard Balladour, profit sharing was given a new impetus through a major reform enacted in 1986. The three aims of the 1986 law were: (1) to simplify and harmonize the various regulations; (2) to strengthen the role of financial participation in company-level bargaining; and (3) to encourage such participation and promote employee share ownership through tax incentives.[5] The legislation did not alter the existing framework of financial participation. Changes were designed to make the law simpler, to reduce administrative approval procedures, and to improve the tax advantages. Three chapters are included in the legislation. One deals with compulsory deferred profit sharing (often referred to as capital sharing); another covers voluntary immediate (cash) profit sharing; and a

---

[4]For these and subsequent statistical data *see* France, Ministre des Affaires Sociales et de l'Emploi, "Dossiers Statistiques du Travail et de l'Emploi," No. 40 (January 1988).

[5]"Government encourages participation," *European Industrial Relations Review*, No. 156 (January 1987), p. 10.

third relates to company savings plans, share ownership plans, and share option plans.

Compulsory Deferred Profit (Capital) Sharing

The 1986 legislation did not significantly change the 1967 compulsory profit sharing system described above. As before, company agreements may provide for different bases and methods for calculating the profit sharing reserve. The result must provide benefits at least equivalent to the statutory formula[6] for the employees, however. Under the provisions of the new law it is no longer necessary to submit a profit sharing agreement to administrative authorities for approval. Now the agreement need only be deposited with the departmental labor authorities, which means greater flexibility and an easier and faster procedure. Payments must be made to all employees including part-time employees and those on fixed-term contracts. A maximum of six months of service may be required for eligibility. The 1986 legislation also provides for a normal blocking period of five years for distribution from the profit sharing reserve, but added a proviso reducing this requirement to three years where there is a company agreement to that effect. (In that case, one-half of the tax advantage to the company and the employee is lost.) The text of the law stresses that the raison d'etre of the vested period is to promote savings and investment. The vesting period applies only to the principal and not to the revenues, and investment alternatives remain the same as described above.

In spite of their compulsory nature, the number of deferred profit sharing plans has remained constant. As of December 31, 1985, approximately 12,000 enterprises, covering 4.5 million employees had profit sharing agreements (see Table VIII-1). Approximately one-third of the 12,000 enterprises had fewer than 100 employees. According to the Ministry of Labor, 10,111 agreements were recorded as of December 31, 1988, covering 12,001 enterprises and approximately 4.5 million employees. Only 2.7 million employees have actually benefited from a profit sharing bonus, however. The

---

[6]The statutory formula is:

$$RSP = \frac{1}{2}\left(\frac{P\text{-}5C}{100}\right) \times \left(\frac{S}{VA}\right)$$

P = Net profit
C = Capital employed
S = Total wage bill
VA = Value added

TABLE VIII-1
*Compulsory Profit Sharing Agreements
(Participation)*

Year	Number of Employees Covered by an Agreement	Employees in Enterprises with more than 100 Employees	Employees in Enterprises with fewer than 100 Employees	Percent in Enterprises with fewer than 100 Employees
1984	4,698,904	4,522,034	176,870	3.76
1985	4,549,940	4,370,507	179,433	3.94
1986	4,524,282	4,345,120	179,162	3.96
1987	4,408,231	4,234,186	174,045	3.94
1988	4,478,214	N.A.	N.A.	N.A.

Source: Ministère du Travail, de l'Emploi et de la Formation Professionnelle.
N.A. = Not available.

average annual payment to employees was 2,900 F (US$483) in 1985 and 3,500 F (US$583) in 1986.[7]

Deferred profit sharing agreements may be concluded in one of four ways: (1) as part of a company collective agreement, or as a separate agreement; (2) between the company's chief executive and "representative" trade unions (there is no requirement that all representative trade unions within a company sign such an agreement); (3) by the works council; and (4) by a two-thirds vote of all employees endorsing a draft agreement put forward by the chief executive. The most popular method for concluding deferred profit sharing agreements has been the works council.[8] For the years 1986 and 1987, for example, more than 77 percent of the agreements were signed by the works councils, while 20 percent were signed by union representatives.[9] Profit sharing agreements must contain the following: the manner in which the agreements were concluded and by whom; their duration; the manner in which payouts are to be distributed; the ways in which employees are to be informed on the implementation of the plan; the formula used for calculating the RSP; and the procedure for conflict resolution.

Although the compulsory profit sharing statute is the most original part of the French system, it has apparently reached a plateau in terms of numbers of enterprises and employees covered. Greater profits among the companies covered would, of course, expand the

---

[7]*Liaisons Sociales*, No. 10535 du jeudi (September 7, 1989).

[8]A works council is mandatory in enterprises with fifty or more employees and is composed of the enterprise head (or his/her representative) and elected representatives of the employees. Although the works council may conclude profit sharing agreements, it is not legally entitled to negotiate collective agreements.

[9]*Liaisons Sociales*, No. 10510 (July 27, 1989).

number of employees who benefit from such plans. In addition, the government in 1990 reduced the employee threshold from 100 employees to 50.

Voluntary Cash Profit Sharing

Arguably, the most significant aspect of the 1986 legislation is the boost it provides for voluntary, cash profit sharing. The concept remains the same in the 1986 law as it has been since first enacted in 1959. Important changes, however, have made these plans more attractive.

(1) Agreements still must be for a minimum of three years, but now agreements may be made following a referendum of all employees in a unit (a two-thirds majority is required for implementation), subject to a joint request from the managing director and from one or more unions represented in the company or from the works council.[10]

(2) Prior administrative approval of a plan is no longer required; plans need only be registered with the local office of the Ministry of Labor and Employment. Agreements must contain: the duration of the agreement; the work units covered; the basis upon which payouts will be calculated (company results, performance, productivity, etc.); the criteria used for the allocation of bonuses among the various categories of workers and work units; the frequency and dates of bonus distribution; the ways in which employee representatives will be informed about the implementation of the plan; and the grievance and review procedures.

(3) A maximum of 20 percent of payroll has been fixed as the ceiling for distribution (the government in 1990 reduced this ceiling to 12 percent, or 8 percent in firms without a pay agreement).

(4) The law now allows bonuses of varying amounts which gives companies greater flexibility to negotiate bonuses for various grades or work units.

(5) Tax relief remains unchanged, i.e., payments are exempt from employers' social security tax and corporate income tax. For the employee, however, the deposit of bonuses into a company savings plan is matched by tax relief on the resulting income up to a maximum of 65,520 F (US$10,920) in 1990, which is one-half of the annual social security ceiling.[11]

---

[10]"Government encourages participation," pp. 10-11.
[11]*Ibid.* p. 11.

The law does not specify who is to benefit from these plans, nor does it specify the definition of profits or productivity, provided the measure rises and falls according to the collective activity of the enterprise (not that of the individual), is objective, and reflects the collective effort of the employees.[12] For example, the link may be to operating profits, profit growth, productivity improvements, or other factors.[13] In contrast to the approach taken in Great Britain with profit related pay where it was designed to replace a significant portion of regular pay, the French have strictly prohibited companies from replacing existing pay with profit sharing bonuses. Since profit-related bonuses are not subject to social security contributions under the French system, many companies were motivated to replace existing bonuses with profit sharing bonuses under the 1986 legislation. Early in 1988 the government ended this practice. In order to qualify for tax benefits, only profit sharing plans based on the 1959 legislation may be replaced by plans updated under the 1986 legislation.

The largest employers' organization, the National Council of French Employers (CNPF), has endorsed the proposition that in no case should profit sharing replace basic pay. At the same time, the CNPF in its 1990 pay guidelines recommended a "flexible and diversified" compensation policy based on three elements: collective profit sharing; individual performance pay; and increases in accordance with economic progress within the sector and the enterprise.[14] The CNPF saw this strategy as having a favorable effect on keeping basic company settlements at an estimated 3 percent during 1989.

Although there is no unanimous trade union view of profit sharing, the French Economic and Social Council in 1988 commissioned M. Jean Bornard, president of the French Christian Workers Confederation (CFTC), to write a report on the "financial aspects of profit sharing."[15] Published in May 1989, the report stressed particularly the necessity of clearly stating the "principle of distinction between profit sharing and wage policy," a distinction which, according to

---

[12]"Boom in profit-sharing agreements," *European Industrial Relations Review*, No. 171 (April 1988), p. 18.

[13]The simplest and most widespread formula used is:

$$\frac{\text{value added}}{\text{wages + nonwage labor costs.}}$$

See *Liaisons Sociales*, No. 10120 (December 24, 1987), p. 17.

[14]"France: CNPF's 1990 Pay Recommendations," *IDS European Report*, No. 336 (December 1989), p. 4.

[15]*See* "Aspects financiers de la participation et de l'intéressement," *Liaisons Sociales*, No. 10510 (July 17, 1989).

Bornard, is presently "insufficiently drawn."[16] Bornard also recommended that a percentage of the tax deductible bonuses be earmarked for financing unemployment benefits, pointing out that a shift toward individualized bonuses exempt from social contributions could endanger the French social security system. In the spirit of the single market of 1993, Bornard advocated the harmonization of profit sharing plans in various EC countries, suggesting the adoption of a community directive for companies with a minimum of 50 to 100 employees.

The number of voluntary agreements has spread rapidly. According to statistics released by the Ministry of Labor, their number doubled between 1985 and 1987 (see Table VIII-2). More than 1,900 new agreements were concluded in 1988, bringing the total to nearly 4,600 agreements covering almost one million employees. By the end of 1989, over 5,000 agreements had been signed. Some surveys predict a further doubling of the number of agreements during the early 1990s.[17] The French Minister of Labor cautioned, however, against the "uncontrolled development" of profit sharing and other types of compensation that are contingent on economic performance since such plans create uncertainty and could endanger both pay bargaining and worker security.[18]

These agreements may be concluded in the same way as deferred plans but must be effective for a minimum of three years. Although the preferred method for concluding deferred profit sharing agreements appears to be the Works Council (77 percent), voluntary (cash)

TABLE VIII-2
Growth of Voluntary Profit Sharing Agreements
(Intéressement)

Year	Number of Agreements	Percentage Increase Compared to Previous Year	Number of Employees Covered by an Agreement	Percentage Increase of the Number of Employees Covered
1984	1,086	+ 18.3	335,180	+ 14.4
1985	1,303	+ 20.0	401,530	+ 19.3
1986	2,162	+ 65.9	589,540	+ 46.8
1987	2,630	+ 21.7	729,295	+ 23.7
1988	4,600	+ 70	1,000,000	+ 37

Source: Ministère du Travail, de l'Emploi et de la Formation Professionnelle.

---

[16]*Ibid.*, p. 2.
[17]"Boom in profit-sharing agreements," p. 19.
[18]"Collective bargaining in 1988," *European Industrial Relations Review*, No. 188 (September 1989), p. 22.

plans are more frequently concluded directly by the employee referendum procedure (52 percent).[19] These figures are not surprising when it is understood that there has been a marked increase in the number of voluntary plans in companies having fewer than 100 employees, and particularly in those with fewer than ten. The direct referendum procedure is likely to be more easily utilized at small firms than in large firms.

Although it is too early to draw any firm conclusions, there is a discernible trend toward the linkage of profit sharing to improvements in productivity and away from company results. From 1985 to 1987 the percentage of agreements based on company results dropped from 82.7 percent to 77.8 percent, while those based on productivity improvement increased from 11.5 percent to 13.8 percent during the same period. There has also been an increase in agreements which combine different formulae.[20]

In 1988, the average profit sharing bonus from voluntary plans reached 4,662 F (US$777), up from 3,385 F (US$564) in 1987. There is a tendency for the average bonus to decrease as company size increases. The total amount of voulntary profit sharing paid annually is estimated at between 4 and 5 billion francs (US$6.7 million to US$8.3 million), or 4.1 percent of the total wage bill.[21]

Savings, Share Ownership, and Share Option Plans

The final chapter of the 1986 legislation covers three types of plans: company savings plans, share ownership plans, and share option plans.

Savings plans were first introduced by legislation in 1967 which provided that companies, on their own initiative or through a collective agreement, could establish employee savings plans. Although these plans were voluntary, they could be linked to the compulsory profit sharing plans which were also introduced in 1967. The link established between the profit sharing plan and the savings plan allowed the employees to deposit all or part of their profit sharing bonus into the company savings plan. The 1986 law continued these provisions and also permits bonuses from voluntary profit sharing plans to be deposited in the savings plan. Employees may also make individual contributions to the savings plan up to one-fourth of their annual income. Finally, the company may also contribute supplemen-

---

[19]*See* "Aspects financiers de la participation et de l'intéressement," *Liaisons Sociales*, No. 10510 (July 27, 1989), p. 12.

[20]"Boom in profit-sharing," p. 19.

[21]"Interessement, Bilan fin 1988," *Liaisons Sociales*, No. 10490, June 27, 1989.

tary payments up to 10,000 F (US$1,667) per employee per year, but this supplementary payment cannot exceed three times the amount of the employee's contribution. The company payment may be increased to 15,000 F (US$2,500) when the employee acquires shares or investment certificates in the company. Employees may obtain discounts on the price of shares up to 20 percent.

Company savings plans offer various tax incentives for employees and employers. For employers, supplementary payments are exempt from capital gains and social security taxes, and for employees, the income from the portfolio is tax free if reinvested. When profit sharing bonuses are transferred into a company's savings plan, they are tax exempt if left for a minimum of five years up to one-half of the social security earnings ceiling.

Part of the purpose of the 1986 legislation was to build links between the various types of financial participation plans; a good example of this is the tie-in between profit sharing and savings plans. Savings plans have thus been playing an increasingly important role as both a source of company capital and as an important means by which employees may build up significant personal capital. A recent survey of approximately 200 firms in the Paris area found that the number of savings plans had doubled since 1986.[22]

Share ownership was introduced by legislation in 1973 and has been amended several times. The essential framework has remained intact in the 1986 legislation. The purpose of these plans is to encourage employees to acquire shares in their companies. Numerous formalities are required when a new share issue is involved, but the procedure is much simpler when existing shares are purchased on the stock market. A plan must be approved by the assembly of shareholders and is only available for companies headquartered in France or in a European Community (EC) country. Shareholders also determine the amount of seniority required for employees to subscribe to such plans, but it may not be less than six months or more than three years. There is a ceiling on the value of shares that can be acquired by an employee, which is fixed at the level of one-half of the annual ceiling on which social security payments are calculated for each of the two methods used (new share issue or purchase of existing shares). The two methods can be used simultaneously. Companies can offer financial assistance to their employees to purchase shares, but contributions may not exceed the employee's annual contribution or the fixed amount of 3,000 F (US$500). Shares are generally blocked for five years with limited exceptions. Within specified

---

[22]"Aspects financiers,", p. 8.

limits, company contributions are deductible for the company and do not constitute income to the employee. Dividends on shares, however, are taxable.

Share option plans, introduced by legislation in 1970, and amended in 1984, allow a company to offer all or a portion of its employees an option to buy its shares at a fixed price over a fixed period of time. These plans have never had broad appeal, being limited largely to senior executives. They are mentioned here only because they are a part of the relatively complex employee financial participation landscape in France.

OTHER LEGISLATION

Although France does not have broad-based employee stock ownership plans (ESOPs) as they exist in the United States and the United Kingdom, the concept of the "leveraged management buyout" has been a part of French law since 1984. Passed by the Socialist government in 1984 and amended in 1987, the law enables employees (particularly managers) to form themselves into a holding company in order to acquire progressively the majority of the stock of the company which employs them, so that they can insure its continued existence, usually in situations in which an owner with no successor wishes to hand over the business to employees. The holding company purchases the assets of the operating company with its own assets and, if necessary, by borrowing additional funds from banks or other financial institutions. The employees must hold at least 50 percent of the voting rights in the holding company. There are a number of statutory incentives such as tax credits, tax deduction for interest on employee loans to purchase shares, and the right to use dividends paid out by the operating company to repay the loans. Subject to prescribed limits, the employee purchasers may deduct from their taxable income the interest on loans contracted to acquire the capital of the holding company.[23]

In the first successful buyout, involving Quercymetal, a garden equipment and do-it-yourself retailer, more than 100 of the company's 186 employees elected to buy shares.[24] In 1987 an estimated thirty-eight leveraged buyouts were undertaken with a total asset value of 3 billion francs. The 1988 figure has been estimated to be

---

[23] Act No. 87-416 of June 17, 1987, sur l'épargne, *Journal Officiel* (Official Gazette), June 18, 1987, pp. 6519-6528.

[24] "New financial participation schemes," *European Industrial Relations Review*, No. 134 (March 1985), p. 12.

at least double the 1987 figure based on the fact that one buyout totalled over 7 billion francs.²⁵

THE PUBLIC SECTOR

Although some workers in the private sector of the economy have benefited from profit sharing, public sector employees have been neglected, arousing discontent among many public sector employees. During the summer of 1989, Prime Minister Michel Rocard outlined guidelines on pay in the public sector. Rocard advocated pay "rigor" (i.e., holding pay increases at the level of inflation) and the use of voluntary profit sharing to relate the workers' pay to company results.²⁶ Although a number of public enterprises operate such plans, including Air France, Renault, and Aerospatiale, unions did not welcome the prime minister's intervention and accused him of attempting to limit the scope of bargaining in the public sector.²⁷

EXAMPLES OF PROFIT SHARING AGREEMENTS

The following examples illustrate the types of plans which have been adopted by various companies in various industries with differing business needs.

Kronenbourg

The Kronenbourg agreement covers 3,300 brewery employees for a three-year duration. It allows the distribution of bonuses not only according to the company's financial results, but also according to efforts made by the employees to achieve sector level targets. The agreement is divided into two parts: *intéressement* and *participation*.

The *accord d'intéressement* (voluntary profit sharing plan) stipulates that a percentage of the results proportional to operating profits (10 percent in 1988, 20 percent in 1989, and 25 percent thereafter) will be added according to whether or not divisional targets have been met. The choice of targets is decided by management at the sector level following consultation with employee representatives. The procedures used to meet the chosen targets are subject to

---

[25] George Graham, "Privatisation proves a fillip for an otherwise disappointing sector," *The Financial Times* (May 5, 1989), p. 19.
[26] "Public sector pay outlined," *European Industrial Relations Review*, No. 188 (September 1989), p. 5.
[27] *Ibid.*

a series of plant level agreements negotiated with either the union representatives or the works council.

The *accord de participation* (compulsory profit sharing plan) creates a special commission charged with the implementation of the agreement and with informing the workforce about it. The commission is made up of thirteen members from either the works council or employees chosen by the works council and must contain the union representatives within the works council. The commission must be informed by management of the financial situation of the enterprise and meets twice a year to analyze the basis of calculation of the RSP. Employees are eligible after six months of employment and distribution is proportionate to each employee's income.[28]

EDF and GDF

The EDF-GDF (nationalized electric and gas companies) profit sharing agreement was the first one to be signed in a nationalized enterprise following the 1986 legislation. The 1987 agreement was signed by all unions present in the company except the communist CGT, which is in principle opposed to the concept of profit sharing. The voluntary profit sharing plan is based on productivity gains and covers 152,000 employees for a three-year period. It is composed of two main elements: one is linked to productivity increases at the central level in both the electricity and gas companies. The other one is also based on collective performance criteria, but at a decentralized level, depending on fulfillment of targets in each individual sector (gas and electricity). Within the framework of the first element, a profit sharing bonus is distributed when a reduction of at least 10 percent in unit cost of electricity and gas over pre-set targets is achieved. Thus, the 1987 payout was based on the average result of the 1985-1986-1987 performance. Within the second element, payout will vary according to fulfillment of targets within each individual sector. One-half of the proceeds is paid on a flat rate basis and one-half according to job grade. The sums paid to each employee will be doubled if deposited into a company savings plan.[29]

Other Agreements

An agreement at the steel firm Sollac in November 1986 includes a collective performance indicator based on product quality, production time, and costs. Maubeuge-Construction Automobile, a subsidi-

---

[28]*Liaisons Sociales*, No. 6045 (January 13, 1988).
[29]*Liaisons Sociales*, No. 5956 (June 3, 1987).

ary of Renault, signed an agreement in 1987 based on four criteria: product quality, output, delivery deadlines, and reject levels. The parent company, Renault, also introduced profit sharing on the basis of product quality, delivery date compliance, and collective attendance records.[30] In 1988, Peugeot, the automobile manufacturer, added a new voluntary profit sharing plan designed to operate parallel to its compulsory profit sharing plan which was first adopted in 1969. Peugeot's voluntary plan provides for profit-related payments up to 2 percent of net results with a ceiling of 100 million francs and a floor of 50 million francs (US$16.7 million and US$8.3 million). At the minimum level each employee would receive a bonus of between 500F (US$83) and 1500F (US$250).[31]

---

[30]*Social and Labour Bulletin* 3/87, pp. 464-465.
[31]"Boom in profit sharing," p. 20.

CHAPTER IX

Federal Republic of Germany

After World War II, the economic system of the Federal Republic of Germany developed into a "social market economy" with the goal of combining the forces of a capitalist market economy (with its freedom of private initiative and the right to private property) with the necessity and principles of social progress. In order to rebuild a destroyed economy, new infrastructures had to be created quickly and this was possible only through government aided private-sector capital formation schemes. The currency reform of 1948 gave preferential treatment to the owners of capital goods whose tangible assets remained untouched, and they were also cleared of 90 percent of their liabilities. The philosophy of Germany's social market economy was to promote economic reconstruction through the enactment of various laws, particularly in the tax area where business investments received generous reductions, but without any direct state intervention. This policy helped achieve a speedy economic recovery and also resulted in considerable capital accumulation and capital concentration, primarily in the corporate sector. For example, almost three quarters of all private assets accumulated between 1950 and 1959 belonged to self-employed households which accounted for only 17 percent of all households.[1]

DEVELOPMENT OF STATE-AIDED ASSET FORMATION PLANS[2]

By the late 1950s, the high concentration of assets had increased political pressure on the government to put more emphasis on the social aspects of the country's successful economic system by introducing measures that would facilitate a broader and more equitable distribution of private assets. A first step in this direction had already been taken in 1952, with the introduction of the Home Savings Law, which aimed to encourage home ownership for those in

---

[1] Hans-Günter Guski, *Vermögensbildung—Bilanz und Perspektiven* (Cologne: Deutscher Instituts-Verlag GmbH, 1975), p. 12.
[2] Hans Nickel, *Staatlich geförderte Vermögensbildung: Das zweite Vermögensbeteiligungsgesetz in der Praxis* (Wiesbaden: Gabler Verlag, 1988), pp. 15-23.

lower income brackets. Since that time, such plans have remained a very popular form of savings, together with tax-privileged life-insurance savings. In 1959, the Savings Premium Law was passed under which the government paid a special premium on certain sums placed in various types of savings plans at financial institutions, provided the savings were frozen in these accounts for periods of five years. As amended in 1975, the Home Savings Law provided a government premimum of 18 percent of savings plus 2 percent for each child under eighteen years of age, while the Savings Premium Law provided 14 percent plus 2 percent for each child under eighteen. In both cases, savings were limited to DM 800[3] per year for an individual and DM 1,600 for a couple. The safeguarding of the family is an important feature of Germany's social policy, which explains the special allowances for employees with children. The allowances are aimed at alleviating the financial burden of raising and educating children. With the enactment of the 1981 Subsidy Reduction Law, the savings premium schemes were phased out (except for savings for the acquisition of private houses or apartments, whose premium entitlement, however, was lowered to 14 percent plus 2 percent per child). By then the government's policy had shifted emphasis to employee asset sharing.

First Asset Formation Law—"DM 312 Law"

With the enactment of the Law for the Promotion of Asset Formation of the Employees (First Asset Formation Law) of July 12, 1961, the German government's socio-political aim was not only the extension of savings options for employees but also a first attempt at promoting their participation in the economy's productive capital (i.e., the combined value of the productive apparatus, including plants, equipment, business buildings, etc.).

The First Asset Formation Law allowed employees in the private sector to save up to DM 312 annually via individual contracts with their employers or company agreements. This amount received income tax relief and was exempt from social insurance contributions for both the employer and the employee. As an additional incentive, the government paid a special bonus of up to 20 percent of the savings if they were held for at least five years and were placed in the following specified asset forms:

- Employee savings contributions under the Savings Premium Law or the Home-Building Premium Law;

---

[3] Exchange rate as of March 23, 1990, was DM 1.7 = US$1.

- Savings by the employee for the construction, purchase, or disencumbrance of specific state- or tax-supported family homes or condominiums;
- Savings by the employee for the purchase of shares in the employee's company at below market prices; and
- Savings by the employee to be transferred to the employer as interest-bearing loans.

The DM 312 law's main aim was to stimulate individual personal savings, but its very limited impact was disappointing. Only about 2 percent of the employees, largely those in higher income brackets, took advantage of the law's benefits. This was chiefly because the law did not provide for collective bargaining on asset formation plans. To remedy this shortcoming, the government introduced legal changes in 1965.

Second Asset Formation Law

Among the changes of the Second Asset Formation Law of July 1, 1965, were the inclusion of asset formation in collective agreements; the obligation on the part of the employer to invest certain amounts of earned wages in asset forming plans at the employee's request; and the extension of the law to cover public sector employees. These changes constituted an improvement of the law as they enhanced its practicability.

Third Asset Formation Law—"DM 624 Law"

The actual breakthrough in the government's asset formation policy was achieved with the introduction of the Third Asset Formation Law of July 27, 1970, whose main features were:

- An increase in the limit from DM 312 to DM 624 on annual asset-forming payments per employee for those earning up to DM 24,000 per year in taxable income if unmarried and DM 48,000 if married, with an additional allowance of DM 1,800 for each child;
- Introduction of income tax and social insurance contributions on the annual savings in exchange for an increase in the government's bonus on savings to 30 percent, or 40 percent with three or more children;
- Extension of asset-forming categories by allowing employees to use their savings as premiums for life insurance policies;
- Creation of a special savings contract for asset-forming savings;

- An increase in tax concessions from DM 3,000 to DM 6,000 annually for employers with up to 50 employees.

The higher savings limit of DM 624, together with the inclusion of life insurance savings and the increased tax concessions for smaller companies led to a growing interest in asset formation plans, particularly through collective agreements. Participating savers who invested the maximum amount and kept their money invested for the prescribed period of at least five years nearly doubled the basic DM 624 annual amount when bonuses and earned interest were added on. The popularity of the DM 624 law can be demonstrated by comparing 1969, when only 1 million employees were covered by collectively bargained asset formation plans, to 1971 when their number had grown to 13.4 million.[4] As impressive as this development may appear, there was little progress in the participation of employees in the economy's productive capital because 98 percent of the asset-forming contributions pursuant to the DM 624 law were invested in cash assets (e.g., savings in ordinary bank accounts; savings to be used for acquiring mortgage loans; and savings used as premiums for life insurance policies) while only two percent constituted productive capital sharing in companies. Where companies offered shares to their employees, they did so usually at a discount on the market price. This discount was limited to a maximum of 50 percent and was tax exempt up to DM 500 per year, provided the shares were held a minimum of five years.

Fourth Asset Formation Law—"DM 936 Law"

As part of a consolidation of the national budget, the Second Budget Structure Law of December 22, 1981, introduced some restrictions in the area of asset formation, including a reduction of the 30 to 40 percent government bonus on employee savings, basing such bonuses, instead, on the risk factor of the chosen method of asset formation. In addition, income tax and corporate tax concessions for small companies were reduced from 30 to 15 percent of the asset forming contributions, or from a maximum of DM 6,000 to DM 3,000; and the income tax exemption on share purchases was reduced from DM 500 to DM 300. In 1982, government policy on asset formation began to shift its emphasis from state subsidized savings plans to the promotion of employee participation in the productive capital of companies, a development that resulted in the *Asset Participation Law of January 1, 1984*. As West Germany's

---

[4]Hans-Günter Guski, *Vermögensbildung—Bilanz und Perspektiven*, pp. 69-70.

incomes policy is strictly voluntary in nature, the asset participation law of 1984, like earlier and later laws in the area of incomes policy, does not impose any mandatory measures. It consists of two parts: the Fourth Asset Formation Law and the specially created paragraph 19a Income Tax Law, *Einkommensteuergesetz* (EStG).

The asset formation law was aimed at the bargaining parties and employees. It increased the DM 624 limit by an additional DM 312 to arrive at the new annual limit of DM 936.[5] In order to discourage the use of regular account savings, the law stipulated that the additional DM 312 would receive special state premiums of 23 percent or 33 percent (for couples on the birth of a third child) only if these amounts were used for company asset participation or savings for the acquisition of mortgage loans (the state bonus for payments into savings accounts or life insurance policies was 16 percent). As a further incentive, the options for forms of asset participation were extended to include cooperative-association shares, silent partnerships, participation certificates, employee participation rights, and "insolvency-protected" employee loans to the employer.

The asset participation law's paragraph 19a EStG was introduced as a means to encourage capital participation iniatives through tax-exempt *company* contributions. Under collective agreements, the employer also may sometimes pay part or all of the amount to be saved. In 1985, a survey showed that approximately 95 percent of the employees surveyed were entitled to some payment from their employer under such agreements.[6] Although such contributions were first made possible with the introduction of paragraph 8 of the 1959 Capital Formation Law (*Kapitalaufstockungsgesetz*), they were mostly limited to large corporations (*Aktiengesellschaften*). The new paragraph 19a EStG, which exists independently from the asset formation law but is designed to supplement it, included all types of companies, thus encouraging smaller firms and their employees to take advantage of tax-exempt capital participation plans.

The asset participation law of 1984 succeeded in moving asset formation into the new direction of employee participation in productive assets. According to a 1986 empirical study[7], some 1,353 companies practiced a model of employee capital participation involving 1.1 million employees holding DM 14.2 billion in company participa-

---

[5]The specified limits are evenly divisible by twelve and fifty-two to accommodate monthly and weekly paid employees.
[6]"Asset formation payments," *European Industrial Relations Review*, No. 148 (May 1986), p. 13.
[7]Hans-Günter Guski and Hans J. Schneider, *Betriebliche Vermögensbeteiligung: Bestandsaufnahme 1986*, (Cologne: Deutscher Instituts-Verlag GmbH, 1986), pp. 6-7.

tion capital, compared to 1983 when there were 980 companies and only DM 5.5 billion in employee-held capital assets. This DM 8.7 billion increase over a three-year period meant an annual growth rate of DM 2.93 billion as compared to an average annual growth rate of DM 457 million prior to the 1984 asset participation law. Although until 1983 only a relatively constant 2 percent of the employees' annual savings had been invested in company assets, 1986 estimates showed an annual 5 to 10 percent participation in productive capital. Furthermore, by 1986, the DM 936 law had led to twenty-one collective agreements, utilizing the new additional DM 312 option on capital participation for some 400,000 employees, and the signing of 131,298 individual agreements on share participation, compared to only 8,702 such agreements prior to the enactment of the DM 936 law. While this constituted a remarkable increase in individual agreements, it was somewhat less impressive when compared with a total of some 12 million employees eligible (i.e., those with an annual income of no more than DM 24,000 if single, or DM 48,000 if married) to receive state premiums on investments in productive capital. Recognizing that the DM 936 law of 1984 was both too complicated and still too limited in terms of investment choices to achieve higher employee participation levels, the government promised in January 1986 to introduce what it termed the "second stage" of its new asset formation policy.

The Fifth Asset Formation Law

This second stage went into effect on January 1, 1987, with the enactment of the *Second Asset Participation Law*. Building upon the 1984 law, it consists of two parts, the Fifth Asset Formation Law and a modified paragraph 19a EStG.

The Fifth Asset Formation Law, while retaining many provisions of the Fourth Law, such as the DM 936 annual ceiling for state premiums and the income requirements mentioned above, introduced some important changes. For example, it simplified the procedure for investing in capital shares by allowing employees to obtain them directly from the employer via special securities purchasing contracts instead of through special saving contracts with a financial institution. What is more important, it enabled employees to exchange their invested shares during the blocking period, giving them a chance to react to drops in share value without loss of state premiums, provided the exchange (e.g., the purchase of alternate shares) was completed by the end of the following month. It also adopted relevant provisions of the former Premium Savings Law so that all necessary legal rules concerning asset forming savings were consolidated into one law. While the 1984 law almost exclusively promoted capital participation in either the employee's own company or in companies listed on the stock exchange, the new law created more external capital participation possibilities by allowing investments in unlisted companies, including companies with limited liability (GmbH-Anteile). Also included were investment certificates in German and, under certain conditions, foreign stock funds, as well as investment certificates in mutual funds, which in addition to stock also offer silent partnerships in unlisted companies.

Paragraph 19a EStG deals with the tax aspects of employee capital participation and is aimed at promoting such participation in company assets by allowing employers to offer their employees certain tax exempt contributions. The Second Asset Participation Law introduced changes to paragraph 19a by matching the forms of asset investments eligible for tax relief with those eligible for state premiums under the Fifth Asset Formation Law and, what is most important, it increased the tax-exemption from DM 300 to DM 500. It states that if employers offer their employees discounted shares, including shares in other companies, the gains realized by an employee are exempt from income tax and social security payments up to one-half of the shares' market price or a maximum of DM 500 per year, provided the legal requirements concerning transactions, depositing, and blocking periods are observed. The employer's share of the social security contribution, of course, would also be exempt. If a company, for example, offers its employees a participation of DM 600, an amount of DM 300 (one-half of the value) would be exempt from income tax and social security payments. If a participation of DM 1,200 is offered, however, only a discount of up to DM 500 would be tax exempt. Discounts exceeding this amount are subject to taxation. In contrast to the provisions of the Fifth Asset Formation Law, the tax advantage offered under paragraph 19a is not subject to any income limits. There is, however, no obligation on the part of the employer to offer discounted company shares. Since any discount granted by the employer has to be shown as liability on the balance sheet, it results in a corresponding reduction in taxable profit. As mentioned before, both the asset formation law and paragraph 19a coexist independently, but encouraging their joint use was one of the goals of the Second Asset Participation Law.[8] This combi-

---

[8]Renate Hornung-Draus, *Mitarbeiter-Beteiligungen: Modelle für die betriebliche Praxis*, published by Bundesvereinigung der Deutschen Arbeitgeberverbände (Bergisch Gladbach: Heider Verlag, 1988), pp. 17-18.

nation of asset-forming payments and tax-exempt contributions is demonstrated in Figure IX-1.

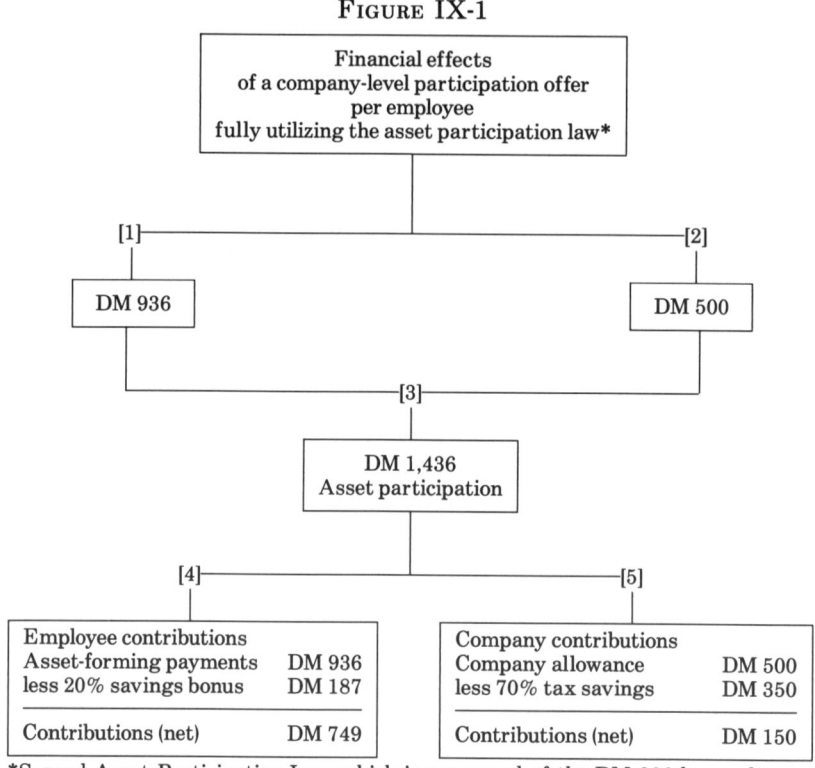

*Second Asset Participation Law, which is composed of the DM 936 law and paragraph 19a EStG:
[1] The Employee pays DM 936 as asset-forming contribution (subject to a minimum blocking period of six years) for a capital participation in his company.
[2] The Employer grants the employee an allowance according to paragraph 19a EStG which is exempt from income tax and social security payments and is added to the employee's own contribution.
[3] With the amounts [1] and [2] the employee starts an asset participation in his company.
[4] On his own asset-forming contribution, the employee receives a 20 percent savings bonus from the state, thus obtaining a capital share of DM 1,436 for only DM 749.
[5] The employer's contribution constitutes a liability which is deducted from company profits which are taxed at an average of 70 percent. This creates liquid funds of DM 1,436, which are paid for by using only DM 150 in own funds (possibly from retained profits).[9]

---

[9] Hans-Günter Guski and Hans J. Schneider, "Kapital für Unternehmen—Vermögen für alle," in *Der Arbeitgeber*, No. 1/42—1990, p. 34.

Federal Republic of Germany

The Amended Fifth Asset Formation Law of 1989/90

There were three major reasons for amending the Second Asset Participation Law so soon after its 1987 introduction. First, the Christian Democratic (CDU/CSU)/Liberal (FDP) coalition government felt a need to concentrate its promotion of employee asset formation even more exclusively on capital asset sharing. The 16 percent state bonus on regular account saving and savings used as premiums for life insurance policies was eliminated, although both have been retained in the amended law as investment possibilities for employees. Second, the government wanted to prevent the misuse with certain external asset participation models. Such models had been increasingly offered since the 1987 enactment of the law by companies especially created for the purpose of selling external silent partnership deals that often included disadvantageous and risky conditions for the employees. Therefore the government stipulated that asset participation contracts concerning silent partnerships, loan claims, and profit participation rights may only be concluded between the employee and his employing company. Third, changes were introduced to further simplify existing legal regulations and reduce government subsidies.

As of January 1, 1990, the following regulations concerning asset-forming contributions are in effect:

The basic structure of the law remains unchanged. First, in addition to normal wages, employers may pay their employees additional amounts of money in specific forms of assets or, independently from that, an employee on his own initiative may use some of his regular pay for asset-forming investments. Second, in order to receive supplementary state bonuses and allowances, the employee may choose among only those forms of asset saving listed in the law's catalogue and the employee must observe a general minimum blocking period of six years (a period of seven years is required for asset savings contracts with financial institutions). These blocking periods commence on January 1 of the year the asset participation was established. As the law establishes only minimum periods, employers are free to negotiate longer blocking periods.

The catalogue of state-aided asset formation investments is divided into negotiable shares (securities) and non-negotiable shares as follows:

Negotiable Shares
Stock in German and, under certain conditions, foreign companies; investment certificates in German/foreign stock funds and mutual funds; convertible bonds; debenture bonds in companies that are

not financial institutions; profit participation certificates[10] in companies that are not financial institutions.

Non-negotiable Shares
Shares in associations; shares in companies with limited liability; silent partnerships (in employee's company only); employee loans to employer; employee participation rights[11] (in employee's company only).

To obtain such shares, the asset formation law requires the signing of specific forms of contract:

—*Securities purchasing contract* between employee and employer for the investment in negotiable securities as mentioned above.
—*Participation contract* between employee and employer for the initial establishment of rights concerning non-negotiable company shares.
—*Participation purchasing contract* between the employee and employer for the investment in already existing non-negotiable share plans (e.g., shares in companies with limited liability).
—*Savings contract concerning securities or other forms of asset* between the employee and a financial institution for the purchase or the initial establishment of negotiable or non-negotiable forms of asset.

In addition to these forms of productive capital sharing, the amended law retains a bonus, albeit reduced, for home savings contracts and other investments in home-building projects.

Although the annual limit of DM 936 on which state bonuses for the above mentioned forms of employee asset formation are paid remains unchanged, the bonus itself has been reduced from 23 percent to 20 percent for investments in negotiable and non-negotiable shares and from 23 to 10 percent for investments in home savings and building projects. The additional 10 percent bonus for couples with three or more children has been abolished.

To increase the number of eligible participants, the income limits have been raised from DM 24,000 to DM 27,000 in annual taxable income for single persons and from DM 48,000 to DM 54,000 for married persons. At the same time, however, the higher threshold for those with children based on a further DM 1,800 per dependent child has been abolished.

Also abolished has been the provision on tax advantages for small companies with fewer than fifty employees, which had allowed them

---

[10]Such certificates are negotiable instruments usually granting the right to a fixed portion of the net profit of a company, but do not represent participation in the company. They have the same creditor claims as bonds.

[11]Employee participation rights are identical in content to profit participation certificates but are nonnegotiable.

to deduct up to 15 percent or a maximum of DM 3,000 of their asset participation contributions from their tax bill.

The employee is entitled to his state savings bonus as of the end of the calendar year in which the asset shares were invested. To claim this bonus, the employee must complete a payment request form at the internal revenue branch of his district no later than December 31 of the following year. The employee forfeits any bonus claim with retroactive effect if he does not observe the legal blocking periods. Early withdrawal of saved assets is possible only under special circumstances, such as the death of the employee or his spouse or unemployment of employee for at least one continuous year.

In what is considered an important time- and cost-saving change for employers, the amended law stipulates that as of January 1, 1990, the payment of employee savings bonuses will no longer be the employer's responsibility but will be handled, instead, by the Internal Revenue Service through the annual income tax return.

CONTRACTUAL AND CODETERMINATIONAL ASPECTS OF EMPLOYEE ASSET SHARING

As noted, there are two ways of establishing employee participation in productive capital: either through additional employer contributions or through an employee's initiative, by requesting the employer to invest certain amounts of earned pay into capital shares. In the latter case, the request has to be in writing and must state the amount to be invested, the time of commencement of the investment, the type of investment, and the institution or company in which to place investments. The employer is obliged to execute such a request, but only if the investments are made in equal amounts of at least DM 25 monthly, DM 75 quarterly, or one annual minimum payment of DM 75. The signing of a special contract for employee-initiated asset savings is not required.

Because West Germany's system of employee capital sharing is voluntary in nature, the employer may (but is not obliged to) offer his employees capital shares and the employees may accept or reject the offer. In order to be eligible for the state savings bonus, the employee must be able to choose freely among the external forms of capital investment, e.g., the various types of negotiable securities listed in the law, and the institution or company in which to invest them. However, capital participation in the company through the non-negotiable shares mentioned above, requires the employer's consent. Where an employer's offer is restricted, for example, to the purchase of company shares, the establishment of silent partnerships, or employee loans, no state bonuses under the Fifth Asset Formation Law will be made available to the employees. The tax concessions provided through the use of paragraph 19a EStG remain available, however.

An employer who wants to offer his employees additional amounts of money in the form of assets may do so on the basis of individual, plant, or collective agreements. The Fifth Asset Formation Law does not contain any regulations about form and content of an individual agreement with the employee, but for legal reasons the written format is the rule. The individual agreement may be concluded with all employees, but the employer does not have to offer them all the same amounts. Although the employer must accord all employees equal treatment and may not discriminate on the basis of race, nationality, origin, religion, political, or union affilition and non-affiliation, or sex and age (Paragraph 75 of the Works Constitution Act), the employer contributions may be differentiated according to the employees' seniority, full-time or part-time status, etc. In individual agreements, the employee may choose between cash payments or asset investments, but only the latter are eligible for state savings bonuses.

Codeterminational aspects play a role if the employer decides to conclude a plant agreement on employee capital sharing. Germany's Works Constitution Act, which regulates the relations between management and employees and extends far-reaching codetermination rights to works councils representing the employees' interests, states in Article 77, Subsection (2) that plant agreements must be in writing and signed by both the employer and works council and that the employer is obliged to display the agreement in a suitable place in the plant. Such plant agreements do not cover managerial employees as the the works constitution law does not view them as regular wage- or salary-earning employees. Like the individual agreement, a plant agreement allows for cash options without the supplementary government bonuses. Today plant agreements are of diminishing importance as they have been replaced by collective agreements established through bargaining with the trade unions. Such collective contracts, which usually take precedence over plant agreements, may not contain any cash deals. The provisions of the collective contract apply only to employees specifically covered by it. If a collective contract on employee asset parcticipation is declared to be generally binding, however, its coverage is extended to all employers and employees in the bargaining region as a whole.

An employer who decides to offer his employees a specific model of capital sharing must inform the works council at the earliest possible time. Formally, the works council is an autonomous agent of the workers' interests and is not dependent on trade unions. Practically, there are close links between the two. The works council's codetermination rights do not extend to: a) the decision whether a participation model should be introduced; b) the amounts involved in the plan; c) the specific form of the participation model; or d) the group of employees to whom the model is to be offered. Paragraph 75 (see above) and Paragraph 78, Subs. (1), No. 10, of the works constitution law, allow, however, for the works council's participation in the structuring of general compensation guidelines, including capital sharing or certain premium pay.[12] Aside from these legal requirements, surveys show that participation models introduced with the active involvement of the works councils were clearly more successful than models established without prior consultation of the employee representatives.[13]

FORMS OF EMPLOYEE CAPITAL SHARING

Of the various state-aided employee participation forms mentioned in the Fifth Asset Formation Law and paragraph 19a EStG, respectively, the most noteworthy in the "negotiable" group are: employee stock plans and, to a much lesser degree, profit participation certificates; and in the "non-negotiable" group: silent partnership (indirect) participation and employee participation rights. The non-negotiable group also includes the very popular form of employee loans. Employee loans, however, are at best only a first step in the direction of employee participation. Employees like them because they are easy to establish and understand. The employee becomes the creditor to his employer, receives a fixed rate of interest and the assurance that his loan will be paid back after an agreed-upon blocking period has expired. It is not genuine asset participation because it is fully insured against risk by the employer and is, therefore, completely detached from success or failure of the company. In addition, employee loans appear to be declining as they represent participation through borrowed capital while companies

---

[12]Hornung-Draus, *Mitarbeiter-Beteiligungen*, pp. 84-86.
[13]Hans-Günter Guski and Hans J. Schneider, *Betriebliche Vermögensbeteiligung in der Bundesrepublik Deutschland, Teil II: Ergebnisse, Erfahrungen und Auswirkungen in der Praxis* (Cologne: Deutscher Instituts-Verlag, 1983), pp. 139-143.

increasingly prefer employee capital participation on the basis of the company's own capital.[14]

Employee Stock Plans. At present, Germany has approximately 1500 companies offering employee capital sharing plans with some 1.3 million, or 11 percent, of their employees participating. In stock corporations, one-third of the employees own shares in their company.[15] Although most of the participating employees are in companies with a workforce of over 1,000, small and medium-sized businesses constitute the majority among participating companies.[16] Of Germany's major private-sector corporations, all offer some form of asset participation, with employee stock purchase plans clearly constituting the most popular form in terms of employees involved. Stock is an ideal instrument for employee participation because it represents company capital, is of optimal fungibility, and is legally clearly defined. Employee participation through company stock is not limited to German companies but is also possible in foreign companies. In other words, the German subsidiary of a foreign company may offer its employees shares of this foreign parent company and may also utilize the tax concessions provided in paragraph 19a EStG. The obvious disadvantage is that this instrument is limited to companies with the legal form of corporation. Experts point out, however, that this disadvantage will become less important because of the growing number of corporations in Germany.[17]

In large corporations, the main reason for introducing capital participation plans is not financial. Instead, these plans tend to be part of a long-range company philosophy that is aimed at increasing the employees' general interest in their company. An exhaustive, four-year study of German companies with at least seven years' experience in employee participation showed that these plans helped to increase the identification of the employees with the company, which, in turn, led to positive developments in areas such as cost awareness, fluctuation, productivity, material situation, cooperation, safety at the workplace, working climate, and attracting new employees.[18]

---

[14]Guski and Schneider, *Betriebliche Vermögensbeteiligung: Bestandsaufnahme, 1986*, p. 21.

[15]Guski and Schneider, "Kapital für Unternehmen—Vermögen für alle," p. 35.

[16]Guski and Schneider, *Betriebliche Vermögensbeteiligung: Bestandsaufnahme, 1986*, p. 30.

[17]Rolf Thüsing, "Mitarbeiter-Kapitalbeteiligung—Rechtliche Rahmenbedingungen," in *Betriebliche Vermögensbeteiligung: Gestaltungsmöglichkeiten der Mitarbeiter-Kapitalbeteilgung—ihre Vorteile und Probleme* (Cologne: Bundesvereinigung der Deutschen Arbeitgeberverbände, 1988), pp. 22-25.

[18]Guski and Schneider, *Betriebliche Vermögensbeteiligung—Teil II*, pp. 44-46.

For example, at *Hoechst AG*, the giant chemical company whose tradition of employee asset participation goes back to the last century, employee shares were introduced in 1960 as an integral part of the company's social policy, as an additional social benefit not as a means of capital increase.[19] According to a special asset formation plan introduced in 1978, Hoechst offers employee shares on an annual basis, provided the dividend is at least DM 5. This is a voluntary social benefit introduced unilaterally by the company, as are most participation plans in German corporations, and is not based on a plant agreement with the works council, which nevertheless is a strong supporter of Hoechst's employee stock plan. Each employee is allowed to purchase stock, up to the equivalent of 1/24 of annual income, or one-half of the monthly salary. Every employee with at least one year of service (a common service qualification in many German plans) receives an individual, salary-based share offer. Employees who come within the prescribed income limits may utilize the DM 936 of the asset formation law for stock investments. Hoechst's executive board determines the purchase price of the employee shares, which is considerably below the actual market price.

The company offers two types of employee stock: 1) four blocked shares with a total participation value of DM 1,000 are offered at a 50 percent discount which is tax exempt under paragraph 19a EStG; the employee pays the other DM 500 and the shares are blocked for six years; and 2) additional unblocked or common stock is offered at a lower discount on the market price (30 percent in 1988), which is, however, subject to taxation. While this lowers the gains, the employee is free to sell this type of stock at any time or use it for speculative purposes at the stock exchange. According to company experience, many employees also hold onto this type of stock. As far as the savings potential of employee stock ownership is concerned, Hoechst calculated that an employee who participated in the share purchase plan fully and continuously between 1978 and 1988 was able to buy 115 shares for DM 13,000. The 1988 value of these shares was approximately DM 30,000, resulting in capital gains of DM 17,000, to which was added the dividend income of DM 6,400 so that the total gain was DM 23,400 for the employee. This savings potential has helped to boost the average participation rate at Hoechst, including subsidiaries, from 22.2 percent in 1978 to 75 percent in

---

[19]Helmuth Schuster, "Betriebliche Vermögensbeteiligung durch Belegschaftsaktien bei der Hoechst AG," in *Betriebliche Vermögensbeteiligung: Gestaltungsmöglichkeiten der Mitarbeiter-Kapitalbeteiligung—ihre Vorteile und Probleme*, pp. 60-77.

1988. Participation among white-collar employees (83 percent) typically is greater than that of blue-collar employees (64 percent).

According to a 1960-1988 overview of employee stock activities at the domestic Hoechst group: 85,000 employees purchased 4.5 million shares, constituting 8.1 percent of the company's capital stock, at a total cost of DM 880 million, of which the employees paid DM 532 million and the company DM 348 million. As do all other large German corporations, Hoechst promotes the interest in employee stock ownership through special information and consultation services. A company survey showed that the employee share concept was highly regarded among employees, being outranked as a social benefit only by company pension and profit sharing schemes.

Siemens AG, the Munich based electronic and engineering company, has promoted the concept of the employee shareholder with increasing success since 1969. Like Hoechst, Siemens has involved its employees in this type of capital sharing as part of its long-term social policy whose aims include the promotion of economic awareness through the ownership of productive company assets. In 1987, some 161,000 employees, or 65 percent, participated in the share purchase plan. According to company statistics, employees who took full advantage of Siemens' share offer between 1969 and 1988 were able to purchase 117 shares which earned DM 16,000, a profit not attainable through any other form of investment.[20]

Daimler-Benz AG and *BASF AG* are also offering discounted employee shares primarily as part of their social benefits policy. They do so with the full cooperation of the works councils. An interesting aspect of the Daimler-Benz participation plan is that employees have the choice between regular company shares or shares of Mercedes-Automobil-Holding AG, which holds 25 percent of the Daimler-Benz capital. Shares of the holding company are traded at a lower price than regular DB shares, but both earn the same dividends.

The BASF chemical company has been offering employee shares to its German workforce since 1955, and has a current participation rate of approximately 80 percent. Of special interest is the fact that the company offers a modified stock ownership plan for the employees of BASF United Kingdom Limited and its subsidiaries. This plan allows British full-time employees with at least twenty-four months of service to become shareholders in the German parent

---

[20]Werner Baake, "Förderung der Vermögensbildung durch die Beteiligung der Mitarbeiter am Produktivvermögen," Sonderdruck aus *Siemens-Mitteilungen*, No. 10/1987.

company and be eligible for dividends. By law, shares are held in trust for a period of two years and employees receive a "certificate of beneficial ownership" with which they establish their right to them. To qualify for full tax exemption, however, shares must be held in trust for three additional years. The UK share plan was the first for BASF employees outside of Germany.[21]

Profit Participation Certificates. Munich based automaker *BMW AG* has offered employee capital participation since 1974 for the similar social- benefit reasons as the aforementioned companies. It is among the relatively few large German corporations that initially chose not to offer company stock to its employees. Instead, in a first phase lasting from 1974 to 1978, the company offered debenture bonds. In 1980, the company launched its second phase, introducing a form of profit participation certificates called registered profit certificates (*Namens-Gewinn-Scheine* = NGS) which are made out to the name of the bearer. NGS are securities granting the right to a portion of company profit equal to the amount of the dividend paid on a DM 50 BMW share, but not less than a 7 percent interest rate on the NGS nominal value. The latter is DM 50 and serves as a basis for calculating the portion of profit per NGS. In 1988, the last year of availability, BMW offered NGS at an issue price of DM 150 per certificate and contributed a tax exempt amount of DM 60, which lowered the actual purchase price to DM 90. The number of NGS obtainable by the employee depended on years of service with BMW and was limited to six for those with one and two years, to a maximum of eight after the second year. NGS, which were subject to a six-year blocking period, were not handed over to the employee but were kept in a special deposit at Deutsche Bank with the costs for this service paid by the company. After the expiration of the blocking period, employees could either retain the NGS or sell them to other employees through an in-house exchange. Those leaving the company had to return their NGS to BMW for the issue price. If they left during a blocking period, the NGS deposit was dissolved and BMW's tax-exempt contribution became retroactively taxable. Similarly, employees utilizing the government savings bonus under the Fifth Asset Formation Law have to pay back this bonus.

In 1989, BMW entered a third phase in its employee participation policy by offering nonvoting employee shares. Over a five-year period, the company will issue employee stock with a total nominal value of DM 15 million. The purchase price of the employee stock is determined by BMW's management board. For 1990, a share has a

---

[21]*Employees take a stake in the company*, BASF News Supplement, June 1985.

value of DM 452. The company offers this share at a 50 percent discount which is tax exempt. The employee pays the other DM 226, and the stock is blocked for six years. As of January 1990, BMW's preferred nonvoting employee shares qualify for full dividends. While issued NGS will continue to exist, BMW will not offer any new ones. Profit participation certificates are an interesting alternative to employee share plans. They offer a high degree of flexibility because they are not subject to the strict legal regulations applied to share plans. On the other hand, their maintenance is very cost intensive and their promotion among employees is more difficult because they lack a clear legal definition. These are the major reasons for BMW's decision to offer an employee stock ownership plan. With this plan BMW is likely both to save costs and achieve higher participation rates among its employees. With the NGS plan, which found very little interest among blue-collar employees, BMW had a total participation rate of approximately 35 percent, while its one-year old employee share plan has already achieved a participation rate of 40 percent.[22]

Employee Participation Rights. Closely related to profit participation certificates is the concept of employee participation rights. While the former are negotiable securities, the latter are nonnegotiable and simply represent certain rights to contractually agreed upon portions of a company's net profits. Typically, this participation form is preferred by small and medium-sized nonstock companies. Participation rights are not defined legally and therefore are well suited for creating individualized employee participation models.

In 1985, the *Andreas STIHL company*, which, with a 26 percent share of the world market, is the leading chain saw manufacturer, chose participation rights as its form of employee capital sharing. STIHL is a second generation family business run as a limited partnership. It operates seven plants in Germany with a workforce of 3,500 and also has manufacturing operations in the U.S., Brazil, Switzerland, and Australia, employing 5,400 people as a group.[23] Its capital participation plan, however, is limited to the employees of STIHL Germany and the purchase of participation rights in the limited partnership Andreas STIHL. From the business point of view,

---

[22]BMW account is based on company information material and on an interverview with a company official.

[23]Wolfgang Meyer, "Betriebliche Vermögensbeteiligung durch Genussrechte bei der Firma Andreas Stihl," in *Betriebliche Vermögensbeteiligung: Gestaltungsmöglichkeiten der Mitarbeiter-Kapitalbeteiligung—ihre Vorteile und Probleme,* pp. 91-104.

the participation plan had to fulfill three basic requirements: 1) it could not lead to a change in the company's legal form of a limited partnership; 2) the decision-making power of the parent company had to remain untouched; and 3) the participation model had to be fully adjustable to the company's prevailing financial situation. From a personnel policy viewpoint, STIHL introduced participation rights as a means of supplementing the employees' income through capital assets, thereby hoping to improve the quality of income distribution and to defuse the conflict of interest between capital and labor. Financial considerations were not an important factor as the company had sufficient equity of its own.

The STIHL participation rights model is characterized by an unusually long blocking period of ten years in exchange for a relatively high company contribution and the involvement of the participating employees in sharing both profits and losses. The profit claim is calculated according to an equation of interest based on STIHL's total net income. Over the years, this has averaged out to a profit claim of 4.5 percent. The maximum profit claim is limited to 10 percent. Loss sharing is cushioned by two social components: it is limited to an annual maximum of 5 percent of the nominal value and even over years may never exceed 25 percent; and while profit claims are paid out annually, possible losses are carried over to future years to be offset against later profits.

Participation rights can be purchased once a year in May. Purchase conditions are determined in an annual written offer and are based upon the company's economic situation. Since the plan's inception in 1985, purchase terms have remained unchanged, i.e., each employee can sign up for a maximum of twenty-seven participation rights at a nominal value of DM 100 each. The employee pays one-third of the nominal value, STIHL contributes two-thirds.

After a ten-year blocking period, STIHL will buy back the participation rights at their nominal value. These rights are neither negotiable nor transferable. Employees who decide to hold on to their participation rights are entitled to a loyalty premium of 4 percent of the nominal value annually, which is paid on return of the rights. The maximum premium of 40 percent is reached after a twenty-year investment period. Depending upon the number of obtained participation rights and such individual circumstances as income earned, tax bracket, etc., and assuming an average profit claim of 4.5 percent, an annual after-tax yield of between 11 and 37 percent can be achieved. In order to ensure continuity, STIHL has pledged to offer profit participation rights even in years in which such an offer is economically not advisable. Under these circumstances, STIHL reserves the right, however, to lower its two-thirds contribution. The interests of those participating in the plan are represented by a partnership committee consisting of five members who are elected from among the participants.

The participation model was introduced over the objections of the metal workers' union, IG Metall, a traditional opponent of company capital sharing plans, and without a plant agreement. Despite this opposition, the company's general works council issued a statement of support for the model and encouraged the employees to take advantage of it. According to the company, the model has worked satisfactorily, reaching a participation rate of approximately 30 percent in its fourth year. This rate is certain to climb with the age of the model, which is one reason why companies with a long tradition of employee capital sharing plans have much higher participation rates than companies with newer plans. STIHL also stresses that it is not its goal to achieve the highest possible participation rate, and that this is why it does not follow the often used practice of giving away profit shares on such occasions as anniversaries or as a substitute for a lump sum payment. Rather, STIHL wants its employees to participate completely voluntarily and with the conviction to use this participation as means of forming a partnership with the company.

Silent Partnership/Indirect Participation. These forms of asset participation usually occur together since the indirect participation refers to a model in which employees share in their employer's capital as silent partners of a special employee participation company, which is usually established as a partnership with limited liability and which invests its capital in the company. Thus, silent partners become indirect participants by acquiring share coupons in the partnership company. To be eligible for the state asset savings bonus of the Fifth Asset Formation Law and to take advantage of the tax exemption under paragraph 19a EStG, the share coupons are subject to a minimum blocking period of six years. This kind of employee participation is typical for small companies because of several advantages: silent partners do not gain any rights to participate in the company's management; partners also share in losses (to the amount of their participation investment); and silent partnerships can be set up in a variety of ways allowing for maximum model flexibility. A survey showed that the combination of indirect participation through silent partnership leads the list of asset participation models with 41 percent.[24] This is not surprising since there is often a greater interest in employee participation models among smaller companies, where cooperation, partnership, and mutual trust, the essentials of creating employee acceptance of asset participation, play a more important role than in larger companies. In other words, the larger the company, the lower the participation rate. For example, companies with more than 1,000 employees have an average employee participation rate of 57.7 percent; those with 51 to 1,000 employees have a rate of 76.5 percent; while the highest rate, 84.4 percent, is found in companies with 50 or fewer employees.[25]

Other forms of employee financial participation used as an instrument of improving motivation, such as profit sharing, are much less common in Germany than in the United States. Where such schemes exist, they usually are used in combination with one of the forms of employee capital participation mentioned above.

With regard to financing the capital participation models, there is a trend toward increased employee contributions. Initially, it was thought that such models could be successful only if companies took on the primary financial responsibilities. Survey results from 1976 show that two-thirds of all nonstock participation models in medium-sized businesses were paid in full by the employer, while in the other third, companies were the major financial contributor. In large corpororations with employee share programs, of course, the employees' own contributions of usually 50 percent were obligatory. According to a 1986 survey, however, barely one-quarter of the companies are still sole financial contributors, and in more than one-half of all cases, combined employer-employee financing has been introduced with the majority of the employees (52 percent) paying the larger share. This development can be attributed to a large extent to the DM 936 law and paragraph 19a EStG whose combined applicability creates an incentive for higher employee contributions. The Christian Democratic/Liberal government's asset participation legislation has therefore not only led to an increase in the number of participation models, it has also helped to bring about considerable change in the financing structure of these models.[26]

---

[24]Guski and Schneider, *Betriebliche Vermögensbeteiligung: Bestandsaufnahme, 1986*, pp. 21-22.
[25]*Ibid.*, pp. 33-34.
[26]*Ibid.*, pp. 35-37.

TRADE UNIONS AND EMPLOYEE CAPITAL SHARING

The German Trade Union Confederation (DGB), the umbrella organization of seventeen affiliated unions, has opposed the concept of employee capital participation from the start, claiming that it could not ensure a fair distribution of wealth in Germany. The DGB maintained that this was only attainable through the creation of union-run collective asset formation funds (similar to those adopted later in Sweden) into which employers were to pay a fixed percentage of profits. The DGB's political ally, the Social Democratic Party (SPD), proposed similar plans. The debate about these collective fund plans, all of which were ultimately rejected, took place in the early- to mid-1970s. With the introduction of a more generous and flexible asset formation legislation and the unions' interest shifting to such issues as codetermination, employment, and shorter hours of work, the topic of collective funds was removed from the sociopolitical agenda. Notwithstanding the increased popularity of employee capital sharing plans, and their contribution towards overcoming the traditional divide between capital and labor, the DGB continues to reject the government's asset formation policy because of fears that over the course of years employee co-ownership will lessen the employees' interest in their unions and subsequently lead to permanent membership losses. Such fears, seem unfounded however. Results of a recent survey show that most companies with employee capital sharing plans, some of which are more than thirty years old, did not experience a decrease in union organization rate (83.2 percent), while others (40.5 percent) even registered a slight increase. In only a few companies (16.8 percent) did a decrease in the number of union members occur over a total period of twenty years. The survey's other important findings include: employee financial participation models do not undermine the rights of works councils, as the DGB has claimed, but rather increase their responsibilties and strengthen their role; the majority of works councils support the concept of employee participation in company capital in spite of union objections; and local union representatives find it difficult to convince rank-and-file members of their leadership's negative views on participation.[27]

The DGB is critical of the fact that the government has shifted its support from the safe forms of account and insurance savings to the more risky capital participation models offered to employees by their companies and is demanding a reintroduction of state bonuses

---

[27]Guski and Schneider, Betriebliche Vermögensbeteiligung—Teil II, pp. 337-348.

Federal Republic of Germany 173

on asset formation through savings plans. As far as the DGB is concerned, employee asset participation is no longer an important collective bargaining issue. One of its major affiliates, the chemical workers union, IG Chemie, has demonstrated, however, that the contrary is true. It signed an agreement with the chemical employers that increased the employers' asset formation contribution from DM 624 to DM 936 as of 1990. Known for its socially progressive bargaining policy, the chemical sector with some 700,000 employees has become the first major industrial sector with a collective agreement on the full utilization of the DM 936 law (for details, see Figure IX-1, above). Banks and some utility companies have also signed collective agreements on DM 936 contributions. While considerable progress has been made in promoting employee participation in the economy's productive capital, much more has to be done to involve broader segments of employees in capital sharing plans. Industry-wide agreements are an ideal tool to accomplish just that and the chemical industry's agreement has set an example for other industries to follow.

CHAPTER X

Sweden

Sweden historically has been a politically homogeneous country, and the Social Democratic Party (SAP) has dominated the political scene since 1932, except for a period between 1976 and 1982. Collaboration between the SAP and the trade union movement has been very close during this entire period, with the dominant trade union organization, the Swedish Trade Union Confederation (LO), offering the SAP unique support during parliamentary elections and support of its economic policy when it is in power. The SAP, for its part, has supported legislation giving the unions additional power in Sweden.

Sweden has attracted attention in other countries for its highly centralized labor market organizations and its high level of trade union membership. Trade union affiliation is approximately 80 to 85 percent, being somewhat higher for hourly workers and slightly lower for salaried employees. Some 80 percent of all salaried employees are members of the Central Organization of Salaried Personnel (TCO), or the smaller Central Organization of Swedish Professional Workers (SACO). In many other countries unions often have problems in taking coordinated action, but in Sweden, until quite recently, decision-making has been highly centralized and coordinated in wage bargaining as well as on general political issues. On political issues the LO acts in a highly centralized fashion, while collective bargaining has become only slightly more decentralized.

During the course of its political dominance, the SAP has constructed an elaborate welfare state offering a wide range of benefits to Swedish citizens. These benefits have been financed by a high level of government expenditure (59.9 percent of gross domestic product in 1987) made possible by a relatively high and progressive personal taxation program. The personal income tax in Sweden makes up 38.5 percent of gross domestic product (GDP), the second highest (behind Denmark) in Europe. The total tax burden of 50.5 percent of GDP remains the highest in Europe. As might be expected, the savings rate of Swedish households is one of the lowest in the OECD area, which is at least partly attributable to the increased importance of compulsory pension schemes which are not recorded as private savings.[1] Sweden is characterized by a high degree of social protection and is predominantly capitalistic. Although state operated businesses are found in public transport, railroads, communications, electricity distribution, and in various enterprises engaged in heavy manufacturing, approximately 95 percent of the employees in manufacturing work in privately run enterprises.[2]

SWEDISH WAGE-EARNER FUNDS

With such strong central trade union power, a sympathetic government, and a highly developed social welfare program, it is not surprising that collective forms of employee financial participation would become the dominant type of capital accumulation system in Sweden. In Swedish, the name of these funds is "lntagarfonder," which literally translated means, "wage-earner funds." The government and the LO choose to refer to them as "employee investment funds," and the Swedish Employers' Confederation (SAF) often refers to them as "trade union funds." Terminology may not always be important, but here the differences are representative of the bitter debate over this concept which has been going on since at least 1971.

The LO views the funds as a way of facilitating its wage policy of "solidarity," a system to increase workers' control over capital formation, and as a means of counteracting the concentration of power and wealth. The SAF and the employers, on the other hand, contend that the funds have not increased the availability of capital and have not moderated wage increases, but have only provided a means for trade unions to assume greater power and control.

Background

Since the early 1950s, the LO has stressed the importance of attaining a more egalitarian wage structure. Its policy of wage "solidarity" is designed to relate pay to the nature of the work which an employee carries out and not to the capacity or ability to pay of his employer. One consequence of this wage policy is that it brings on a more rapid structural transformation by eliminating noncompetitive companies. Another consequence is that the more profitable companies are not asked to pay higher wages and, therefore, generate what

---

[1]Organization for Economic Cooperation and Development, *OECD Economic Survey, 1986/1987: Sweden* (Paris: OECD 1987), p. 12.
[2]Price Waterhouse, *Doing Business in Sweden* (Price Waterhouse 1987), p. 5.

the union calls "excess profits." During the 1960s, the LO discussed ways of benefiting from, or "skimming off," the excess profits without jeopardizing the wage solidarity policy. In 1971, the LO created a committee headed by Rudolph Meidner, an LO economist, to study the problem. The aims of this study were: to complement the wage policy based on the principle of solidarity; to counteract the concentration of wealth which stems from industrial self-financing; and to increase the influence which employees have over the economic process.[3]

After four years Meidner introduced his proposals, and in 1976, the committee proposed to the LO congress a scheme involving collective investment plans which would be financed by company profits. Meidner and the committee rejected any plan that would transfer funds from efficient to inefficient companies, since that type of arrangement would not fit with the LO's desire to allow the system to eliminate the weak and to develop a strong, efficient, and competitive business sector. The committee also rejected individual profit sharing plans as incompatible with solidarity in wage policy. At no time did the proposals make provision for individual employees to withdraw and dispose of their shares since that would tie workers to their company and undermine the solidarity of wage earners as a whole. It also would not offer any significant increase in worker influence over decision making within the companies.

Briefly, the original Meidner proposal meant that each private sector company would be bound to issue new shares worth an amount corresponding to 20 percent of each year's profits. The companies would turn over the shares to a central fund controlled by a board composed solely of union representatives. As the fund accumulated shares, its stake in the individual companies would, of course, increase. Meidner estimated that it would take between twenty and seventy-five years, depending on the company's profitability, for the fund to acquire 50 percent ownership in a company.[4] The shares could not be traded, but the income from the shares could be used to purchase other company stock, to finance union members' education, or a host of other welfare activities.

The Meidner proposals aroused substantial opposition from employers which centered on the apprehension that these proposals would bring about too great a concentration of power among politicians and trade union leaders. SAF made clear its belief that the

---

[3]Rudolph Meidner, *Employee Investment Funds: An Approach to Collective Capital Formation* (London: George Allen & Unwin, Ltd., 1978), p. 15. (English translation of the 1976 report).

[4]*Ibid.*, p. 59.

wage-earner fund concept would bring about the end of the free market economy and would precipitate the flight of capital and undermine an already weak willingness to invest. Protests even took the form of street protests by employers and others. October 4 of each year has become the unofficial "free enterprise" day in Sweden since several demonstrations have occurred on October 4.[5] In 1976, the issue of wage-earner funds played a large part in the parliamentary election which resulted in the Social Democrats stepping down after forty-four years in power.[6]

The Meidner proposals were modified several times and heatedly debated between 1976 and 1983. The final proposal was announced in 1983 after the Social Democrats returned to power in the 1982 election, and despite resistance, the fund concept was adopted in December 1983. The SAF cites numerous public opinion polls which purport to show that, both before and after adoption, collective investment funds are favored by a small minority of Swedes, including LO members and members of the Social Democratic Party.[7]

Present Operation

The 1983 enactment established five regional wage-earner funds within the framework of the National Pension Insurance Fund. Each fund is managed by a board of directors of nine members (appointed by the government), at least five of whom are to represent the workers' interests. The funds are financed from two sources: (1) a payroll levy on all employers in the private and public sector—0.2 percent in 1984 and increasing to 0.5 percent in 1990; (2) a "profit sharing" tax of 20 percent on each company's (joint stock companies, cooperatives, savings banks, and insurance companies) annual profit, after adjustment for inflation, with a deduction of SEK 1,000,000 (U.S.$158,000)[8] or alternatively, an amount equal to 6 percent of its payroll as a tax free sum. Deductions are also allowed for income tax and allocations to investment funds. The five funds share the money equally. For each fund there is a ceiling of SEK 400 million (U.S.$63.1 million) for the annual allocation of capital. Over the seven years of the funds' operation, through 1990, the total allo-

---

[5]"Protests against employee investment funds," *European Industrial Relations Review*, No. 130 (November 1984), p. 9.

[6]Lennart Forsebacks, *Industrial Relations and Employment in Sweden* (The Swedish Institute, 1980), p. 125.

[7]Leif Widen, *Trade Union Funds in Sweden* (Stockholm: Swedish Employers' Confederation, 1988), pp. 6-8.

[8]SEK = Swedish Krona. The exchange rate used in this chapter is the 1987 average, SEK 6.3404 = U.S.$1.

cated was SEK 2.8 billion (U.S.$.44 billion). At the end of 1990, money will no longer flow into the funds, but the boards will continue to operate, with income after 1990 deriving from interest on capital invested. The profit sharing portion of the funds is so designed that it will apply essentially only to the large companies.

Fund managers may buy shares in any Swedish company. There is a short-term and a long-term profit requirement for the funds. The long-term profit requirement means that allocations must be made for the purchasing power of the base capital. In the short-term the funds are required to pay 3 percent of the current value of the capital received each year to the public pension fund. Each fund is permitted to hold at most 8 percent of the total voting rights in any limited liability company quoted on the stock exchange. Together the five funds may own a maximum of 40 percent in one of these companies. To this may be added another fund which was established earlier and which is entitled to control 10 percent of a company's voting shares. There is no limit on the shares which may held in non-listed companies. At the request of a local trade union a fund management board may be required to turn over to that local union 30 percent of the voting rights of the company involved for one year.

Results

When the wage-earner funds were established, there were five official objectives stated: to facilitate the wage policy of solidarity, to counteract the concentration of power and wealth, to increase workers' influence in enterprises, to increase capital formation, and to strengthen the pension system. There is a wide divergence of opinion about whether or not those objectives have been achieved. The LO officially states that they have been achieved, and the employers claim the only target that has been reached is increased union control of business.

Although the funds have failed to live up to expectations, a fact which is acknowledged by LO leaders, none of the dire predictions of the opposition have come about either. Trade union criticism stems, in part at least, from a lack of communication with individual employees who reportedly do not understand what the funds are all about.[9]

Effect on Wages and Profits. If the wage-earner funds were designed to reduce "excess profits" in Swedish businesses, they have been something less than successful. First quarter, 1988,

---

[9] "Employee investment fund renews controversy," *European Industrial Relations Review*, No. 159 (April 1987), p. 7.

results of major Swedish companies show profits averaging a third higher than those of the same period in 1987.[10] The LO acknowledges that profits during the 1983 to 1987 period have been high, but it also points out that the excess profit problem would have been greater without the profit sharing tax. Wage rates have also been increasing faster than prices since 1985,[11] fuelled by a shortage of skilled labor and favorable profit levels.

Concentration of Wealth and Power. The LO states the value of quoted companies in Sweden at SEK 600 billion (U.S.$94.6 billion) and laments the dominating influence in these companies exercised by a limited circle of private individuals or representatives of large institutions such as insurance companies and foundations. Wage-earner funds were seen as a way of decreasing that concentration. According to a 1988 LO study, the five wage-earner funds, plus the fourth pension fund, which also is permitted to buy shares, own jointly approximately 4 percent of the companies quoted on the stock exchange. By 1990, it is estimated that they will own 6 or 7 percent.[12] The employers claim that trade union control currently exceeds 5 percent, and that the largest private shareholder in Sweden, the Skandia Insurance Company, holds only 6 percent of all listed equities.[13] Since the institutional investors are relatively passive, the argument goes, the trade unions will be able to exert more power at general meetings. Although trade union control is relatively weak, it is greater by approximately 4 percent than it would have been in the absence of the wage-earner funds. There is no evidence that the exercise of share ownership by the trade unions has been abused or has been detrimental to the Swedish economy.

Increase Workers' Influence. The objective was to provide a new opportunity for increasing worker influence within enterprises and influence company decisions as they relate to the community as a whole. A LO survey showed that in 1985 and 1986 local trade union representatives in large numbers exercised their option to obtain 50 percent of the voting rights of shares held by the wage-earner funds. The voting rights were utilized by the local unions to enable them to participate in corporate general meetings.[14] Since the voting shares held in listed companies seldom exceed 1 percent, the influence

---

[10]The Economic Intelligence Unit, *Country Report: Sweden*, No. 3 (1988), p. 9.
[11]Supplement, *Industrial Relations Europe*, Vol. XVI, No. 188 (August 1988).
[12]Landsorganisation i Sverige (LO), Trans Erica Stempa, *3 Years with Employee Investment Funds: An Evaluation* (Stockholm: LO, 1988), p. 33.
[13]Widen, *Trade Union Funds in Sweden*, p. 9.
[14]LO, *3 Years with Employee Investment Funds*, pp. 27-28.

exerted by the union is limited, but may be substantially greater in non-listed companies.[15]

Increase Capital Formation. At the time the wage-earner funds were being debated and introduced, there was a need for new venture capital in Sweden. The theory of the funds was that money taken in from large, profitable companies and from the public sector would be invested in vigorous, goods-producing export industries. The 1983 devaluation of the Swedish krona, the introduction of an economic adjustment program, and lower oil prices improved the Swedish economy and business investment grew markedly, at least until 1986 when it slowed significantly. The contribution of the wage-earner funds to that investment growth has been relatively small. In the first year of operation, 98 percent of the money spent by the funds was used to buy shares from previous shareholders, and only 2 percent was used to create new capital.[16] At the end of 1987, less than 10 percent of the funds' assets had been used to form new equity capital.[17]

Strengthen the Pension System. The contribution of the funds to the public pension system has been modest. From 1984 through 1986 the five funds transferred some SEK 200 million (U.S.$31.5 million) to the pension fund, a small addition to a fund whose assets are valued at over SEK 190 billion (U.S.$45.8 billion).[18] The LO, however, maintains that the funds' capital will increase enormously.[19] The funds were to be phased out after 1990, and government officials have indicated that there will be no move to extend the deadline.[20] Debate will center on what to do with the assets of the funds after 1990. Some trade union leaders have been openly critical of the funds' performance and have even advocated company-based profit sharing which is clearly favored by employers.[21]

VOLUNTARY PROFIT SHARING IN SWEDEN

It should be clear that the Swedish wage-earner funds are not profit sharing plans in the sense that term has been used in this study. The most significant difference is that the wage-earner funds

---

[15]*Ibid.*, pp. 33-34.
[16]"Employee investment funds retained," *European Industrial Relations Review*, No. 141 (October 1985), p. 8.
[17]Widen, *Trade Union Funds in Sweden*, p. 10.
[18]LO, *3 Years with Employee Investment Funds*, pp. 36-37.
[19]*Ibid.*, p. 37.
[20]"Swedish Tax and Incentive Regime Will Tighten," *Business Europe*, Vol. XXVII, No. 4 (October 5, 1987), p. 4.
[21]"Sweden," *IDS/PA European Report*, No. 304 (December 22, 1987), p. 9.

do not make provision for individual employees to receive a share of the profits of their employer—profits which presumably they have helped to create. The wage-earner funds have been presented here as a contrast of a collective approach to profit sharing versus an individual approach. In Sweden we are able to see both approaches working side by side.

Although there are few statistics available, one source estimates that twenty companies (out of 150 companies) listed on the Stockholm Stock Exchange have formal profit sharing plans involving all employees. Covered employees are estimated at 200,000 or approximately 4 to 5 percent of the work force.[22]

Two types of voluntary profit sharing schemes have evolved. One is based on annual bonus payments (cash profit sharing), and the other involves deferred payment to the individual employee—both similar in concept to plans existing in the United States. Central trade union organizations oppose individual profit sharing because it does not comport with their wage solidarity policy which seeks to eliminate pay differentials based on company profitability. At the local union level, however, there is mounting evidence that attitudes toward company-based profit sharing plans are enthusiastic. A 1987 poll showed that 90 percent of the employees had a positive attitude toward such plans.[23]

Taxation of profit sharing is similar to that in the United States. In both cash and deferred plans the employer treats the sums allocated as an operating expense which is tax deductible. The individual receiving a profit sharing bonus is taxed on receipt. With deferred plans, tax is deferred, except that recent legislation imposes the social security tax on deferred funds but at a rate of 27 percent as compared with the usual 37 percent. Some employers threatened to drop their plans as a result of this tax imposition.[24]

Employers are interested in promoting the principle of shareholding among their employees, and deferred profit sharing is a way of accomplishing that objective. The deferred profit sharing sums are normally invested in a trust with the trust purchasing shares in the principal company. Swedish employers have found also that profit sharing is a tool for communication and a device for educating employees in the economics of the business.[25] Each company, how-

---

[22]"Profit sharing schemes," *European Industrial Relations Review*, No. 166 (November 1987), p. 15.
[23]*Ibid.*
[24]"Profit-share tax angers firms," *Industrial Relations Europe*, Vol. XV, No. 172 (April 1987), p. 7.
[25]"Profit sharing schemes," p. 16.

ever, has its own reasons for establishing a profit sharing plan designed to meet the needs of that business. Consequently, details vary from one plan to another. The three plans outlined below represent three generations of plans and, of course, three different sets of objectives.

Åkermans

Åkermans, a company that manufactures excavating machinery, has the oldest and best known profit sharing plan in Sweden. When the plan was introduced in 1946 the company was small, with approximately fifty employees. It now has 1,300 employees, all of whom are covered by the plan. The plan was inaugurated in an attempt to find a method for retaining employees in a labor-competitive area. In essence the plan is a combination plan in which half of the allocated funds is paid out as an annual bonus, and the other half is placed in a trust fund for deferred payment. Currently, the trust owns approximately 6 percent of the shares of Åkermans itself. Benefits claimed by the company include improved productivity, improved labor turnover rates, decreased absenteeism, and improved corporate spirit.[26]

Svenska Handelsbanken

With 6,000 employees, Svenska Handelsbanken is the second largest commercial bank in Sweden. Profit sharing was introduced in the early 1970s as a way of recognizing the contribution of the bank's employees to its success. Profits are compared with those of other commercial banks; if they are higher, one-third is allocated to the employee trust fund which is managed jointly by management and the employees. The trust invests in the bank's shares, and by 1986 it became the largest shareholder. Employees receive a payout at retirement or when they leave employment at the bank.[27]

Volvo

More recently, in 1982, Volvo introduced a profit sharing plan for all of its 54,000 employees at all levels in Sweden. Funds are transferred to a trust through an agreed upon method. (Although initiated by management, the plan was negotiated with the unions.) Employees receive shares based on time worked during the year, and have individual shares in the trust subject to a maximum that can

[26] Ibid.
[27] Ibid.

be withdrawn after five years. The fund is prohibited from acquiring more than 5 percent of the voting stock of Volvo.[28] Volvo also has a number of payment-by-results plans at various plants which are in the nature of gain sharing plans designed to improve productivity and quality.

GAIN SHARING IN SWEDEN

The SAF encourages employers to develop new wage systems and to improve their existing systems. It undertakes to do this by offering suggestions, solutions, and shared experiences with firms attempting to make their wage systems responsive to their own particular business. This is all a part of a desire by the SAF to continue to decentralize wage determination in Sweden. A recent study sponsored by SAF summarizes thirteen "payment-by-results" plans,[29] each of which is an example of a single, private company experimenting with a highly individual gain sharing approach appropriate to its own peculiar problems and needs. The following four case studies illustrate the diversity of applications of gain sharing to a variety of business situations.

Scan Väst

Scan Väst is a cooperative association which has two business areas: slaughtering and meat processing. Although Scan Väst had evolved a number of results oriented wage payment schemes, it had struggled to find a way of introducing a payment-by-results system for its distributors.

Under the old system, sales representatives canvassed customers, while the distributor/drivers delivered meat products to the large number of small customers. The company's goals were to improve service to its small customers by providing full service on the spot, with the job of the driver being expanded to include selling as well as delivery. The solution was to convert the drivers to business managers responsible for their "own" store. Under the new system, the salesman/driver was given full responsibility for buying goods from stock, inventory control, selling, service, returns, etc. In order to do this a revised accounting system was developed to provide for internal accounts for each van and a minicomputer system was installed on each van.

---

[28]*Ibid.*
[29]Swedish Employers' Confederation, *Payment by Results: 13 Case Studies from Sweden*, Lena Ostman, ed., (Stockholom: Swedish Employers' Confederation, 1987).

Results from the new system are measured by several business factors which can be influenced by the salesman/driver, such as sales, inventory control, returns, and discounts. The bonus earned is based on these total business results. By decentralizing responsibility and by enabling these employees to share in the results of their efforts, the company reports it has achieved its goals. The salesman/drivers apparently are also pleased with the new system.

Scan Väst pointed out that its pay system could not have been changed without changing other aspects of the business, such as accounting and purchasing so that results could be monitored at the point they were achieved. This is an important advantage that well-planned gain sharing plans have over profit sharing plans. The gain sharing plans can be tailored to measure results at a much more circumscribed level in the organization.

Volvo Kalmar Plant

Volvo's plant at Kalmar, Sweden, is one of three assembly plants in Sweden. The Kalmar plant's assembly system consists of a series of automatic trolleys which carry each vehicle past a number of production groups, with each group having responsibility for assembling a homogeneous function of the vehicle, such as the electrical system. Workers are paid on a piece rate system, but it measures only a limited portion of overall productivity. In order to improve efficiency, the company sought a payment-by-results component to supplement individual wages and to relate pay more closely to its objectives.

The company's most important criteria for improving efficiency were quality and assembly costs.[30] In 1981, a new Scanlon-type, multi-factor, productivity bonus plan was introduced in an effort to improve quality and to lower assembly costs. The plan established seven measures or factors which all related to quality or to assembly cost and were compared to base values:
- man-hours per car for direct and indirect production workers;
- man-hours per car for office workers;
- capital cost for the inventory of components and finished cars;
- consumption of materials and tools;
- consumption of other input materials, such as oil, gasoline, and rust-proofing agents;
- cost of rejects and adjustments per car;
- quality is measured by allocating points for each vehicle inspected.

---

[30]Warren C. Hauck and Timothy L. Ross, "Sweden's Experiments in Productivity Gainsharing: A Second Look," *Personnel*, Vol. 64, No. 1 (January 1987), p. 64.

The employees (except for the plant manager) receive 25 percent of the improved results as a bonus. Each employee receives an identical amount of money per hour worked and is paid semi-annually. The results are calculated fortnightly, and employees are informed about what went well and not so well. A bipartite committee also reviews the results. All factors have exhibited improved results since the plan was introduced, and, of course, the bonus has also increased sharply. In 1984 it reached three kronor per hour (approximately $.50), which was more than had been expected. Both management and the trade unions agree that this is a good payment-by-results system. According to a recent employee survey, the "plan appears to be favorably received by most of the employees."[31]

Swedish Farmers' Union (LRF)

The Swedish Farmers' Union (LRF) plan is notable because it is a results-related program in a strictly white-collar, service operation. The LRF is a trade association for Sweden's farmers and is a central body within the farmers' cooperative movement. A legal affairs unit (JB), provides legal counselling services for members and for LRF itself. JB is an independent profit center within LRF which is expected to pay its own way. Its personnel consists of lawyers and secretaries in eight branch offices. Two separate trade unions are also involved.

Costs and an agreed upon yield (2.5 percent) are deducted from revenues generated by JB. The resulting surplus is shared one-quarter to LRF, one-quarter to the personnel in JB, and one-half is allocated to the branches which have achieved a result better than standard. Each employee's bonus comes out of JB's share as well as from the branch office's share and is proportionate to the time worked by each individual. Chargeable hours are weighted by a factor of two in order to stimulate a high number of debitable hours. The bonus is paid on top of a fixed salary.

The general opinion is that the system has helped to bring about several improvements. Debited services have increased, and the accounting for time spent on various activities has improved. There is also a greater awareness of results and changes in results—almost a profit-oriented interest is reported by the company.

---

[31]*Ibid.*, p. 67.

Sweden

Alufluor

This heavy chemicals manufacturing company represents an example of the application of gain sharing in a continuous process operation along with an ambitious information sharing program. The factors which form the basis of the payment-by-results system are output, raw material usage, and hours worked.

Output is measured as production in tons and is compared with an index based on 1980 production. Raw material yield is measured as the consumption of raw material per ton of product. Usage is also compared with a base figure. Hours worked is the total number of hours worked by the company's own and sub-contract personnel—also compared with an index value. These factors are measured for three-month periods, and the bonus is paid twice a year. Each factor is rewarded with a bonus when an improvement is achieved compared with the 1980 base year. Improvement is converted to kronor, and 10 percent is shared out among all employees except the president and his deputy.

The information sharing program is considered to be a very important part of the payment-by-results system. Information sharing is based on the premise that all employees should feel that they are members of the company's team and that they understand the company's situation. There are three types of meetings:

1. Management meetings (monthly) which involve shift representatives and the unions. These are problem solving meetings as well as information-sharing sessions.
2. General information meetings (monthly) for all employees, in small groups, are used to present the results of operations to everyone in the company. The emphasis is on results of each employee's work area.
3. Every other month there are workplace meetings which are oriented toward production and which may involve related groups such as maintenance. Problems and projects are discussed.

Alufluor is pleased with the results since the program was started in 1984. It has led to better profitability, improved coordination, greater contentment, a lower employee turnover, enhanced motivation, less absenteeism, and strong feelings of belonging.

TRENDS IN SWEDEN

Employers in Sweden, as in other countries, are increasingly recognizing the need for pay plans which are more flexible and which are more closely related to the economic fortunes of the individual business. Many companies are working on result-based wage systems and methods of appraisal as a basis for wage differentiation. A recent research study by the SAF indicates that, over the three years preceding the study, a smaller proportion of total pay of workers was made up of base wages and a larger share by bonuses related to productivity, quality, company results, and other factors. Base wages, as a percent of total pay, dropped from 45 percent to 39 percent over a three-year period of time. There is also a trend toward more flexible pay for white-collar workers as well.[32]

Opposition to the wage-earner funds appears to be growing even within the unions and the Social Democratic Party. Although the government has stated that there are no plans to extend the collection of the profit sharing tax beyond 1990, the question of what to do with the money in the funds after 1990 remained as a major issue in the late 1980s and can be expected to be hotly debated.

---

[32]"Wages increasingly determined by performance," *European Industrial Relations Review*, No. 149 (June 1986), p. 7.

CHAPTER XI

Other EC and European Countries

THE NETHERLANDS

The Netherlands, like a few other Western European countries, offers employees a number of individual statutory wage-savings plans. These plans are voluntary and often contain some type of tax benefit. At the same time, a few large employers have adopted a wide range of nonstatutory company profit sharing or bonus plans. The Netherlands has debated and rejected a collective asset formation plan like that adopted in Sweden in 1984. Generally, employee financial participation in the Netherlands is similar to that in the Federal Republic of Germany.

Statutory Savings/Profit Sharing Plans[1]

Since 1965 the Netherlands has had three types of statutory, voluntary savings plans, only one of which is related to the profits of the employer. Employees may participate in one or more of these plans at any time and may also be covered by a voluntary company profit sharing plan. The three statutory plans are discussed below.

Bonus Savings Plans. With this type of plan, the employee may agree to have up to 750g (US$397) deducted annually from his or her pay for a minimum of four years (tax free). The employer pays no social security tax on these amounts. These funds are placed either in a special savings account administered by the employer or by a designated agency such as a bank or a building society. Investments may include shares of the employer's stock or that of other companies, subject to certain limitations. A "bonus" payment by the employer also accrues to the employee's account. If the employee keeps the entire sum invested for four years, the bonus is 50 percent of the employee's own savings. An investment for ten years qualifies for a bonus of 200 percent. These sums are free of tax for the employer. There are limited instances (such as marriage, emigration,

---

[1]The discussion of these statutory plans which follows is extracted largely from Loontechnische Dienst (LTD), Ministerie Van Social Zaken en Werkgelegnheid, "Onderzock Gefacilieerde Bedrijfsspaaregelingen," June 1987 (a report on a survey by an agency of the Dutch government).

and purchase of a home) in which the employee may withdraw funds before the end of the specified period.

Profit Sharing Plans. This type of statutory plan is the only one which is related to the profits of the employer and is available only in companies which have a profit sharing plan. The employer agrees to allocate from profits up to 750g (US$397) annually for each employee in return for tax and social security exemptions. There is, of course, no guarantee of regular payments for employees. The money is invested under the same conditions as the bonus savings plans mentioned above, except the money paid in is frozen for a seven-year period (subject to the same exceptions noted above). The minimum holding period does not apply to the yield on money invested this way.

Wage Savings Plans. These plans are based on a collectively bargained agreement under which the employer deducts up to 2 percent of the maximum social security taxed earnings (approximately $725) for each employee. The fund is jointly administered by the company and the union. Participation is compulsory for those employees covered by the collective bargaining agreement and savings are frozen for seven years. Employees do not pay income or social security tax on their contributions. Although employers are exempted from paying social security tax on these amounts, they do pay a 15 percent tax on the amount saved.

A 1985 survey by an agency of the Ministry of Social Affairs and Labor reported that 404,000 employees were participating in one or more of these statutory plans (see Table XI-1). Since the survey included approximately 3.25 million employees, this indicates that approximately 12 percent of the employees covered in the survey were participating in one or more of the plans. The most popular plan by far is the bonus savings plan. The survey also indicated that larger companies (those with 100 or more employees) are more likely

TABLE XI-1
Number of Employees and Actual Participants in Companies with Savings Plans (thousands)

	Number Employed in Companies with Savings Plans	Number of Eligible Employees	Number of Actual Participants
Bonus Savings Plans	565	466	280
Profit Sharing Savings Plans	144	140	76
Wage Savings Plans	53	48	48

Source: Loontechnische Dienst (LTD), Ministerie Van Social Zaken en Werkgelegnheid, "Onderzock Gefacilieerde Bedrijfsspaaregelingen," June 1987, p. 6.

to have one or more of the plans and that approximately 50 percent of the companies with such plans are manufacturing companies. Interestingly, profit sharing savings plans are more prevalent in the banking, insurance, and service sectors. Average bonus payments to participants in 1985 were: 446g (US$236) per participant for bonus savings plans; 777g (US$411) for profit sharing savings plans; and 535g (US$283) for wage savings plans.

Employers and employee representatives agree generally that the bonus and profit sharing savings plans are desirable employee financial participation tools. There is less agreement on the wage savings plans. Some attempts have been made to integrate the three plans into one super plan, but to date this has not occurred. Employee representatives apparently wish to keep the wage plans, while employers prefer the more flexible (and voluntary for employees) plans. Consequently, the three plans will probably remain separate until some accommodation on integration is concluded. There is a fourth very small plan which is available for young workers exclusively.

Company Profit Sharing

In 1970, legal restrictions were lifted on the establishment of savings and profit sharing plans other than those in the 1965 legislation. The plans which have resulted are varied. Some relate bonuses to company profits, others may pay a fixed bonus regardless of profit level, and others may combine the two along with one or more of the statutory savings plans.[2] Most of the nonstatutory profit sharing plans are found in large, widely recognized companies.

Philips, the international electronics firm, for example, has a typical array of financial participation plans for employees. The company's "fixed" bonus plan pays employees 10 percent of total earnings—7 percent paid in June of each year and 3 percent paid in December. This payment includes the legally mandated minimum vacation bonus. Another plan is more closely related to company performance and relates the employee bonus to the dividend paid to shareholders. If the dividend on a 10g share is 18 percent, then the employees receive a bonus of 6 percent of their earnings. If the dividend exceeds 18 percent, the employee receives an additional bonus of .015 percent for each 1 percent the dividend exceeds 18 percent, or if the dividend is less than 18 percent, the bonus is reduced by .010 percent for each 1 percent the dividend falls below 18 percent. The

---

[2]"Savings and Profit-Sharing Schemes in the Netherlands," *European Industrial Relations Review*, No. 45 (September 1977), p. 14.

employee cannot receive an amount greater than the amount of the dividend, however. Employees must have one year of employment for full participation, but employees hired during the year receive a prorated bonus. In addition, the company makes available to employees the right to purchase "debentures" (*personeelobligaties*), up to a specified maximum, which may be converted into company shares.[3]

Stock Ownership/Share Option Plans

Share options for management and professional personnel are spreading rapidly in the Netherlands as a way of attracting and retaining highly qualified employees, particularly in growing, high technology firms. A recent study indicates that twenty-one companies are known to include *all* employees in their share option plans. Share option plans, according to the authors of this study, are often viewed as a means of providing more flexible remuneration, particularly for management employees.[4]

Although not unique, the share option plan of Amro Bank, a large financial institution, is illustrative of the type of share option plan applied to a total employee population. The employees are offered an option for 60 shares (at 90g (US$48) per option). In 1985 over 50 percent of the bank's workforce subscribed to the plan. In 1986, the above study reported that 90 percent of the employees participated.[5]

Collective Asset Formation Plans

Since the early 1960s, there have been several proposals for a compulsory levy on company profits (*vermogensaanswasdeling* or VAD), similar to the Swedish Wage Earner Funds. The basic concept is to create a fund (by levying a tax on company profits) which would be managed largely by the unions and used to accumulate shares or "worker capital" for eventual distribution to employees or to provide increased pensions or other benefits. The uses of the funds have been a source of much debate. The Christian National Trade Union Federation (CNV) insists that such funds should be used to reduce working time to create jobs. The employers oppose compulsory, collective programs of this type and contend that the various savings

---

[3]Taken from Article 17 and Article 18 of the company statutes of N.V. Philips' Gloilampenfabrieken.

[4]H.G. Eijgenhuijsen, J.G.J.F. Oudenejans, and G. Rietkerk, "Aandelenopties voor management en personeel sterk in opkomst," *de Naamlooze* Vennootschap, No. 6511 (January/February 1987), p. 5.

[5]*Ibid.*, p. 6.

plans should by improved instead. Although the main political parties favor the idea in principle, nothing has yet been enacted into law.[6] The Dutch apparently are not ready to follow Sweden where such funds have been much less than effective and have satisfied no one.

In 1987 the tripartite advisory body, the Social and Economic Council, recommended that pay should be linked more closely to company profits in order to make the labor market more flexible. Firm proposals to implement this recommendation have not yet been forthcoming.

BELGIUM

Since the late 1970s the Belgian unions have been most concerned with employment security, while the employers have sought to control labor costs. The resulting issues are wage restraint, social security reform, reduction of working time, and recourse to part-time work. In the United States similar conditions led to an increase in collectively bargained profit sharing, the employees receiving a variety or employment security provisions and at the same time accepting profit sharing as a trade-off. In Belgium that has not yet occurred.

Profit Sharing Legislation

Employers have exhibited interest in the flexibility offered by profit sharing. The government, however, has not offered encouragement in the form of tax relief. At the same time, the trade unions have expressed opposition to profit sharing and the distribution of company shares to employees. Legislation to provide for profit-related pay (*dividende du travail*) was introduced in parliament in 1987. The proposed bill would have permitted employers to allocate up to 10 percent of profits as profit-related pay if the employer agreed to increase total employment by 1 percent. Such plans could only be concluded through collective agreement, and profit-related pay could never replace normal pay. A special tax rate of 25 percent was to be utilized and thus to exempt the employee from the progressive taxation system.[7] In the face of strong union opposition, the bill was not enacted. The General Labor Federation insists that profit

---

[6] "Profits levy debate resumes as pay pressure grows," *Industrial Relations Europe*, Vol. XII, No. 139 (July 1984), p. 5.

[7] "Belgium: Profit-related pay," *European Industrial Relations Review*, No. 156 (January 1987), p. 2.

sharing and the distribution of company shares to employees are acceptable only if wages continue to be negotiated collectively and all aspects of profit sharing are negotiable also.[8] Similarly, there exists little encouragement of share ownership plans for employees in Belgium.

Company Profit Sharing

Recent surveys in Belgium provide some evidence that at least in the top and middle management ranks there has been a substantial increase in the incidence of variable or flexible compensation.[9] Below the management level there are relatively few plans.

In only one rather exceptional case, that of HBK-Spaarbank, has a profit sharing plan led to any significant degree of employee share ownership. HBK-Spaarbank is a private financial institution which has operated its plan since 1979. No unions are involved. Under the plan, profits are shared equal to the return on capital paid to the shareholders. The funds are handled by a "cooperative" managed by a board composed of equal numbers of employee representatives and shareholder representatives. HBK shares are purchased, or those of other companies may be purchased if sufficient HBK shares are not available. The employees receive a dividend each year. In the eight years of operation the proportion of employee-owned shares has reached nearly 11 percent. There are no tax advantages to the company or to the employee participants.[10]

A slightly different approach was taken by Agfa-Gevaert, the photographic giant, in 1986. The plan was developed as a way of avoiding the effect of the mandatory wage freeze. Profits are shared at a rate of .001 percent of the distributable profits. The shares generated do not have voting rights, are not transferable, and do not leave with the employee at death or termination of employment. The return to the employee comes in the form of a dividend on the shares in the fund. The payments were treated by the tax authorities as dividends and thus escaped the wage freeze.[11]

Although plans such as these are technically a form of deferred profit sharing, there is no tax relief, as there is in the United States, to act as an incentive to encourage the spread of the concept to large numbers of firms and employees. That situation is not likely to

---

[8]R. Blanpain, "Firm Productivity and Wages Policies: Management Iniitatives To Gain Workers' Participation," pp. 22-23 (paper dated October 28, 1988).
[9]*Ibid.*, pp. 11-17.
[10]*Ibid.*, pp. 21-22.
[11]*Ibid.*, pp. 20-21.

change soon because of the government's austerity program and its interest in reducing the deficit. Trade union opposition to profit sharing and employee share ownership also remains as a deterrent to the spread of those plans in the heavily unionized sectors. Variable or flexible remuneration has shown a sizable increase in the late 1980s for executives and middle managers. The labor force in Belgium, as in many other countries, is becoming more white-collar, more individually oriented, and better educated—factors which could eventually result in more performance related compensation systems. For the present, Belgium is still in the "starting blocks"[12] with regard to profit-related pay systems.

ITALY

Economically, Italy is composed of two divergent regions, the North, which has a number of prosperous, modern enterprises, and the South, known as *Mezzogiorno*, which remains more agricultural and has numerous pockets of deprivation. Partly because of the continuing economic lag of the South, business in the region has shown little interest in profit sharing. Indeed, small firms in general have shown little interest in profit sharing and performance-related pay. The companies which have moved in the direction of performance-related pay are the large, widely known multinational companies such as Fiat, Montedison, Olivetti, Pirelli, and Zanussi. They have been able to compete successfully in international markets by restructuring and modernizing which has spurred the growth of productivity. In 1988, however, performance-related pay plans began to appear among these companies as an additional tool designed to increase labor cost flexibility as well as to boost productivity improvement. The performance-related pay plans, although negotiated with unions, have split the three major trade union confederations and may threaten the longer term unity of the Italian trade union movement.

Trade Unions and Politics

The three major trade union confederations are: the Italian General Confederation of Labor (CGIL), which has been closely allied with the Italian Communist Party, with a Socialist minority; the Italian Confederation of Workers' Trade Unions (CSIL), which was originally a Roman Catholic movement with a strong orientation to

---

[12]*Ibid.*, p. 24.

the Christian Democratic Party; and the Italian Union of Labor (UIL), aligned toward the Socialist Party, and generally representing higher paid workers.

After World War II, the CGIL was the only trade union confederation in Italy, and it grew to a peak membership of six million by the late 1940s. In 1948 the CGIL split into the three confederations noted above and along political lines. The unions, however, have never had direct political representation in government through party affiliations. After 1950 the unions were quite successful in persuading various governments to enact a number of protective laws, but these have not favored any one union over another.[13] During the 1960s and 1970s collective labor relations developed independently of legal intervention by the government. By 1972 the three confederations established a Unitary Federation requiring joint formulation of policies at the national level and leading to detailed internal bargaining. In 1984 the CGIL disagreed with the CSIL and the UIL over wage indexation policy, and the federative pact dissolved.[14] Although there were political and structural factors that tended to deter labor unity, cultural causes were perhaps more to blame. Many union leaders simply did not understand or respond to the economic and social changes occurring in the early 1980s. They had difficulty in moving from a confrontational stance to one more cooperative and supportive of improved productivity. The result has been divergence, with the more moderate members more willing to accept flexible working conditions and performance-related pay experiments. Decisions have been often compromises and attempts to avoid a complete break among the three confederations.[15]

Performance-Related Pay

Since 1984 performance-related pay has increased substantially, although there have been no government initiatives to encourage it. Between 1984 and 1988, sixty of such agreements were negotiated at company level, covering 400,000 employees.[16] The first firms to introduce performance-related pay were in the retail and engineering

---

[13]T. Treu, "Italy," in *International Encyclopaedia for Labour Law and Industrial Relations*, R. Blanpain, ed. (Netherlands: Kluwer, 1986), p. 23.

[14]Gino Giugni, "Recent Trends in Collective Bargaining in Italy," in *Collective Bargaining in Industrialized Market Economies: A Reappraisal*, John P. Windmuller, et al., ed. (Geneva: International Labour Office, 1987), pp. 226-227.

[15]*Ibid.*, pp. 227-228.

[16]"New flexibility in company-level agreements," *European Industrial Review*, No. 190 (November 1989), p. 13.

sectors. In the manufacturing sector Fiat, Zanussi, and Olivetti led the way in 1988.

The introduction of performance-related pay in 1988 in collective bargaining by some of the largest employers has widened the differences between the Communist CGIL on the one hand and the other two confederations on the other. Fiat, Italy's largest company, led the way in 1988 by introducing the first large-scale agreement linking wage increases to company performance. The CSIL and the UIL signed the agreement, but the CGIL refused to sign on the grounds that the membership did not authorize the negotiators to negotiate a fundamental change in pay practice.[17] The Fiat agreement gave approximately 170,000 employees a lump sum payment in 1988. The average bonus in 1989 was 359,000 lire (US$284). Beginning in 1990, a group performance bonus will be calculated according to each group's performance taking into account productivity, company financial results, and a quality index. A fixed amount will be paid out in monthly payments and consolidated into base pay. A remaining, variable portion will be paid as a lump sum each year in July. This new premium payment will be considered as distinct from regular compensation.

Zanussi, the electrical goods manufacturer, followed Fiat by awarding lump sum bonuses of $500 per employee in 1988 and $660 in 1989. The new pay system, which will not be fully operative until 1990, provides for two bonuses; an annual bonus tied to individual unit productivity and a quarterly bonus linked to the attainment of production targets. By 1990 the annual bonus will vary between $462 and $532 and the quarterly bonus will be fixed at $140.[18]

Olivetti also introduced a performance-related pay program in 1988. This plan also consists of two parts. One portion is a guaranteed bonus payable each June which is then offset against another payment based on an index of company competitiveness payable in January. The index measures Olivetti's performance against its competitors in the computer industry. The profit-related bonus will be triggered when operating profit exceeds consolidated revenue by 6 percent, with a ceiling of 10 percent. Olivetti has established this ratio as the minimum it needs to remain competitive in the world computer market. The guaranteed bonus provides for transitional payments through 1991. Profit-related payments will be added if the index exceeds 6 percent, but if in a given year the index fails to reach

---

[17]"Fiat Reaches Uneasy Agreement," *IDS/PA European Report*, No. 318 (July 26, 1988), p. 3.

[18]"New Pay Approach at Zanussi," *IDS/PA European Report*, No. 322 (October 1988), p. 5.

6 percent, employees will not lose the guaranteed bonus. It has been estimated that the two elements combined could reach approximately 10 percent of pay.[19]

Another profit-related plan was introduced at Italgel (1,350 employees). It provides a flexible bonus in addition to the normal wage increases if the company reaches its target for gross operating profit. The bonus will make up about 40 to 45 percent of the total pay increase.[20]

Among the recent performance-related pay agreements, only 25 percent link the variable portion of pay to company performance indicators such as gross operating profit or sales. In 30 percent of the agreements the variable portion is tied to general performance indicators measuring productivity, quality, and waste reduction (more closely related to gain sharing as defined in this study). Other firms combine the two criteria of company results and productivity improvement. Employers cite improved productivity, greater labor cost flexibility, and employee motivation as the chief motives for the introduction of these plans.[21]

Performance-related pay is, however, expected to have a relatively small effect on total pay. In Italy, the proportion of an employee's pay determined at company level (*superminima*) is relatively small. For example, in the engineering industry in Lombardy, the company determined portion of total pay is only 4.46 percent for blue-collar workers and 14.27 percent for white-collar workers. The largest component of pay is accounted for by cost-of-living payments (54 percent), followed by the contractual minimums (32 percent) which are established by national collective agreements usually renewed every three years. Thus, performance-related pay does not necessarily result in a substantial impact on total pay even if it should completely replace company level pay.[22]

A recognition of this minimal impact on pay may explain the willingness of at least two of the unions to go along with the concept. All three major confederations signed the Olivetti and Zanussi agreements.[23] Internal disagreements brought new leadership to the

---

[19]"Company deals offer pay for performance," *IDS/PA European Report*, No. 325 (January 1989), pp. 12-13.
[20]"Profit-Related Pay Settlements," *IDS European Report*, No. 322 (October 1988), p. 5.
[21]"New flexibility in company-level agreements, p. 13.
[22]"Italy: Manufacturing pay reflects national deals," *IDS/PA European Report*, No. 318 (July 26, 1988), p. 7.
[23]"Company deals offer pay for performance," p. 13.

CGIL late in 1988, and it appears that performance-related pay may be slightly more acceptable to this new leadership.[24]

Although the three performance-related pay systems discussed above cover approximately 260,000 employees, such agreements are still relatively rare in Italy. A few companies have followed Fiat's lead, but many will be observing the results before jumping into profit sharing. The employers' association, Confindustria, favors a wider application of profit sharing as a way of increasing cooperation between employers and employees.[25]

Employee Share-Ownership Plans

Italian employers see employee share ownership plans as a way of increasing employees' interest in their companies. Again, the unions are divided. The Communist-oriented CGIL is cautious while the other two confederations, CSIL and UIL, see them as a way of increasing workers' participation and would like to negotiate them.[26]

The Stock Exchange Control Commission reported that from 1985 to 1987 over twenty companies offered shares to their employees. There are no tax incentives to encourage employers to introduce employee stock ownership plans. Shares allocated to employees and held in trust for two years are free of tax to the employee, however.

Montedison recently introduced a savings plan which calls for an employee contribution of 1 percent of pay matched by 1.1 percent by the company. Fund capital will be invested 50 percent in government bonds, 30 percent in equity, 15 percent in real estate, and 15 percent in cash. The fund is managed jointly by company-appointed individuals and representatives elected by the participants and by the unions.[27]

The UIL has expressed interest in a system of "unit trusts," such as those common in Great Britain, which would enable employees to invest in shares of their own and other companies. Employee contributions would be negotiated with employers, and the trusts would be managed by independent experts. The unions' role would be limited to general direction and supervision. The investors receive units representing equal shares in the diversified portfolio, and shares can be sold to the trust at any time. Of course, the value of the units

---

[24]*Ibid.*
[25]"New Style Italian Pay Deals: Watch Fiat's Performance Pact," *Business Europe*, Vol. XXVIII, No. 32 (January 1988), p. 3.
[26]"Employee share-ownership scheme at Montedison," *European Industrial Relations Review*, No. 161 (June 1987), p. 7.
[27]*Ibid.*

depends upon the performance of the portfolio as a whole. None of the British unit trusts are under union auspices. The UIL sees such plans as providing unions and their members with information and supervisory rights of minority shareholders and not as an attempt to gain union control of firms.[28]

DENMARK

Like Sweden, Denmark has a highly unionized labor force, approximately 80 percent, with some estimates as high as 90 percent. The dominant federation is the Federation of Danish Trade Unions (LO). Denmark is perhaps unique in having a union solely for women, the General Female Workers' Union (KAD), although there are women in other unions. Supervisory and salaried employees have a separate central organization equivalent to the LO. Politically, the LO is closely tied to the social democrats, although the relations now are somewhat looser than they were a few years ago.[29]

Denmark was one of the first European nations to embrace the welfare state concept. Government expenditures as a percentage of GDP are third among major Western nations, exceeded only by Sweden and the Netherlands. Denmark also ranks behind only Sweden in the proportion of government employees in the total labor force, and government social expenditures are among the highest in the Western world. One result is high marginal tax rates which mean inevitably the lowest level of disposable income among major Western countries. This factor, along with a relatively high level of pension benefits as compared with income during the working years, has retarded the level of private savings.

Denmark in 1957 was the first Scandinavian country to enact legislation to encourage profit sharing. The 1957 legislation created a profit sharing board with the responsibility for advising companies which contemplated the introduction of such plans. Little has been achieved under this program. In 1973 the Social Democrats and the LO proposed a collective investment fund similar to those in Sweden, but opposition from employers and a lack of support from union members led to the defeat of this proposal. The Social Democrats and the LO have continued to press for a compulsory levy on profits with the money going to a central investment fund similar to the Swedish wage-earner funds. The government and the Danish

---

[28]"Unions 'should create trusts' to boost share ownership," *Industrial Relations Europe* (April 1987), p. 4.

[29]Aage Tarp (B.C. Roberts, ed.), *Industrial Relations in Europe: The Imperatives of Change* (Stockholm: Swedish Employers' Confederation, 1985), p. 41.

Employers' Confederation (DA) favor voluntary profit sharing, and the Radical Party has endorsed company-based funds which would allow employees considerable discretion in how the money is eventually distributed.[30] A government sponsored report, the Hassenkam Report, released in 1986, found that at most only 5 to 10 percent of Danish employees benefited from profit sharing; obviously, a small proportion after many years of limited encouragement of voluntary profit sharing.[31] Finally, in 1987, the Danish parliament enacted profit sharing legislation. Companies may give their employees shares in the company worth a maximum of Dkr6,000 (US$877) tax-free to the employee and tax deductible to the firm. Additional shares at favorable rates may also be given or sold to employees, but they will be liable for normal tax. The shares must be retained for five years. The scheme is voluntary and does not include public sector companies. The same law provides for employee board representation in companies with over thirty-five employees.[32]

One year after enactment it was reported that only ten profit sharing plans had been adopted. The employers' association, DA, claims that the reason such plans are few is that there have been no profits.[33] It is certainly too early to determine success or failure of the legislation. Some time may be required before the unions, the employees, and the employers can begin to experiment with the profit sharing and employee ownership concept. The employers, of course, are hoping for success of voluntary plans as a counteraction to the LO's demand for wage-earner funds.

SWITZERLAND

Development of Employee Financial Participation

First attempts were made by Swiss employers to provide for employee profit sharing in the early 19th century, but for the most part these early forms of participation were collective in nature. A portion of a company's profits would be put into an internal employee savings bank or be used for such social benefits services as soup kitchens, factory schools, cafeterias, or health insurance.

---

[30]"Compulsory profit-sharing drafts are rejected," *Industrial Relations Europe*, Vol. XVI, No. 161 (May 1986), p. 4.
[31]"Profit sharing plan due this autumn," *Industrial Relations Europe*, Vol. XVI, No. 164 (August 1989), p. 6.
[32]"Legislation enacted on employee share-ownership," *European Industrial Relations Review*, No. 164 (September 1987), p. 3.
[33]"Voluntary profit sharing fails," *IDS/PA European Report*, No. 320 (August 23, 1988), p. 4.

Individual employee profit sharing and capital participation in Switzerland[34] began in the late 19th century with a program introduced in 1871 by Billon & Isaac, a Geneva-based manufacturer of music-box components. Its employees were entitled to a premium of which one-half was paid out in cash while the other half was put into an obligatory "depot" or depository that was then converted into participation certificates of SF 100.[35] The Dr. A. Wander AG introduced an employee profit sharing scheme in 1912, whose total amount was based on annual dividends. This plan was continued until 1968 when Wander became part of the Basel-based Sandoz AG.

Influenced by neighboring France, the western part of Switzerland, known as Suisse Romande, began to show some interest in labor participation models that combined regular profit sharing and employee stock participation to issue labor shares, in contrast to the regular capital shares. During the 1920s there were several experiments with this type of share. This concept, which was based on the equality of capital and labor, found no lasting adherents, however. Even "regular" employee shares remained a seldom used tool of employee capital participation until the early 1960s. A breakthrough occurred in 1964, when J. R. Geigy AG of Basel (which later merged with Ciba to become one of the world's leading chemicals and pharmaceuticals group) introduced a share participation plan based on periodic share offers for all employees. In order to ensure the broadest possible participation, the company offered financial assistance and allowed the purchase of certificates worth one-fourth of a share at a price of SF 100 that eventually were converted into regular shares when four-fourths had been accumulated. This initiative was highly successful (yielding a participation rate of 85 percent) and led to the establishment of a host of participation plans in other Swiss companies, including Mövenpick-Holding AG, Zurich, in 1967, and Sandoz AG, Basel, in 1969.

Many of the employee participation initiatives of the mid-1960s to mid-1970s were either limited to a one-time occurrence or were discontinued after several years, often because of a lack of interest on part of the employees. For example, in 1973, Nestlé, the country's largest multinational, introduced a profit sharing plan that was based on both cash payments and the distribution of bonds that rep-

---

[34]Reto A. Lyk, *Die Mitarbeiteraktie in der Schweiz* (Zurich: Verlag Organisator AG, 1989). This study is the first and only comprehensive account of employee stock ownership in Switzerland. Unless otherwise specified, the subsequent report on Swiss employee participation, including all figures, is based on this source.

[35]The exchange rate used throughout is US$1 = SF 1.52, as of March 27, 1990.

resented one-tenth of a share and could be converted into actual shares when ten-tenths had been accumulated. Because of low employee interest in these bonds, the latter were cancelled in 1983. Since then profit sharing has taken place on a cash-distribution basis without a capital participation system.

Still, the early 1970s witnessed a growing interest in employee capital participation and by the end of 1975 there were some forty Swiss companies offering employee shares, including participation and bonus certificates,[36] involving some 50,000 employees. In the second-half of the 1970s and during the early 1980s there was a noticeably slower rate of increase in participation programs, but interest in them began to rise again in the mid-1980s.

Present Situation

While there are no official surveys of the number of companies offering employee shares or of the number of employee shareholders, the following account provides a reasonably accurate picture of the present situation.[37] There are some 130 domestic Swiss companies offering their employees various types of shares and more than 110,000 employees participating in these share plans. The estimated market price value of all employee shares (early 1989 rates), including participation certificates (Partizipationsscheine = PS), exceeds SF 1 billion. This compares to some 70,000 employee shareholders holding a total of approximately SF 400 million in 1979. Within a decade, the average value of the capital participation per employee rose from SF 6,000 to 9,000. Employee financial participation is more common in manufacturing and service-oriented companies, particularly banks, than in merchandising enterprises. Medium-sized and smaller companies are more inclined to initiate employee capital sharing plans than are larger enterprises.

Unlike the Federal Republic of Germany, Switzerland has no employee share ownership legislation and except for some tax concessions for blocked shares, there are no government incentives for employee asset participation plans. It is therefore surprising that in terms of numbers of companies and employees as well as in terms of employee capital shares held, Switzerland is on equal footing with Germany. In both countries, every 65th inhabitant owns employee stock.

---

[36]These are profit participation certificates, granting the right to a fixed portion of a company's net profit. Unlike regular stock, they do not represent a direct participation in the company.

[37]Based on private surveys and research by Reto A. Lyk, note 34, *supra*.

Although employee shares, just like all other share investments, are subject to risks because of potential stock exchange losses, they constitute the preferred form of employee capital participation because they are easy to understand and offer above-average savings possibilities. First, they are obtained from the employer at a discount on the market price of up to 50 percent (in some instances, shares are offered free), and second, the value of employee shares held (for example, for ten years under normal business conditions), may be four to five times higher than the original purchase price. Employee participation rates depend upon the specific participation conditions. With free share offers the participation rate is, of course, 100 percent. It also tends to be near 100 percent where employees must co-pay for shares, provided the shares are not subject to any blocking periods. In the case of unblocked shares, the employee must pay taxes on the full difference between the reduced employee price of purchase and the market price at purchase time. If shares are blocked (i.e., if their sale is restricted for several years) and there is no obligation for the employee to resell the shares prior to the expiration of the blocking period, Swiss tax law grants a 10 percent discount on the market price for each blocked year, up to a maximum of 50 percent. In other words, what is actually subject to taxation is the difference between the reduced employee purchase price and the discounted market price according to the following table:

Blocking Period (Year)	Discounted Market Value (Percent)
1	90.91
2	82.64
3	75.13
4	68.30
5	62.09
6	56.45
7	51.32
8 and more	50.00

Applying this discount table, for example, a share with a market value of SF 600 that has been purchased for SF 200 and has been kept for a period of five years is not subject to taxes on the total difference between SF 200 and SF 600, that is SF 400, but only on SF 172.50, which is the difference between the discounted market value of 62.09 percent, or SF 372.50, and the purchase price of SF 200.[38] Gains on employee shares are subject to social security taxes,

---

[38]Lyk, *Die Mitarbeiteraktie in der Schweiz*, p. 88.

Other EC and European Countries

but they are not due until after the expiration of the blocking period.

Swiss employee stock plans are rarely introduced as a means of additional company financing but rather to promote the idea of co-ownership in the productive capital among employees. It is believed that the employees are more inclined to defend a capitalist economy as "co-capitalists" than as non-owners. Of the two major types of shares used in Switzerland, bearer shares (Inhaberaktien) and registered shares (Namensaktien), the registered ones are more frequently used in the context of employee participation. Unlike bearer shares, which are principally anonymous and may be held by foreigners, registered shares bearing the name of the holder can be used to ensure in a documented fashion that the capital majority—or at least the voting majority—is Swiss. For example, the Zurich-based Oerlikon-Bührle Holding Company has had a share participation plan covering twenty-two subsidiaries in Switzerland and Liechtenstein since 1977, according to which every five years Swiss citizens may obtain 3 to 6 registered shares, while foreigners may purchase 1 to 2 bearer shares. In both cases, the shares are obtainable through a special foundation, the "Oerlikon Bührle Foundation for Employee Participation" at a 30 percent discount on the market price. These shares are unblocked and therefore freely disposable. The participation rate has been approximately 65 percent for years. An especially attractive feature of this plan is that the employees may sell back their shares at any time to the foundation at the original purchase price, so that there is practically no risk involved.

Examples of Employee Share Plans

Ciba-Geigy AG, Basel, maintains a successful participation plan according to which employees with four years of service can purchase one registered share every two years at a cost of SF 200. The employee can sell every third share, while the other shares must be kept until retirement. The employee may also request, however, that the free shares be blocked until retirement. With some 14,500 employees participating, Ciba-Geigy's plan is second in importance only to the one at Zurich-based Union Bank of Switzerland (UBS). The bank's plan consists of three parts: first, all employees receive one registered share annually; second, managerial employees have a rank-related right to purchase more shares; and third, there is a loyalty bonus after each five years of service. For many years, shares have been offered for SF 200. These shares are blocked and employees may choose between a five-year blocking period or blocking until retirement. It is UBS's experience that employees up to approximately forty years of age prefer the five-year period. The plan is very successful and approximately 97 percent of the 17,300 employees participate. At the Swiss Credit Bank in Zurich, employees with five years of service may obtain four discounted registered shares annually. They are also entitled to additional loyalty shares after each fifth service year completed. Shares are blocked for five years. An interesting example of a company with employee participation on the basis of participation certificates (PS) rather than shares is the computer service company Also-Holding AG in Hergiswil. At the time of joining the company, full-time employees receive an option to purchase a certain number of PS (at 60 percent of the PS's value at the time of joining) which may be exercised at the earliest after two years.

It should also be noted that an increasing number of foreign-based companies offer their Swiss employees participation opportunities by making the parent company's share participation plan internationally available. Prominent among these companies are Caterpillar Tractor Company, Peoria, Illinois, and IBM Corporation, New York, as well as such German companies as Rosenthal AG, Commerzbank (Switzerland) AG, Deutsche Bank (Suisse) S.A., and Dresdner Bank (Switzerland) AG.

As alternatives to the share or PS plans, there are employee loan plans (employees extend a credit to their employer for a higher than usual interest rate) and fund-like participation possibilities such as that practised at Basel-based Hoffmann-La Roche & Co. AG. The company invests annually an amount equal to the dividends paid on one company share for its employees into a special internal fund administered by a Profit Sharing Foundation. At Brown, Boveri & Cie, Baden, there is an asset formation fund into which employees contribute amounts between SF 50 and SF 300 per month, which are then supplemented by the company up to a fund investment of SF 6,000 per employee. This plan was continued after the recent merger with Asea AB.

Switzerland's trade unions, although not totally rejecting employee capital sharing, have adopted a very cautious attitude toward such plans. While some of them still would prefer the introduction of collective Swedish-type wage earner funds, there is a growing number of open-minded union officials within the Swiss Trade Union Confederation, who realize that employees are increasingly willing to take on financial co-responsibilities by becoming shareholders in their companies. Even though the SF 1 billion in total market value of employee shares is impressive as it shows that a step in the right direction has been undertaken, it pales compared to the over SF 200 billion worth in shares of domestic companies quoted at the Zurich stock exchange at the end of 1986, and at the same time demonstrates the full potential for Swiss employee capital sharing.

THE EUROPEAN COMMUNITY

With the exception of Sweden, Switzerland, the United States, Canada, and Mexico, all of the countries studied here are members of the EC. Although the EC has been playing an increasingly interventionist role in the economic and social affairs of its members, it has not yet introduced any strong initiatives on the subject of employee financial participation. However, in 1979, the Commission of the European Communities did issue some basic guidelines for asset formation plans.[39] Chief among these were:

- Such plans should be directed toward those with relatively modest incomes;
- Premiums should be preferred to tax benefits;
- Sums invested should be frozen for at least five years with provision for release under certain circumstances;
- There should be some protection against inflation;
- There should be a choice of types of investments.

In 1983, the European Parliament requested the Commission to make recommendations on the subject of employee participation in asset formation. With this background, the action program adopted in 1989 to support the Commission's social charter contained a declaration to present an unspecified "instrument" on equity sharing and financial participation by workers. The Commission would leave the choice of types of programs to the member states, to be either legislated or left to negotiation by employers and employees or their representatives. It is likely that the final instrument will avoid favoring any particular system, but at the same time it may be expected to encourage the spread of programs which either allow employees to share in the profits or the capital of firms or which provide for a redistribution to the workers of some share of the results of the enterprise.

---

[39]Commission of the European Communities, *Employee Participation in Asset Formation*, Com (79) 190 final, Brussels, August 28, 1979, pp. 31-32.

CHAPTER XII

Summary and Conclusions

Although there is considerable variation from one country to another, there is clearly an overall trend toward increasing the financial participation of employees in the fortunes of their employers. At least in numbers of plans and employees involved, the United States leads the way, but in several European countries employers have recently introduced forms of gain sharing, profit sharing, share ownership, or savings plans. With few exceptions, the initiative for most plans has come from employers or governments. Apparently there has been little upward pressure from employees or their representatives, and in most countries trade unions have been and remain skeptical (if not openly opposed) of the concept of financial participation for employees. Indeed, there are skeptical employers around the world, many with reputations as human resources innovators, which have not adopted the more controversial programs such as profit sharing and employee stock ownership plans (ESOPs).

Savings plans have been the least controversial of the various types of financial participation plans. In the United States, savings plans are largely an addition to the employee benefit package. In Europe, they are more likely to be a means by which governments seek to influence the savings patterns of employees. West Germany and the Netherlands, for example, have developed savings plans to a fine art. In neither context have they been a source of major controversy, but judgments on the degree to which they meet their differing aims are not easy to make. As an aid to savings they are a positive factor, yet a marginal one in view of the amounts of money involved. From the employer's standpoint, they are a low cost fringe benefit and require less of a continuing employee education program than other types of plans. From a policy standpoint, the United States has tended increasingly to treat savings plans as a source of retirement income by restricting the availability of the funds to the employee and by deferring tax liability. European countries have tended to freeze the accounts for a period of years (usually two to seven) but to free the saver from tax liability after the frozen period, thus placing less emphasis on retirement and at the same time encouraging employees to save.

Profit sharing plans are viewed by most employers as something more than a mere fringe benefit. They represent an ideological policy based on an underlying assumption that employees who contribute effort resulting in profit for the employer should share in the profit they help to generate. The objective of such plans is to increase labor-management collaboration and to develop employee attitudes favorable to the firm while giving employees a share of the fruits of capital productivity. Many firms undoubtedly establish deferred profit sharing plans as a method for funding an employee retirement plan without locking the company into fixed annual contributions which would be required in a qualified defined benefit pension plan. In a rather individualistic country like the United States, profit sharing generally has found greater acceptance by employers and employees than it has in the more collectivist countries of Europe. In addition, the U.S. government, in the past at least, has been more supportive of profit sharing than most European and Asian governments have been. During the 1980s, however, there was a tendency for the U.S. government to place additional restrictions on deferred profit sharing plans through the tax laws, while countries such as the United Kingdom and France have made substantial efforts to encourage the spread of profit sharing and employee ownership.

At least three levels of government involvement in profit sharing can be identified: (1) the absence of any legislative or regulatory action; (2) encouragement with or without tax incentives; and (3) mandatory profit sharing. Some proponents of profit sharing believe that tax incentives are inappropriate. The rationale for this view is that profit sharing should be installed only in companies that have carefully developed a sharing, participative climate with a management that sees profit sharing as an integral part of all aspects of the business. Tax incentives, according to this view, may persuade employers to introduce profit sharing before they are ready for it, limiting the chance of plan success. Other observers believe that incentives are necessary to encourage firms to adopt profit sharing and that few will do so without some economic incentive. Experience around the world indicates that profit sharing is generally less prevalent in those countries that have not enacted tax incentives for firms or employee participants. (Major countries in this study which fall in this category include Belgium, Italy, the Netherlands, and Switzerland.)

The second category includes countries which have either enacted tax incentives for employers and/or employees or those countries which provide encouragement short of tax breaks. Countries which

Summary and Conclusions

lead in adopting tax incentives for profit sharing plans are France, the United States, the United Kingdom, Canada, and Denmark (see Table XII-1). Countries which officially encourage the adoption of profit sharing but which stop short of tax incentives are Singapore and Finland. The government of Denmark for many years provided only advice and assistance to companies in establishing profit sharing plans, but recently Denmark enacted legislation to provide at

TABLE XII-1
Tax Incentives for Employer and Employee by Country

	Savings Plans	Employee Stock Ownership	Deferred Profit Sharing	Cash Profit Sharing	Gain Sharing
France					
Employer	x	x	x	x	
Employee	x	x	x	x	
U.S.					
Employer	x	x	x		
Employee	x	x	x		
U.K.					
Employer			x		
Employee	x	x	x		x
Germany					
Employer	x	x			
Employee	x	x			
Netherlands					
Employer	x	x			
Employee	x	x			
Canada					
Employer			x		
Employee		x[a]	x		
Denmark					
Employer		x	x		
Employee		x	x		
Sweden					
Employer			x		
Employee			x		
Switzerland					
Employer					
Employee		x			
Italy					
Employer					
Employee		x			
Mexico					
Employer					
Employee					
Belgium					
Employer					
Employee					

[a]Quebec only.

least some minimal tax incentive for employers and employees. Whether directly because of tax incentives or other reasons, countries that have tax incentives have been those in which profit sharing has expanded more rapidly, such as the United States, the United Kingdom, France, and Canada. The European Community (EC), insofar as it has expressed itself on the subject, has recommended "premiums" rather than tax incentives to encourage the growth of asset formation plans.

Tax incentives for employers are probably more important than tax incentives for employees as a motivator for the establishment of a financial participation plan for employees. Generally, most payments to employees are deductible for the employer at the time those payments are made to the employee. In the case of deferred distribution to the employee under qualified plans, the employer is permitted to take a deduction at the time the accrual is made although the employee may not receive the payment until many years later. The advantage to the employer is a current reduction in tax liability, the amount of which may vary from country to country. The principle, however, is the same.

In the case of the employee, the situation is different. The United States has uniformly *deferred*, not excused, tax for the employee until some future time when a distribution is made to the employee, usually at retirement, death, or termination of employment with the employer. If tax rates are lower at the time of distribution, the employee will benefit; if tax rates are the same at distribution the employee gains nothing; and if tax rates are higher at distribution the employee loses. There is usually a presumption that at retirement the employee will be in a lower tax bracket, but that is not a certainty in every case. Lower paid employees may not be in a lower tax bracket than they were prior to retirement, and they may perceive any possible tax savings as a relatively minor consideration.

European countries have generally taken a different approach to employee tax incentives. Instead of deferring taxes, as in the United States, many European countries excuse the tax if the employee does not take distribution for a specified period of years, often referred to as a "blocking" period. There is also a tendency for European countries to place actual shares of stock into the employees' hands as opposed to a trust arrangement that is characteristic of U.S. deferred profit sharing plans and employee stock ownership plans.

The U.S. system is a reflection of the emphasis on profit sharing and share ownership as retirement vehicles, or at least as retirement supplements. In Europe, share ownership in particular has been viewed as a way of closing the gap between capital and labor—as a way of ending class warfare or of redistributing wealth.[1]

In the case of incentives for cash profit sharing plans, European countries have moved ahead of the United States. During the 1980s, both France and the United Kingdom enacted legislation to provide tax incentives for both employers and/or employees in their cash profit sharing plans. A bill to provide limited tax incentives for employees in cash profit sharing plans was introduced in the U.S. Senate in 1987 but made little headway and has not been reintroduced. Lacking employer incentives it is unlikely that wide support can be obtained for a small tax benefit to employees, a great percentage of whom have little interest in tax savings.

Although Table XII-1 indicates that no country provides tax incentives for gain sharing plans, the French law allows voluntary profit sharing plans to link pay to "productivity improvements" or "other" factors. Such plans are more closely related to what has traditionally been referred to as gain sharing.

The third category of government involvement includes those countries that mandate profit sharing for at least some employers either by legislation or, as in the case of Mexico, by the constitution. Countries in this category include Sweden (which also has voluntary deferred profit sharing with tax incentives), Mexico, some South American countries, and France (which has both voluntary and mandatory programs with tax incentives for both types). There is an important difference between the Swedish Wage Earner Funds and the mandatory profit sharing of France, Mexico, and the South American countries. The Swedish model involves collectively (union) administered funds. Individual employees do not receive a direct stake in their own company. The French, Mexican, and South American systems do provide for the payments to be distributed to the employees from their own employer. Although these plans cover significant numbers of employees, the degree of success in achieving objectives set for them has been debatable. In these countries there is often a strong interest, as in Sweden for example, in decreasing the concentration of wealth, while increasing workers' influence on company decisions. Although the French operate both mandatory and voluntary profit sharing plans, it appears that voluntary plans

---

[1] *See* George Copeman, "Employee Share Ownership in the European Community," paper delivered to the ESOP Association, 12th Annual Convention, May 24-26, 1989, at Washington, DC.

are going to be the wave of the future, particularly among the smaller companies.

Cash profit sharing predated deferred profit sharing in many countries, but until the 1980s cash plans were not widespread. The spread of cash profit sharing has been fueled by a desire of employers to develop more flexible compensation programs which will accommodate more rapid pay adjustments in the face of economic downturn. The flexibility issue raises the question of the extent to which variable pay should replace fixed pay or fringe benefits. Traditionally, profit sharing payments were seen as add-on bonus payments which should not replace any portion of base pay or fringes, and there are many observers (particularly trade unionists, but including many others) who continue to hold that view. At least one U.S. study has concluded that there is no evidence that cash profit sharing is "offset elsewhere in the pay package."[2] The same study found no evidence that the presence of profit sharing, cash or deferred, reduced the value of other benefits.[3] Unfortunately, the wage study is based on data from the 1970s, and the benefits study is based on 1950s data. We do not know the results of several large cash plans which were inaugurated, often as part of concession packages, in the 1980s. It is possible that there has been more substitution, but proof will have to await further research.

Although the U.S. government has taken no position on the issue of profit sharing payments replacing a portion of regular pay, the French government has made it clear that such payments are not to replace base pay. The view from the Conservative government in the United Kingdom is opposite that of the French. There are no statistics yet from the United Kingdom to indicate whether substitution has occurred, but it appears unlikely that there has been any large scale substitution, largely because the trade unions have strongly opposed it.

Deferred profit sharing plans in the United States have profit sharing trusts that usually hold substantial amounts of employer stock in employee owned accounts. In that sense, ESOPs have much in common with deferred profit sharing plans. They are both programs which give employees a stake in the ownership of their employer. The major difference is that company payments to the ESOP are not tied to profit levels in the company, and profit sharing

---

[2]Daniel J. B. Mitchell, David Lewin, and Edward E. Lawler III, "Alternative Pay Systems, Firm Performance, and Productivity," Alan S. Blinder (ed.), *Paying for Productivity: A Look at the Evidence* (Washington, DC: The Brookings Institution, 1990), p. 61.

[3]*Ibid.*, pp. 60-61.

Summary and Conclusions

payments usually are related to profits in some way. Both types of plans, however, provide economic incentives for employees after a somewhat extended period of time. From the employer's standpoint, the reasons for the establishment of ESOPs are much the same reasons for which they might establish deferred profit sharing plans, but ESOPs have much broader appeal for employers because they may used for a variety of other purposes, usually with substantial tax advantages. With such perceived advantages it is easy to understand the growth of ESOPs during the 1980s.

The available evidence indicates that employee ownership and profit sharing may have a positive effect on productivity, particularly if they are combined with organized problem solving employee participation programs. Although additional research is needed to establish more precise relationships between employee participation and both share ownership and profit sharing, virtually all observers agree that management must do something more than install profit sharing or employee ownership and walk out the door. At a minimum there must be an employee communication program designed to provide a basic understanding of the plans. At the other extreme are those companies which use the financial participation program as a starting point for an information sharing program for their employees along with an extensive employee involvement program.

Employee stock ownership in Europe has developed more slowly, but there are indications that this may be changing. Privatization of state owned businesses in countries around the world offers unprecedented opportunity for employee share ownership to grow even in Eastern Bloc countries where it has been almost unheard of before. Although employee stock purchase plans are common in Japan as part of the Japanese-style management policy of "sharing the fruits" of corporate performance, American-type ESOPs are not common. According to a study made by the Tokyo Stock Exchange, 88 percent of all Japanese publicly held companies, a total of 1,588, have employee stock purchase programs.[4] The method by which employees acquire shares is less important in Japan than the special nature of corporate control. Corporations are viewed as organic collections of people rather than collections of physical assets or as shares of stock. The result, particularly in larger companies, is more control by employees, including both management and labor, and

---

[4]Tsutomu Hado, "Employee Stock Ownership Plans," The Nikkei Industry Research Institute, February 10, 1986, p. 6.

less control by outside shareholders.[5] This is a cultural phenomenon that in itself may result in greater employee motivation than has yet been achieved in many ESOP companies in the United States.

As a group incentive plan to motivate employees to improve performance, gain sharing offers a more direct route than other employee financial participation plans since rewards are more closely related to extra productive effort and are less influenced by extraneous factors beyond the control of employees. There are strong indications, however, that the more successful gain sharing plans in the United States are accompanied by active employee involvement programs. Participation by employees in the decision making process is more important with gain sharing than it is with profit sharing or employee ownership because the employee has a more direct stake in the performance of the unit or business and thus has a stronger incentive to become involved in improvement activities. The need for sharing information with employees also increases with greater employee involvement in the business. Unless management is willing to share some of the decision making power, is ready to share information with employees, and is willing to commit sufficient time and resources, the success of a gain sharing program is at risk. Of course these activities might also increase the chances of success for other programs such as profit sharing and employee ownership, but they are acknowledged to be more important in supporting gain sharing.

Numerous scholars have concluded that employee participation, or more simply how employees are treated, is as important, if not more so, than how they are paid. This should come as no surprise since the Hawthorne studies some sixty years ago showed that a change in the customary supervision of employees to encourage consultation and feed-back and to allow employees to express reactions, hopes, fears, etc., about their jobs accounted for better attitudes and improved productivity.[6] With the growth of financial participation we are now seeing the importance of joining financial and decision making participation to make both more successful.

---

[5]David D. Roberts and Walter L. Ames, "U.S. Leveraged Buyouts Spawn Japanese-Style Strategy," *The Japan Economic Journal*, Vol. 24, No. 1232 (October 18, 1986), p. 7.

[6]*See* F. J. Roethlisberger, *Management and Morale* (Cambridge, MA: Harvard University Press, 1955), pp. 14-15. The complete report on the Hawthorne studies is contained in F. J. Roethlisberger and William J. Dickson, *Management and the Worker* (Cambridge, MA: Harvard University Press, 1939).

Index

Achievement sharing, 52
Aerospatiale, 148
AFL-CIO, 100, 103, 109
Agfa-Gevaert, 194
Air France, 148
Air Line Pilots Association, 109
Åkermans, 183
Also-Holding AG, 206
Alufluor, 187
Aluminum Company of America, 49
Aluminum, Glass & Brick Workers, 49
Amalgamated Clothing and Textile Workers Union, 43
American Compensation Association, 29
American Federation of Labor, 31
American Motors, 42, 43-44, 45
American Productivity Center, 29, 37, 55
American Velvet, 42, 43
Andreas STIHL, 168-70
Approved Deferred Share Trusts (U.K.), 120-21
Argentina, 2
Asset accumulation plans, 3
Association for the Promotion of Profit Sharing, 30
Association of Western Pulp and Paper Workers, 51

Balladour, Edouard, 139
Bankers Trust, 58
 survey of savings plans, 59-68
BASF AG, 166
Belgium, 1
 profit sharing in, 193-95
Bethlehem Steel, 48
Billon & Isaac, 202
BMW AG, 167-68
Boise Cascade, 79
Bonus pools, 22
Bornard, M. Jean, 143, 144
British Coal, 132
Brotherhood of Carpenters and Joiners, 50
Brown, Boveri & Cie, 206
Bullock, R.J., 26
Bureau of Labor Statistics (U.S.), 38
 savings plans survey, 59-68

Canada, 1, 211
 deferred payment plans, 113
 economic indicators, 111
 equity sharing, 113
 gain sharing in, 112
 profit sharing in, 112
 productivity index, 111
 stock option plans, 114
 tax incentives, 212
 union reaction to gain sharing, 115
Canadian Auto Workers, 115
Cash profit sharing, 6, 39-40, 214
 incentive value of, 6
Caterpillar Tractor Company, 206
Central Organization of Salaried Personnel (Sweden), 175
Central Organization of Swedish Professional Workers, 175
Ciba-Geigy AG, 205-206
Chile, 2
China, 2
Christian Democratic Party (Italy), 196
Christian National Trade Union Federation (Sweden), 192
Chrysler Corporation, 18, 27, 45-46, 48
CODA, see qualified cash or deferred arrangement
Collective profit sharing
 aims of, 7-8
Combination plans, 40
Commission of the European Communities, 207
Commerzbank (Switzerland) AG, 206
Communications Workers of America, 98
Confederacion de Trabajadores de Mexico, 118
Concession bargaining, 15
Curran, Joseph, 98

Daimler-Benz AG, 166
Danish Employers' Confederation, 200-201
Dan Rivers Mills, Inc., 82, 101
Data Services, 124
Deferred Profit Sharing Plan (Canada), 113
Deferred profit sharing plans, 4-5, 33, 34, 113, 214

217

Deferred tax liability, 7
Deficit Reduction Act of 1984 (U.S.), 72, 89
Defined contribution plans, 34
de Gaulle, Charles, 137
Denmark, 1, 211
  profit sharing in, 7, 200-201
Department of Employment (U.K.), 129
  study of firms with ESOPs, 133
Department of Labor (U.S.), 83
Department of National Savings (U.K.), 129
Deutsche Bank (Suisse) S.A., 206
Dresdner Bank (Switzerland) AG, 206
Du Pont Fibers Division, 52

Eastern Airlines, 99, 106
Eastern Bloc, 2, 215
Eastman Kodak, 31, 119
EDF-GDF, 149
Electricity Supply Trade Union Council, 132
Employee Profit Sharing Plan (Canada), 113
Employee Retirement Income Security Act (ERISA), 41, 60, 66, 69, 83, 86
Employee savings plans, 57-68
Employee stock ownership plans (ESOPs), 1, 5, 69-109, 214-16
  allocation of stock in, 70-71, 74
  in buyouts, 80-81
  in Canada, 114
  and collective bargaining, 104
  company contributions to, 35-37, 74
  conflicts with labor law, 106-108
  definition of, 69-70
  distribution of shareholder stock, 84
  distribution schedules, 75-76
  disadvantages of, 82-85
  dividend payments, 75
  economic results, 90-91
  eligibility for, 73-74
  equity financing, 81, 88-89
  establishment of, 70
  evaluation of, 95-97
  history of, 69
  as hostile takeover defense, 81
  incentive value of, 5
  labor-management cooperation, 92-93
  leverageable, 72-73
  leveraged, 70-72
  in leveraged buyouts, 78, 82
  non-leveraged, 72-73
  objectives of, 77-78, 79
  organizational structures, 95
  ownership of capital, 85-86
  participation rates, 13, 14, 73
  pension plans, 101
  performance of companies, 85
  repurchase liability, 83
  risks, 83-84
  set up and operating costs, 83
  studies of, 91-92
  tax advantages of, 5, 72, 79
  types of, 71-72
  and unions, 74, 98, 101, 108-109
  in the United Kingdom, 130-35
  vesting schedules, 75
  voting rights, 76
  and worker control, 76-77
  worker participation, 92-93
Employee Stock Ownership Trust (ESOT), 70
Employment Gazette, 133
ERISA, see Employee Retirement Income Security Act
ESOP Association, 87, 93, 94, 102
ESOPs, see Employee Stock Ownership Plans
ESOT, see Employee Stock Ownership Trust
European Parliament, 207

Federal Republic of Germany, 1, 151-73
  Capital Formation Law 1959, 155
  Christian Democratic Liberal coalition, 159
  codeterminational aspects of asset sharing, 162
  contractual aspects of asset sharing, 161-62
  currency reform of 1948, 151
  development of asset formation plans, 151
  employee participation rights, 168-70
  employee stock plans, 164-65
  Fifth Asset Formation Law, 156-59, 162, 163
  Fifth Asset Formation Law, amended, 159-61
  First Asset Formation Law, 152-53
  forms of capital sharing, 163
  Fourth Asset Formation Law, 154-56
  Home Savings Law, 151-52
  profit participation certificates, 167
  proposal for collective profit sharing, 7
  Savings Premium Law, 152
  Second Asset Formation Law, 153, 156-58
  silent partners/indirect participation, 170-71
  social market economy, 151

Index

Third Asset Formation Law, 153-54
trade unions and employee capital sharing, 172-73
Fiat, 195, 197
Finland, 2, 211
Finance Act of 1978 (U.K.), 119-21
Fixed formula plans, 35
Fixed plus discretionary plans, 35
FMC, 83
Ford Motor Company, 46, 48
Foreign Subsidiary Buyback Program, 114-15
France, 1, 137-50, 214
   compulsory deferred profit sharing, 6, 140-41
   leveraged buyouts in, 147-48
   1959 profit sharing law, 137
   1967 profit sharing law, 138
   1986 profit sharing law, 139
   number of profit sharing agreements, 140-41
   profit sharing in, 137-50
   savings plans, 145-46
   share option plans, 147
   share ownership, 146-47
   tax incentives, 212-13
   voluntary cash profit sharing, 142-45
French Christian Workers Confederation (CFTC), 143

Gain sharing, 1, 6, 9-28
   in Canada, 112
   in industrial firms, 23-25
   level of employee involvement, 15-16
   management attitudes towards, 15
   results of, 26-27
   in Sweden, 184-87
   in the United Kingdom, 135
Gallatin, Albert, 29
General Accounting Office (U.S.), 27, 73, 77, 78, 82, 86, 93, 94
   ESOPs study, 91
General Mills, 81
General Motors, 46-48
General, Municipal, Boilermakers and Allied Trades Union, 125-26
German Trade Union Confederation (DGB), 172
Germany, see Federal Republic of Germany
Gilman, Nicholas Paine, 30
Glasgow University Centre for Research in Industrial Democracy and Participation, 120-21
Gompers, Samuel, 31

Hassenkam Report, 201

HBK-Spaarbank, 194
Hewitt Associates, 33, 39
   survey, 11-12
Hewlett-Packard, 119
Hoechst AG, 165-66
Hoffmann-LaRoche & Co. AG, 206
Hyatt-Clark Industries, 80, 99, 105-106, 107

IBM Corporation, 206
IG Metall, 170
Improshare, 112
Incentive pay, 13, 22-23
Inland Revenue (U.K.), 124
Inland Steel, 49
Internal Revenue Code (U.S.), 32, 34, 40, 57, 86
   and ESOPs, 71, 73
   Section 401 (k), 57-60, 68
Internal Revenue Service (U.S.), 32, 33, 39, 61, 68
International Association of Machinists, 99
International Brotherhood of Electrical Workers, 51-52
International Brotherhood of Teamsters, 99, 107
International Woodworkers of America, 50
Itagel, 198
Italian Confederation of Workers' Trade Unions, 195-96
Italian General Confederation of Labor (CGIL), 195, 199
Italian Union of Labor (UIL), 196
Italy, 1, 195-200
   employee share ownership plans, 199-200
   performance-related pay, 196-99
   profit sharing in, 195-200

Japan, 2, 215-16
J.C. Penney, 81
Joint Economic Committee, U.S. Congress, 85
J.R. Geigy AG, 202

Kronenbourg, 148-49
Kruse, Douglas Lynn, 54, 55
KTM, 132

Landrum-Griffin Act, 101, 106
Lawler, Edward E., 26
Lawson, Nigel, 122
LeClair, Jean, 137
Lockheed Corporation, 81

Long, Senator Russell B., 77
Lowe's, 83
LTV, 48, 49

Mateos, Lopez, 116, 118
Maubeuge-Construction Automobile, 149-50
McAdams, Jerry, 9, 11-12
Meidner, Rudolph, 177-78
Mercedes-Automobil-Holding AG, 166
Metzger, Bert, 54, 137
Mexico, 1, 213, 116-18
  organized labor and profit sharing, 118
  profit sharing in, 116-17
Montedison, 195, 199
Motorola, 97
Mövenpick-Holding AG, 202

National Center for Employee Ownership (NCEO), 69, 76, 77, 87, 102-103, 105, 106
National Civic Federation, 30
National Council of French Employers (CNPF), 143
National Economic Development Council (U.K.), 121
National Freight Consortium, 131
National Labor Relations Board (U.S.), 107
National Labor Relations Act (U.S.), 101, 106, 109
National Maritime Union, 98
National Profit Sharing Commission (Mexico), 116
National Steel, 48, 49
Nationwide Anglia, 124
NCEO, see National Center for Employee Ownership
Nestlé, 202-203
Netherlands, 1, 189-93
  bonus savings plans, 189-90
  company profit sharing, 191-92
  profit sharing in, 189-92
  proposals for collective profit sharing, 7
  wage savings plans, 190-91
New York Stock Exchange, 94

O'Dell, Carla, 9, 11-12
Oerlikon-Buhrle Holding Company, 205
Olivetti, 195, 197, 198-99

Pacific Telesis, 52
Pan American, 106
People's Provincial Bus Company, 132
Performance factors, 13-14
Performance goals, 9

Peru, 2
Peugeot, 150
Philips, 191-92
Pirelli, 195
Poland, 2
Polaroid, 81
Proctor, Col. William Cooper, 30
Proctor & Gamble, 30, 81
Profit-Related Pay (U.K.), 121-25
  criticisms of, 125
  legislation, 123-24
  risks involved, 122
Profit sharing, 1, 29-55
  in Belgium, 193-95
  in Canada, 112, 114
  and collective bargaining, 42
  combined with gain sharing, 27-28
  in Denmark, 200-201
  distribution, 38-39
  in the European Community, 207-208
  in France, 137-50
  in Italy, 195-200
  investments, 38
  in Mexico, 116
  in the Netherlands, 189-92
  origins of, 29-30
  plan administration and management, 38
  results, 52-55
  in steel and aluminum industry, 48-49
  in Sweden, 181
  in Switzerland, 201-207
  trends, 209-210
  in the United Kingdom, 119-36
  in wood products industry, 50
Profit Sharing Council of America (PSCA), 4, 33, 35, 39
Profit Sharing Research Foundation, 54
PSCA, see Profit Sharing Council of America

Qualified cash or deferred arrangement (CODA), 57-58
Quality circles, 21
Quebec Securities Commission, 114
Quercymetal, 147-48

Ralston Purina, 79
Rath Packing Co., 80, 85, 105
Raymond International Inc., 82, 101
Regional Bell Operating Companies, 51-52
Renault, 148, 150
Retirement Equity Act of 1984, 37
Reuther, Walter, 98
Reynolds Metals Co., 49
Robertshaw Controls Co., 109

Index

Rocard, Michel, 148
Rosenthal AG, 206
Rucker plans, 10-11, 26, 112

Sandoz AG, 202
Save as You Earn (SAYE), 127-30
  evaluation of 129-30
  features, 127
  tax aspects, 129
SAYE, see Save as You Earn
Savings plans, 1, 58-68, 209
  advantages and disadvantages of, 58-59
  coverage, 60
  eligibility, 60
  employee contributions, 60-61
  employer contributions, 62-63
  features and trends, 59-60
  forfeiture allocations, 66
  forms of distribution, 67-68
  in France, 145-46
  hardship withdrawals, 67
  in-service withdrawals, 66-67
  investment of contributions, 63-64
  investment transfers, 64-65
  loans, 67
  post-tax withdrawal penalties, 66
  pre-tax withdrawals, 66-67
  trends, 68
  vesting, 65-66
  voluntary suspensions, 63
Scan Väst, 184-85
Scanlon plans, 10-11, 26, 112
  in Sweden, 185
Scottish Transport Group, 132
Sears, Roebuck, 31, 85
Shepard, Edward Morse, 55
Siemens AG, 166
Singapore, 2-3, 211
Skandia Insurance Company, 180
Social Democratic Party (German), 172
Sollac, 149
South Bend Lathe, 99, 105
Southern Pacific Railroad, 109
Soviet Union, 2
Svenska Handelsbanken, 183
Sweden, 1, 175-88
  collective asset formation plans, 192-93
  Swedish Employers' Confederation (SAF), 176, 177-78, 184
  gain sharing in, 184-87
  National Pension Insurance Fund, 178-79
  profit sharing in, 181
  proposals for collective profit sharing, 7
  results of wage earner funds, 179-81
  Social Democratic Party (SAP), 175
  Swedish Farmers' Union, 186
  Swedish Trade Union Confederation, 176
  taxation of profit sharing, 182
  trends in flexible pay plans, 187-88
  wage earner funds, 176-81, 192, 213
Swiss Credit Bank, 206
Swiss Trade Union Confederation, 206
Switzerland, 1, 201-207
  employee financial participation in, 201-201
  share ownership statistics, 203
  tax advantages of employee stock ownership, 204-205

Tax Reform Act of 1986 (U.S.), 34-35, 38, 65, 71, 72, 75, 83, 84
Texaco, 81
Toronto Stock Exchange, 114
Trans World Airlines, 106
Team-based pay systems, 9, 12, 21-26
  clerical employees, 21
  in financial services, 22-23
  white-collar applications, 22-23

Unions
  control over investment funds, 7
  response to team concept, 16-18
Union Bank of Switzerland, 205-206
United Airlines, 109
United Auto Workers, 18, 43, 45, 46, 98, 105, 109
  reaction to profit sharing, 47-48
United Electrical Workers, 99
Unity Trust, 131-32
United Kingdom, 1, 119-35, 211, 214
  ADST plans, 127
  and ESOPs, 5, 131
  payment by results, 135
  profit sharing, 119-36
  PRP plans, 127
  savings plans, 128
  study of ESOPs, 133-34
  tax incentives, 6-7, 212-13
USX, 49
United Steelworkers of America, 42, 49, 98, 100, 103, 107, 109, 115

Vandenberg Subcommittee, 31-32
Venezuela, 2
Vesting, 37-38
  cliff vesting, 38
  graduated vesting, 38
  immediate vesting, 27

Vickers, 132
Volvo, 183-84
  Kolmar plant, 185-86
  gain sharing, 185-86

Welfare and Pension Plans Disclosure Act
  of 1958, 40-41
Western Council of Lumber Production
  and Industrial Workers, 50

Weyerhaeuser, 50-51
Weitzman, Martin L., 44, 55, 121
Wierton Steel, 80, 97, 105
Williams, Lynn, 103
Whitman, 79

Yorkshire Rider, 132

Zanussi, 195, 197, 198-99